Intelligence and National Security

Intelligence and National Security

A Reference Handbook

J. Ransom Clark

Contemporary Military, Strategic, and Security Issues

PRAEGER SECURITY INTERNATIONAL
Westport, Connecticut • London

Library of Congress Cataloging-in-Publication Data

Clark, J. Ransom.
Intelligence and national security : a reference handbook / J. Ransom Clark.
p. cm. – (Contemporary military, strategic, and security issues, ISSN 1932–295X)
Includes bibliographical references and index.
ISBN-13: 978–0–275–99298–9 (alk. paper)
1. Military intelligence—Handbooks, manuals, etc. 2. National security—Handbooks, manuals, etc. I. Title.
UB250.C53 2007
327.1273–dc22 2007016119

British Library Cataloguing in Publication Data is available.

Library of Congress Catalog Card Number: 2007016119
ISBN-13: 978–0–275–99298–9
ISBN-10: 0–275–99298–5
ISSN: 1932–295X

First published in 2007

Praeger Security International, 88 Post Road West, Westport, CT 06881
An imprint of Greenwood Publishing Group, Inc.
www.praeger.com

Printed in the United States of America

The paper used in this book complies with the Permanent Paper Standard issued by the National Information Standards Organization (Z39.48–1984).

10 9 8 7 6 5 4 3 2 1

Contents

Preface

In his memoir, veteran Cold Warrior Milt Bearden quotes Leonid Nikitenko, counterintelligence chief of the KGB First Directorate, on the subject of working in intelligence: "[T]here is no business like it. We are politicians. We are soldiers. And, above all, we are actors on a wonderful stage. I cannot think of a better business than the intelligence business."[1] Whether the thoughts are the Russian's or Bearden's is not material, the sentiment rings true for those who fought the intelligence wars of the last half of the twentieth century. However, the business of intelligence changed with the demise of the Soviet Union in 1991, and it changed even more after the terrorist attacks of September 11, 2001. It will be interesting to watch the next generation of intelligence challenges play out in the hands of a new generation of practitioners.

Much ink has already been spilled (and even more can be expected) seeking to assign blame for what "went wrong" on 9/11 and to argue multitudinous points of view as to what should be done to "fix" American intelligence. Neither area is the focus of what I have sought to accomplish here. The goal of this book is to provide those who are interested in watching or even participating in the intelligence business enough background and context to assist in making reasoned evaluations of ongoing and future activities. The approach to the subject matter is meant to be illustrative and explanatory—and to prompt more questions than are answered. The careful reader should find many leads in the text, chapter endnotes, and bibliography to additional reading and research across a wide spectrum of subjects related to the role of intelligence in maintaining U.S. national security.

In the mid-1960s, the Central Intelligence Agency took in a Tennessee country boy and sent him out to travel the world—and paid him to do it! My gratitude for that opportunity remains quite real. Thanks are due to Hayden Peake for opening my mind to the possibility that intelligence was something that could be studied, not just done. The careful and caring mentoring of my department chair, Dr. Stacia Straley, immeasurably smoothed my move into the academic world. The brand-new President of Muskingum College, Dr. Anne C. Steele, stood by me in the awful months following my wife's death; I will never be able to thank "my President" enough for challenging me to move forward. I did so and found the loving and ever positive Helen. She has been at my side through multiple months of putting this work together word by word, offering encouragement at every obstacle along the way. Thanks are due to Praeger/Greenwood editor Alicia Merritt for offering me the opportunity to write a book that I did not even know was bottled up inside me. Adam C. Kane and the Praeger Security International crew have seen this book through to completion. And most of all, I thank my Mother, Sue Shelton Clark, for all that she has given me.

All statements of fact, opinion, or analysis expressed are those of the author and do not reflect the official positions or views of the Central Intelligence Agency (CIA) or any other U.S. Government agency. Nothing in the contents should be construed as asserting or implying U.S. Government authentication of information or CIA endorsement of the author's views. This material has been reviewed by the CIA to prevent the disclosure of classified information.

Note

1. Milt Bearden and James Risen, *The Main Enemy: The Inside Story of the CIA's Final Showdown with the KGB* (New York: Random House, 2003), 457.

Abbreviations

A-2	Air Force Intelligence Staff
ABM	Anti-Ballistic Missile
ACS	Automated Case Support system (FBI)
AFSA	Armed Forces Security Agency (NSA predecessor)
AIB	Allied Intelligence Bureau (World War II)
ASD	Asian Studies Detachment (U.S. Army)
BBC	British Broadcasting Corporation
CA	Covert Action
CBI	China-Burma-India Theater (World War II)
CCF	Congress for Cultural Freedom
CI	Counterintelligence
CIA	Central Intelligence Agency
CMS	Community Management Staff
COI	Coordinator of Information (OSS predecessor)
COINTELPRO	FBI Counterintelligence Program
COMINT	Communications Intelligence
COMPUSEC	Computer Security
COMSEC	Communications Security
CSE	Communications Security Establishment (Canada)
DCI	Director of Central Intelligence (abolished 2004)
DCIA	Director, Central Intelligence Agency (established 2004)
DEA	Drug Enforcement Administration
DHS	Defense HUMINT Service
DHS	Department of Homeland Security
DIA	Defense Intelligence Agency
DNI	Director of National Intelligence (established 2004)
DSD	Defence Signals Directorate (Australia)
ELINT	Electronic Intelligence
FBI	Federal Bureau of Investigation
FBIS	Foreign Broadcast Information Service (now OSC)

FRUMel	Fleet Radio Unit, Melbourne (World War II)
FRUPac	Fleet Radio Unit, Pacific Fleet (World War II)
FTD	Foreign Technology Division (USAF)
G-2	Army Intelligence Staff
GCHQ	Government Communications Headquarters (British)
GEOINT	Geospatial Intelligence
GRU	Soviet/Russian Military Intelligence Service
HF/DF	High-Frequency Direction-Finding ("huffduff")
HPSCI	House Permanent Select Committee on Intelligence
HUMINT	Human Intelligence
I&W	Indications and Warning Intelligence
IC	Intelligence Community
IMINT	Imagery Intelligence
INFOSEC	Information Security (COMSEC/COMPUSEC)
INR	Bureau of Intelligence and Research (State Department)
ISR	Intelligence, Surveillance, and Reconnaissance
JCS	Joint Chiefs of Staff
JMIP	Joint Military Intelligence Program
KGB	Soviet Intelligence Service
MASINT	Measurement and Signature Intelligence
MI5	British Internal Security Service
MI6	British Foreign Intelligence Service
MID	Military Information Division (established 1885)
N-2	Navy Intelligence Staff
NALT	Northern Afghanistan Liaison Team (CIA)
NASIC	National Air and Space Intelligence Center
NCPC	National Counter Proliferation Center (established 2005)
NCS	National Clandestine Service
NCTC	National Counterterrorism Center
NGA	National Geospatial-Intelligence Agency
NIC	National Intelligence Council
NIE	National Intelligence Estimate
NIMA	National Imagery and Mapping Agency (now NGA)
NIO	National Intelligence Officer
NIP	National Intelligence Program
NIS	National Intelligence Survey
NOC	Non-Official Cover
NPIC	National Photographic Interpretation Center
NRO	National Reconnaissance Office
NSA	National Security Agency
NSC	National Security Council
NTIS	National Technical Information Service
ONE	Office of National Estimates (CIA, 1950-1973)
ONI	Office of Naval Intelligence (established 1882)

OSC	Open Source Center (established 2005)
OSINT	Open-Source Intelligence
OSS	Office of Strategic Services (World War II)
PDB	*President's Daily Brief*
PFIAB	President's Foreign Intelligence Advisory Board
PHOTINT	Photographic Intelligence
PSYOPS	Psychological Operations
R&A	Research and Analysis Branch (OSS—World War II)
RFE	Radio Free Europe
RL	Radio Liberty
SCI	Sensitive Compartmented Information
SEIB	*Senior Executive Intelligence Brief*
SIGINT	Signals Intelligence
SIS	Secret Intelligence Service (British—MI6)
SMO	Support for military operations
SOCOM	Special Operations Command
SOE	Special Operations Executive (British—World War II)
SOF	Special Operations Forces
SOG	Studies and Observation Group (Vietnam War)
SSCI	Senate Select Committee on Intelligence
SVR	Russian Intelligence Service
TECHINT	Technical Intelligence
TELINT	Telemetry Intelligence
TIARA	Tactical Intelligence and Related Activities
UAV	Unmanned Aerial Vehicle
USIB	United States Intelligence Board
VCF	Virtual Case File (FBI)
WHSR	White House Situation Room
WMD	Weapons of Mass Destruction

CHAPTER 1

What Are We Talking About?

What Is Intelligence?

In its simplest form, intelligence is about information. Who needs or wants certain information, where that information is to come from, the manner in which it is to be handled, who will learn about it, and how it is going to be used are all matters central to a discussion of intelligence.

In more modern times, intelligence has also come to mean process and the organizations that are part of that process. Intelligence as process is exemplified by the so-called intelligence cycle. The classic intelligence cycle begins with requirements, information is collected against those requirements, the collected information is processed, the processed information is subjected to analysis and a product results, and that product is then distributed to those individuals or organizations that have requested the intelligence or have a need for it and are appropriate to receive it. This is an idealized depiction; but it does represent the process as it is supposed to happen.

Two additional disciplines—counterintelligence (CI) and covert action (CA)—are also associated with the intelligence function. Just as we want to know things that other countries or groups do not want us to know, so others want to know things about us that we prefer to remain unknown. Protecting our intelligence operations and other secrets against the actions of those who want to learn about them (or who would betray them) is the function of counterintelligence. Covert action is a catchall term for activities by which national security policy is carried out in secret. It has been around for a long time. The idea is to do things in a way that the hand of the instigator is not visible. Although covert operations are not intelligence in the informational sense, they have in modern times largely been carried out by intelligence organizations. This is because they are the organizations that operate primarily in secret and are most likely to have the means to conduct such activities.

The drive to determine what potential adversaries are doing is as old as human conflict. The eyes of the two spies Joshua sent into Jericho were performing essentially the same function as the sophisticated cameras of an Unmanned Aerial Vehicle (UAV) flying in the skies of Afghanistan or Iraq. Just like Joshua, America's political and military leaders from George Washington to the present have all had to make decisions based on available intelligence about the disposition and intentions of an enemy.

The Development of American Intelligence

The Revolutionary War

Although the development of intelligence in America is not a straight line from the Founders to today's multifaceted activities, George Washington is generally acknowledged as an astute intelligence officer who worked directly with many of his spies. And, as early as November 1775, the Continental Congress established the Committee of Secret Correspondence to collect foreign intelligence.[1] However, the new nation did not create an intelligence establishment that survived the end of the war.

This, in fact, would be one of the major themes in America's relationship with intelligence for the next 160 years: No permanent, national-level intelligence organization or structure. That does not mean, however, that the United States, and specifically its early presidents, did not engage in activities that involved both the collection of intelligence and the use of agents to influence the course of events on its expanding borders and overseas. In addition, in times of extreme difficulty, the political and military leaders would create ad hoc organizations to perform the intelligence function.

Although much of his intelligence experience dealt with military matters—dispositions of British troops, planned lines of march, and the like—Washington clearly understood the value of secret agents to the job of being President. In 1790, Congress granted the President a Contingency Fund. Sometimes referred to as the "secret fund," Washington was expected to use the money to pay for activities that he preferred not become public, such as for agents to obtain and report back information not otherwise available.

The first president's successors would also use secret funds and all manner of secret agents as they worked to expand the frontiers of their new country. Nonetheless, such covert activities continued to be on an as needed, rather than institutionalized, basis.

The Civil War

In pursuit of military and political advantage, the two sides to the American Civil War each used spies (men and women), irregular forces, and clandestine agents both directly against the other's forces and in Europe and Great Britain.

Behind the great battles of that conflict, a clandestine war was waged, although the effect intelligence had on the overall progress of the war appears limited.

An early "secret service" emerged when Allan Pinkerton, a private detective, joined Gen. George McClellan's staff as chief of intelligence. However, the commander of the Army of the Potomac was not well served, as Pinkerton was out of his element in dealing with the intelligence necessary to support an army in the field. He resigned when Lincoln fired McClellan in 1862. In Washington, Lafayette Baker formed another intelligence body, focused on catching Confederate spies, under the auspices of the War Department. Although he had some success against Confederate spies and agitators, Baker's function as a kind of secret police with wartime powers did not survive the end of the war. In 1863, Gen. Joseph Hooker tasked Col. George H. Sharpe with setting up a new intelligence unit for the Army of the Potomac. Sharpe's Bureau of Military Information was generally well regarded among Union commanders for its network of spies and the information on Confederate forces that the network produced. Military commanders beyond the Eastern campaign were largely left to organize their own intelligence organizations, leaving success in information collection and handling to the skills of individual officers. Despite its success, Sharpe's Bureau was dissolved at the end of the war, as the nation returned to its posture of no continuing intelligence structure.[2]

The Civil War saw the beginning of some technological innovations in intelligence gathering. Although balloons had been used for aerial reconnaissance for over half a century in Europe, their first use in America came from the efforts on the Union side of ballooning pioneers John Wise and Thaddeus Lowe. Their work from these airborne platforms, especially identifying enemy troop movements beyond the immediate area of a battlefield, won some adherents early in the war. However, supporters were apparently not sufficient to sustain the activity as the Army disbanded the balloon corps in May 1863.

The Civil War also saw the first use in this country of wiretaps for gathering military intelligence. The telegraph was a relatively new means of communication, and both sides used the existing networks to speed long-distance communication of instructions and information to military commanders in the field. Recognizing the telegraph's importance, the U.S. government promptly established a Military Telegraph Service within the War Department. The Service assumed responsibility for the Union's telegraph communications, for gathering intelligence through tapping the Confederacy's lines, and for communications security. Since telegraphic communication between the Union and the Confederacy was cut off early in the hostilities, tapping into the other's telegraph links often involved risky covert penetrations behind enemy lines. While both sides tried to protect their communications by the use of codes and ciphers (see sidebar "*Codes and Ciphers*"), it is generally accepted that the Union was the better at both protecting its messages and breaking those of the Confederacy. The Military Telegraph Service was phased out after the war and its functions assumed by the U.S. Army Signal Corps, created a year before the war began.

Codes and Ciphers

Codes consist of words, numbers, or symbols that are used to replace the actual or plain text of a communication. A code value of 3579 could be used to stand for whatever has been agreed on, from a word (airplane), to a phase (enemy sighted to the north), or even a sentence (The agreement will be signed on Tuesday). In a cipher, another letter usually replaces each letter in a text. For instance, "major" might be enciphered as "lzinq." A code can be enciphered for even greater security. Obviously, in either a code or a cipher, the recipient of the communication needs to be working from the same "book" as the sender. The discipline of making and breaking codes and ciphers is called cryptology.

The war gave birth to a unit in the Treasury Department, which continues to the present. Formed in 1865 and charged with catching counterfeiters, the Secret Service would eventually be tasked with protecting the President and other officials. Performing the protective function would also involve the Secret Service in counterintelligence activities by the end of the nineteenth century. Since 2002, the Secret Service has been part of the Department of Homeland Security. However, it remains primarily a user—a consumer—of the intelligence collected by other departments and agencies.

The Beginning of Organization

It would be almost twenty years after the Civil War before the first institutionalized intelligence units would emerge in the U.S. military. In the meantime, the war that was fought on America's frontier was carried out with localized and ad hoc intelligence collection. The primary intelligence-gathering instruments in the Army's long campaign against the Plains Indians were the "scouts." Keeping track of the mobile Indian forces required wide-ranging reconnaissance activities. These were conducted by a combination of freelance frontiersmen, adventurers, and friendly Indians. If Gen. George Armstrong Custer had paid more attention to the location and strength of his potential opponents, he might have prevented his death and that of a portion of his command at the Battle of the Little Bighorn in 1876. By the 1880s, the American military had come to realize that it was trailing the major European nations in incorporating the weaponry and technology of the day into the U.S. force structure. At the same time, some in the country were beginning to look beyond the continental United States for areas of continued national growth and expansion.

In 1882, the Navy created the nation's first peacetime and continuing bureaucracy for intelligence gathering—the Office of Naval Intelligence (ONI). The Army followed suit in 1885 by establishing the Military Information Division (MID). And in 1888, Congress authorized assigning military attachés to diplomatic posts abroad. Thus, as the 1880s drew to a close, the United States had gone from basically ignoring the rest of the world to creating multiple wedges into information held by other nations that might be useful to a country readying itself to play on the international stage.

The Spanish-American War

When war with Spain broke out in 1898, neither ONI nor MID could be called professional intelligence organizations. However, both units played a role (although not a determinative one) in the U.S. victory. ONI agents and naval attachés in Europe quickly built up extensive networks to track the actions of the Spanish fleet. MID officers performed covert reconnaissance duties in Puerto Rico and Cuba and maintained contact with the Cuban insurgents. The famous "Message to Garcia" is an overblown version of one such trip into the interior of the island. In addition, both the U.S. Army Signal Corps and the Treasury Department's Secret Service contributed to the intelligence effort. A Signal Corps captain who had previously been the manager of the Western Union telegraph office in Key West enlisted the telegraphers in Havana as secret agents. In a triumph for what would later be termed communications intelligence (COMINT), they provided access to all the cables passing between Havana and Madrid. As rumors of war began to circulate in the United States, the Secret Service was called upon to investigate potential cases of Spanish espionage. While Spanish spying activities in the United States appear to have been minimal, an alert Secret Service was able to short-circuit the so-called Montreal Spy Ring, an effort by the former Spanish naval attaché in Washington to organize an espionage network from the safety of neutral Canada.[3]

World War I

Because the capabilities developed to deal with hostilities were allowed to atrophy following the Spanish-American War, U.S. intelligence entered World War I in worse shape than any of the major belligerents. The emerging world power did not have even a third-rate intelligence capability. That situation would begin to change as America was deciding to go to war.

Massive German covert action operations, ranging from propaganda, to subversion in labor unions, to economic and physical sabotage, together with the horrors of unrestricted submarine warfare, certainly prepared President Woodrow Wilson to abandon his stance on neutrality in the European war. There is some small irony, however, in the fact that for a country with so little intelligence capability the last push to change America's position would come through an intelligence coup. That coup came from Great Britain's codebreaking activities.

Like their adversaries, the British had been active with propaganda activities in the United States. The goal was to pull the administration and American public opinion to their side. The British were also active in passing to the Americans intelligence about German operations. Such came both from British agents and the codebreaking unit (usually referred to as Room 40) of the Admiralty's Naval Intelligence Department. On January 16, 1917, German Foreign Minister Zimmermann sent the German Minister in Mexico an enciphered message ("The Zimmermann Telegram") proposing a German-Mexican alliance in the event of war with the United States. The payoff would be Mexico's recovery of Texas, New Mexico, and Arizona, lost in the Mexican-American War. Room 40 intercepted and deciphered the message, and turned it over to the Americans on February 24. President Wilson went to Congress for a declaration of war on April 2, 1917.

When America entered the war, intelligence received renewed attention. With assistance (some suggest guidance) from the British in the person of William Wiseman, Maj. (later Maj. Gen.) Ralph Van Deman resuscitated a moribund Military Intelligence Division (MID). Under Van Deman, MID took on the form of a modern intelligence organization: collecting, processing, and disseminating military and other intelligence; supervising the military attachés; managing counterintelligence operations; conducting liaison with the Allies' intelligence services; and making and breaking codes and ciphers. Heading the latter unit was the colorful Herbert O. Yardley, part genius and part con artist. MID and the similarly revivified Office of Naval Intelligence (ONI) were heavily committed to counterintelligence and countersubversion activities in the United States. Both organizations worked together with the Justice Department's Bureau of Investigation (established in 1908) and Treasury's Secret Service in trying to cut down on the propaganda, political agitation, strikes, fires, and explosions that flowed from the German covert campaign.

Rather than relying on MID and ONI, the U.S. forces sent to Europe organized their own intelligence units. Admiral Sims, commander of U.S. naval forces in Europe, set up a miniature ONI within his staff in London; and the naval officers worked closely with their British counterparts on intelligence matters. General Pershing's American Expeditionary Force (AEF) in France had a full-fledged field intelligence staff (G-2 in Army terminology). The staff created the AEF's own order of battle intelligence, prepared maps for the commanders, handled censorship of the mail to and from the troops, performed general counterintelligence activities, created cipher systems, and monitored German military communications.

From an intelligence point of view, one of the distinguishing developments in World War I was the substantial use of wireless radio for communication. In that environment, Army and Navy intelligence were able to enhance their skills in communications intelligence—intercepting radio signals, seeking to determine from where the signals came (direction finding), analyzing the nature of the signals (traffic analysis), and breaking the codes and ciphers in which the messages were sent (cryptanalysis). World War I also saw the widespread use of the airplane for aerial reconnaissance. Pairing the airplane with the camera meant that it was no longer necessary to rely just on the observational abilities of a pilot or passenger. Thus, the intelligence discipline of photographic intelligence (PHOTINT) began its infancy.

Between the Wars

The United States emerged from World War I with the beginning of an intelligence community. Its components included the Justice Department's Bureau of Investigation and multiple intelligence-related units within the Army and the Navy. However, neither MID nor ONI controlled the full spectrum of intelligence activities in its respective service. Despite cooperation among the various entities on some matters, such as counterintelligence, substantial rivalries existed, both between the two military services and within the services themselves. MID and ONI sustained substantial decreases in staffing and funding after 1919, but they were not cut back to the minimalist existence that had been the case before the war. Despite the drawdown, U.S. intelligence overall was stronger than it had been in 1917. In fact, lessons learned in the last war would yield some of intelligence's greatest accomplishments in the next war.

Army Intelligence. In the aftermath of the war, MID continued to collect foreign intelligence through military attachés and officers serving in overseas commands in Hawaii and the Philippines. MID also worked closely with the Bureau of Investigation on counterespionage and countersubversion matters. In the 1920s, some overzealousness or heavy-handedness in investigating domestic political and labor groups produced a public backlash against military counterintelligence. It would be revived, however, as war drew near in the late 1930s.

MID's codebreaking operation was kept alive after the war by Yardley's salesmanship, as he was able to convince the War and State departments to jointly fund the activity. The unit, which became known as the American Black Chamber, proved its worth when Yardley's team broke the Japanese code prior to the opening of the Washington disarmament conference in 1921. Aware that Japan would back down from its initial demands, the U.S. negotiators could press hard for terms favorable to their side.[4] Despite its successes, the Black Chamber was shut down when Secretary of State Henry L. Stimson withdrew the State Department's funding for the project. Although Stimson would later change his opinion as war approached, his action in 1929 was predicated on his disapproval of the dirty business of reading the correspondence of ostensibly friendly countries ("Gentlemen do not read each other's mail").

The Army was not significantly hampered in its cryptologic endeavors by the disappearance of the Black Chamber, as it was already moving to set up its own operation. Heading the effort was William Frederick Friedman, hailed by David Kahn as the world's greatest cryptologist. Friedman had served in World War I with the AEF's Radio Intelligence Section. Shortly after the war he joined the Signal Corps as a civilian employee, working primarily on devising cryptographic systems. In 1929, Army codemaking and codebreaking was consolidated in the Signal Corps; and Friedman was given the leadership of the Signal Intelligence Service (SIS). He would lead the SIS team in "one of the most arduous, grinding, extended, and ultimately triumphant cryptanalyses in history"—the solving in 1940 of the Japanese Purple machine-cipher system.[5] The output from this breakthrough was disseminated under the code word of MAGIC.

Navy Intelligence. The overseas intelligence networks established by ONI during the war were largely dismantled by the budget cuts following the war. ONI directed its remaining resources primarily toward Japan, and used the naval attaché system to develop a core group of officers knowledgeable in the Japanese language and culture. The latter was a very foresighted program. Many of its graduates played key roles in Navy intelligence successes during World War II. Efforts to establish human intelligence networks in Japan during this period proved fruitless. In this information-starved environment, the Navy came to rely heavily on communications intelligence in following developments in the expanses of the Pacific region.

In 1924, a radio intelligence organization was set up in the Office of Naval Communication (ONC). Heading the organization was Lt. Laurance F. Safford, who would devote much of his career to building the unit (best known as OP-20-G) into an integral component of U.S. naval victories in World War II. Radio intercept sites were established in Hawaii and the Philippines and on Guam, and mobile intercept stations were placed on warships. To take advantage of the take from this eavesdropping on Japanese naval communications, the Navy began to hone its codebreaking skills. In the 1930s, OP-20-G was able to read Japanese naval systems with some regularity. Although ONI tried on several occasions to wrest the highly productive OP-20-G away from the Office of Naval Communication, it was not successful. This left Navy intelligence-gathering split between two commands rather than centralized in a single intelligence command. The same situation existed in the Army, with MID lacking any command authority over the Signal Intelligence Service.

FBI. Congress gave the Bureau of Investigation (after 1935, the Federal Bureau of Investigation or FBI) authority to conduct counterintelligence investigations in 1916. However, the Bureau's role immediately after World War I was less a matter of chasing foreign spies than it was addressing internal concerns associated with the violence being promulgated by anarchist and other radical political groups. As the potential for conflict in Europe and Asia rose through the 1930s, the focus tilted back toward the activities of foreign intelligence services in the United States. In 1939, President Roosevelt placed coordination of counterespionage activities with a committee consisting of the heads of the FBI, MID, and ONI, a move recognizing the military's counterintelligence responsibility with regard to service personnel and military bases.

In 1940, the President expanded the FBI's responsibilities to collecting nonmilitary foreign intelligence for the western hemisphere, except for the Panama Canal Zone. At the same time, the Army assumed responsibility for intelligence collection in Europe, Africa, and the Canal Zone; and the Navy took charge of collection in the Far East-Pacific region. In response to this new charge, FBI Director J. Edgar Hoover created a Special Intelligence Service to collect and analyze intelligence from the countries in Central and South America. Some of the FBI agents served in Latin America as "legal attachés" at U.S. embassies and consulates; others concealed their intelligence function, appearing to work at such jobs as journalists or salesmen for trading or other companies.

World War II

Even with a glaring gap in the collection of human intelligence, U.S. intelligence entered World War II on a stronger footing than had been the case in 1917. However, it was no better organized. Thanks to the assistance of a German-American double agent ostensibly working for German military intelligence, the FBI had neutralized the German espionage network in the United States by June 1940. This meant that America avoided the troubling level of subversion and sabotage encountered pre-World War I. In addition, both the Army's SIS and the Navy's OP-20-G were intercepting and reading substantial volumes of Japanese diplomatic and military traffic. Why, then, such complete surprise when the Japanese launched their attack on Pearl Harbor on December 7, 1941? That question will probably be debated as long as historians study war. Despite a wealth of conspiracy theories surrounding United States' lack of preparedness on that day, the plainest answer to the "Why" question has two parts. First, there was no single piece of intelligence that revealed the Japanese were going to attack Pearl Harbor on a specific date. And, second, no one was putting together the pieces of intelligence that did exist and that might have served as a warning. Or, to state it differently, there was no structure to coordinate the work and pull the product together into an analytic whole.

Perhaps, the best example of this dysfunctional situation is that, by agreement and to reduce the rush by each to be first to put their decrypts in front of the President, SIS was processing Japanese material on even-numbered days and OP-20-G on odd-numbered days. The take from that work, much of it focused on Japanese diplomatic traffic enciphered by the Purple system, was hand-carried to a small number of recipients in Washington, DC. The political and military leaders read the decrypts and returned them to the waiting messenger. The material then went back to its originating office where it was burned. As author James Bamford has noted, the technical side of intelligence, "particularly in the breaking of Purple, had been performed with genius, [but] the analytical side had become lost in disorganization."[6] Whether an intelligence failure, a failure of military command at multiple levels, or failure by the senior political leadership, the experience of Pearl Harbor has framed how Americans have thought about intelligence ever since. The theme of a lack of coordination and even cooperation among U.S. intelligence organizations would continue through the war and carry forward all the way to the present.

By the time America entered the fray, the war had been underway for over two years. Germany and the Soviet Union had divided Poland; the German army had occupied Belgium, Luxembourg, the Netherlands, and most of France; the German air force had launched a massive aerial assault on London; Germany had invaded Russia; and Japan had seized French Indochina and was deep into its four-year-old war in China. Following their attack on Pearl Harbor, the Japanese overran Burma, Hong Kong, Malaya, Thailand, the Dutch East Indies, and the American possessions of Wake Island, Guam, and the Philippine Islands. The war fought by the United States between 1941 and 1945 was in some ways two wars—one in Europe and another in the Pacific. Each war can also be seen as consisting of multiple levels that were influenced by different intelligence components and activities.

The War for Europe. Intelligence by itself cannot be said to win wars. It can, however, do much to ease the load of those who must fight the wars. Such was the case in Europe, where Britain's ability to read German military communications played a significant role. During the 1930s, Polish intelligence had been able to read the German military's communications enciphered on the Enigma machine. The Poles passed their knowledge to the British before Germany and Russia dismembered their country. Working from this base, the Government Code & Cypher School (GC&CS, later GCHQ) devised electromechanical machines (Bombes) that, together with reconstructed Enigma machines and some captured cipher materials, allowed the British to read Germany's most secret military communications. The take from the Enigma machine spawned a new code word for high-level communications intelligence—ULTRA.

The sharing of the British ULTRA and the U.S. MAGIC began in early 1941, before the United States entered the war. The cooperation between the countries also included Australia and Canada, and would grow into a full-scale agreement on sharing communications intelligence technology, product, and workload (the BRUSA Agreement). The basic thrust of this agreement remains in effect. The intelligence from Enigma played a major support role in the Battle of the Atlantic. The transatlantic shipping lanes were vital to the war effort in terms of supplying Britain and in moving the U.S. Army to its Mediterranean and European staging areas. Germany's effort to break that link was led by its submarine forces ("wolf packs"). Because the U-boats had to surface to communicate by radio with the naval commander, their transmissions and those of German headquarters could be intercepted. The intelligence obtained from reading the German ciphers, especially when combined with the ability of OP-20-G's network of high-frequency direction finding (HF/DF or "huffduff") stations to quickly pinpoint the location of transmitters, was a potent weapon. The Allies could direct convoys away from where the U-boats were and target the submarines and their supply vessels with antisubmarine ships and airplanes.

Earlier, as war engulfed Europe, President Roosevelt had sent William J. Donovan, a World War I hero and Wall Street lawyer, to Europe to assess Britain's ability to survive the German onslaught. Donovan's recommendation—developed with support from the head of British intelligence in the United States, William Stephenson—was to establish a centralized organization to control foreign intelligence activities, including covert action. Roosevelt stopped short of such a sweeping move, instead creating the position of Coordinator of Information (COI) and giving Donovan the job. However, the continuing absence of coordination is illustrated by the fact that, at the time of Pearl Harbor, Donovan was not receiving the MAGIC decrypts. He was, however, in the process of building an organization designed to produce strategic intelligence (collection and analysis) and to initiate clandestine operations. In June 1942, Donovan and his office formally became the Office of Strategic Services (OSS), working under the Joint Chiefs of Staff.

Although the existing players in the intelligence game opposed its creation, OSS would grow into a full-service human intelligence and covert action organization. In the process, it added significantly to U.S.-British intelligence collaboration—but not particularly to cooperation among American intelligence components. The FBI, Army, and Navy all retained their specific intelligence functions; and Gen. Douglas MacArthur had his own intelligence units in the Southwest Pacific. One of the first tests for the OSS was supporting Operation TORCH, the British-American invasion of North Africa in November 1942. OSS officers recruited agents from among local tribal leaders and sympathetic French military, police, and administrative personnel; and their reporting helped frame the landing areas. In addition, OSS provided guides at beaches for the landing troops. At one of the landing areas, an OSS agent removed the fuses from demolition charges in a tunnel connecting the beach with the city. The tunnel "was vital to Allied movement and it was estimated that it would have required three months to rebuild."[7]

Often working with their counterparts in Britain's Special Operations Executive (SOE), OSS teams used both parachutes and rubber rafts to infiltrate the German-occupied countries of Europe, from Greece, to Italy, to the Balkans, to Norway, and to France. These teams worked with local resistance groups in mounting opposition to the occupiers. OSS personnel provided these groups training and arms, coordinated the local groups' sabotage and guerrilla-style operations, and when necessary fought alongside them. The best known of the teams are the combined SOE-OSS-French Jedburghs. Both before and after D-Day, the Jedburghs parachuted behind German lines in France to meet up with the resistance forces. As a future Director of Central Intelligence, William E. Colby, described it years later, the mission of his Jedburgh Team Bruce was to organize "an uprising of French resistance groups so as to wreck the maximum havoc in the German rear and undermine German defense against the advancing Allied armies."[8]

The OSS also enjoyed success in intelligence collection against the Axis states. The stations in the neutral countries of Sweden, Spain, and Switzerland created agent networks that reached into the occupied countries and into Germany itself. Future Director of Central Intelligence Allen Dulles, working out of the Bern station in Switzerland, managed agents providing a wide range of intelligence on Italy and Germany. Reporting from Bern included German order-of-battle; technical information on submarine production, aircraft defenses, and work on the V-1 and V-2 missiles; and early reports about Germany's research in gas and germ warfare. Fritz Kolbe (codenamed "Wood"), who worked in the German Foreign Office, provided thousands of documents of significant military and political value.[9] The breadth of the roles of the OSS is illustrated by one of Dulles' last acts in Bern, when in April 1945 he arranged negotiations for the surrender of the German forces in northern Italy.

Beyond supporting resistance groups and gathering on-the-ground information in Germany and the occupied countries, Allied intelligence was also an integral part of the success of D-Day. The British made many contributions to that endeavor, but two intelligence coups and the relationship between them stand out. Achieving tactical surprise was an essential ingredient in the planning for Operation Overlord. Hitler knew the attack was coming, but he did not know where. Intelligence helped keep it that way.

In the earliest days of the war, British counterintelligence had completely rolled up the German espionage network in Britain. In addition, a number of the German agents were "turned"; that is, they went to work for the British. Thus was born the now famous Double-Cross System of the British Security Service (MI5). Throughout the war, these double agents provided a mixture of true and false information to the German military intelligence service. As Sir John Cecil Masterman, who headed the Twenty or XX Committee, put it, "by means of the double agent system *we actively ran and controlled the German espionage system*" in Great Britain.[10] The Double-Cross System worked with precision because of Britain's other great coup—the intelligence product from reading German military communications. ULTRA allowed the Allies to confirm that German intelligence believed and was acting on the information being sent by the Double-Cross agents. The reporting of these agents was part of an elaborate deception plan (Bodyguard) designed to hide the date, time, and place of the D-Day landing. The plan was so successful that even after the landings took place in Normandy, the German High Command continued to look for the main invasion force well away from the actual landing sites.

Another area where World War II saw significant advances in intelligence collection was in photographic intelligence (PHOTINT). This came about through the marriage of the airplane and photography and the accompanying development of the art and science of photointerpretation. In 1941, the Army centralized management of its air units in the Army Air Forces, with a separate intelligence division (A-2). During the war, A-2 and the air staffs of subordinate commands provided commanders with a range of reconnaissance intelligence from both high-altitude bombers (target identification and bomb-damage assessment) and high-speed interceptor aircraft (tactical intelligence support to ground forces).

The War in the Pacific. The alternating-day method of producing the MAGIC decrypts of Japanese diplomatic traffic did not last much beyond Pearl Harbor. The Navy agreed that SIS would be solely responsible for working on Japanese diplomatic traffic. The Army, then, centralized the whole process for handling MAGIC from interception to analysis under the control of the Special Branch of Military Intelligence (G-2). OP-20-G was left to focus on naval communications, but that was not a small task. Before the year was over, naval codebreakers would be producing intelligence of such importance that it helped shorten the war.

Immediately after the Japanese attack, OP-20-G directed a unit at Pearl Harbor (later named Fleet Radio Unit, Pacific Fleet—FRUPac) to concentrate on the latest variant of a Japanese fleet cryptographic system known as JN25. By April 1942, the cryptanalysts under Lt. Cdr. Joseph John Rochefort were reading enough of the traffic to understand that the Japanese were planning to seize Port Moresby in New Guinea and, thereby, threaten Australia. At the battle of the Coral Sea in May, this thrust was turned back. And, then, came the big breakthrough—the discovery that Japan's next target was Midway Island, a small but strategic atoll in the middle of the North Pacific. Within a week of when the battle plan was broadcast to the Japanese fleet, Adm. Chester W. Nimitz, Commander in Chief of the U.S. Pacific Fleet, had virtually the full text in his hands. Nimitz placed his much smaller force of three carriers north of Midway, and on the morning of June 4, 1942, launched his planes against the Japanese fleet. The battle of Midway was won by the men in the U.S. ships and planes—four Japanese carriers lost to the Americans one—but the fleet was in place at the right time because of the work of the Navy codebreakers. Two months later, the U.S. Army landed in Guadalcanal in the first step of the island-hopping offensive that would take it ever closer to the Philippines and Japan itself.

Even before the fall of the Philippines to the Japanese, Gen. Douglas MacArthur had reconstituted his headquarters for the Southwest Pacific Theater in Australia. Rejecting a role by the OSS in coordinating Allied intelligence in the Southwest Pacific, MacArthur established his own intelligence agency. The Allied Intelligence Bureau (AIB) was a joint venture with the Australians and was responsible for coordinating intelligence and covert action activities for American, Australian, British, and Dutch units throughout the area of operations. The AIB answered to MacArthur's chief intelligence officer, but was headed by the Australian Army's Director of Intelligence. Among the units under AIB's jurisdiction was the Australian Navy's Coastwatching Service. The coastwatchers made a singular contribution to the Allied offensive from Guadalcanal to the Philippines. Coastwatchers included Australians who had worked in the islands before the war—missionaries, farmers, and schoolteachers, among others—as well as natives of the Solomon and other islands. They reported by radio on their observation of Japanese ship and aircraft movements. These observations were a critical component in the intelligence available to Allied planners as they prepared and executed the Pacific campaign. Coastwatchers also aided in the rescue of American air and naval crews downed or sunk in Japanese-held territory. For example, a coastwatcher was involved in the rescue of John F. Kennedy and his crew after the sinking of PT 109.

The Navy cryptanalysts who had evacuated from Manila in January 1942 were already operating from Australia (Fleet Radio Unit, Melbourne—FRUMel) when MacArthur arrived. Nevertheless, he established his own communications intelligence unit—the Central Bureau. The unit combined Australian Army and Air Force codebreakers with personnel from the Signal Intelligence Service (SIS). Central Bureau cryptanalysts, together with their stateside SIS colleagues, were part of the breakthrough in January 1944 that finally provided continuing access to the Japanese Army's communications. Although the Central Bureau would disappear at the end of the war, its successes "rivaled similar efforts in any theater in World War II."[11]

While blocked from working in the Pacific (Nimitz) and Southwest Pacific (MacArthur) theaters, the OSS was active in the China-Burma-India (CBI) Theater. Detachment 101 parachuted into northern Burma in early 1943 and spread out from there. In cooperation with indigenous Kachin tribesmen, the OSS group engaged in an effective guerrilla war against the Japanese occupation forces. By mid-1944, Detachment 101 and its Kachin warriors had helped Gen. Joseph W. Stilwell gain control of the territory needed to link up China to the Burma Road and a land connection to the outside world. In China, an OSS target analysis group produced vital data for Gen. Claire Chennault's Fourteenth Air Force in its bombing campaign against the Japanese. Other OSS personnel operated with mixed success in Indochina and Thailand. When the war ended, OSS teams were dropped into Manchuria to gather intelligence and assist in the release of Japanese-held prisoners of war, including Gen. Jonathan Wainwright, captured when Corregidor fell.

As impressive as intelligence's contribution to the overall war effort was, it is still possible to wonder what might have been achieved if there had been greater coordination among the services. Continual foot-dragging and outright hostility from the FBI, Army, and Navy marked the organizational life of OSS. The services, in turn, carried on turf battles among themselves throughout the war. British liaison personnel involved in the MAGIC-ULTRA exchanges often felt that they achieved better cooperation from their American counterparts than the U.S. services accorded each other. Some historians have suggested that Army Air Force intelligence (A-2) might have performed better if it had not faced continuing jurisdictional disputes with the main Army intelligence staff (G-2) in Europe and with the Navy (N-2) in the Pacific. Most of these disputes were settled by compromises that allowed the work to go forward, but really did not resolve the core issues. The period after the war saw this approach repeated.

The Intelligence Community

The Cold War

The Cold War was waged on many fronts, in many ways, and by many different components of the American government. It ranged across the world—from

Europe, to Asia, to Latin America, to Africa, to the American home front. It included shooting wars, the overthrow of governments, monetary support to other governments and to independent groups, assistance in aid and training to peoples in countries that many had trouble finding on a map, help from human beings on the other side, and initiative and innovation in technology. Its heroes came from among Presidents, diplomats, all ranks of the uniformed services, American industry, and the members of what we now call the Intelligence Community.

As World War II ended, America faced the question of what to do with its enormous war machine. It initially reacted in its traditional pattern—it demobilized. Simultaneously, it began to dismantle the elaborate intelligence structure that had been created to help wage a world war. President Truman and his advisers grappled with the question of whether the country needed an intelligence structure and, if so, what kind. Truman's initial answer seemed to doom the role of centralized intelligence in postwar America. He dismembered OSS. The analysis unit was sent to the State Department (where it became the Bureau of Intelligence and Research—INR). The secret intelligence and counterintelligence activities were housed, first, in a caretaker organization in the War Department and, later, in the Central Intelligence Group (CIG) under the joint control of the State, War, and Navy departments. The ensuing chaos in the intelligence getting to the President's desk, the legacy of the surprise attack on Pearl Harbor, and growing concerns about expansion by the Soviet Union into Western Europe overcame Truman's antipathy toward a permanent intelligence organization.

In addition to the debate about what do with the intelligence function, the period immediately after the war was a time of intense bickering among the armed services. While military budgets were shrinking, it was becoming clear that the United States needed a new national defense strategy to accommodate the changed situation in the world and the coming of the atomic age. The Air Force wanted to be a separate service, equal to the Army and Navy; and it wanted a national strategy that put the emphasis on air power. The Navy was fearful of losing its air arm and the opportunity to build supersized carriers. The Army believed that any new war would require a mass army, which meant that universal military training (and the costs attendant to it) was a necessity.

Recognition of the need for coordination between the War and Navy departments and for a system for coordinating intelligence led to passage of the National Security Act of 1947. Together with its amendments in 1949, the Act transformed the U.S. national security structure. However, the decisions made then were the result of compromises, and further bureaucratic and political compromises have followed. On the military side, the legislative actions created an independent Air Force; established the position of Secretary of Defense, with the three services existing as individual departments within the unified Department of Defense; and linked the three services through a system of joint committees coordinated by the service chiefs sitting as the Joint Chiefs of Staff (JCS) and presided over by the JCS Chairman. Other reforms followed in succeeding years, almost all aimed at increasing the authority of the Defense Secretary and improving coordination and cooperation among the services—at increasing "jointness," in today's terms.

The 1947 Act also created the Central Intelligence Agency (CIA), America's first peacetime, civilian intelligence organization, and established the position of Director of Central Intelligence (DCI). For the next fifty-seven years, until passage of the Intelligence Reform and Terrorism Prevention Act of 2004, the DCI would head the CIA, serve as the President's chief intelligence adviser, and theoretically coordinate U.S. intelligence activities. Success in the latter endeavor was highly dependent on circumstances and personalities, as the DCI controlled neither the personnel nor the budgets of the greater part of the Intelligence Community. The original legislation assigned the CIA the function of serving as the nation's primary organization for gathering, processing, analyzing, and disseminating foreign intelligence to policymakers. As tensions grew in the early Cold War years, that role expanded to include responsibility for covert political and paramilitary activities abroad and for the research and development of such technical collection systems as the U-2 and SR-71 spy planes and reconnaissance satellites.

The entity created in 1947 to integrate national security policy matters was the National Security Council (NSC). A part of the Executive Office of the President, the NSC reviews, guides, and directs the conduct of the nation's foreign intelligence and counterintelligence activities. The director of the NSC is the Assistant to the President for National Security Affairs (also referred to as the National Security Adviser). The manner in which the NSC and its staff have been used over the years has changed multiple times to meet the needs of individual presidents, but it remains at the center of the national security coordination process.

At the same time, other changes were taking place in the organizational arrangement of U.S. intelligence. In 1949, the military services lost much of their communications intelligence and communications security responsibilities to the Armed Forces Security Agency (AFSA), a unit formed under the Joint Chiefs of Staff. However, a poor performance before and during the Korean War led to the transformation of AFSA into a civilian agency directly under the Secretary of Defense. An executive order in 1952 created the National Security Agency (NSA), the largest agency in the U.S. Intelligence Community. NSA's responsibilities include exploiting foreign signals intelligence and making the nation's communications secure. Thus, NSA is the nation's primary codebreaking and codemaking organization.

Confronted with communist expansionism in Europe and Asia in the first fifteen years after the war, Presidents Truman and Eisenhower countered with covert operations supporting groups opposing the communists. Psychological and political activities in Italy in 1948 were instrumental in preventing a communist victory in that country's national elections. A similar success in arming anticommunist forces during the civil war in Greece raised the hopes of policymakers that they had a "third option" to diplomacy or war in preventing the spread of communism. However, efforts to support anticommunist groups in Poland, Ukraine, the Baltic States, and Albania failed to limit the control of those areas by either the Soviets or their surrogates.

It is difficult to place precisely the blame for the failure to anticipate the North Korean attack in June 1950. General MacArthur, commander of U.S. forces in the Far East, had excluded the CIA from working in Japan and Korea. AFSA had not made North Korea a priority target for collection of communications intelligence. (Intelligence agencies normally do not make up their own requirements but respond to the needs of their main "consumers"; for AFSA, this was the Joint Chiefs of Staff.) There is little indication that Army intelligence at MacArthur's headquarters in Tokyo had a significant human collection program targeted on Pyongyang. There were certainly bits and pieces of information that might have tipped off that an attack was coming, but there was no one place where these pieces came together. The "surprise" of the Chinese intervention as MacArthur's forces approached the Yalu River border with China is easier to identify as a field intelligence and command failure. The Korean War lasted until 1953, but it became clear early in conflict that demobilization had severely drained the military services of trained intelligence personnel. There were shortages in linguists capable in the Korean and Chinese languages to support interrogation of prisoners of war or to translate the take from the interception of enemy communications. Even aerial reconnaissance suffered from too few personnel, planes, and facilities. Nevertheless, aerial reconnaissance saw a number of innovations in the Korean War. These included the use of aerial color photography (which aids photointerpreters in differentiating types of terrain) and of the panoramic camera (for a broader, horizon-to-horizon picture).

During and after the shooting war in Korea, U.S. policymakers remained committed to the use of covert tactics to resist communism elsewhere in the world. In 1953, the CIA backed a coup d'etat in Iran, toppling a communist-supported prime minister and returning the Shah to power. The next year, the CIA was the funding source for a military junta that overthrew a Guatemalan president seen in Washington as under communist influence. The United States also assisted the Filipino armed forces in developing the counterinsurgency program that defeated the communist Huk insurgents' effort to overthrow the Philippine government. However, in 1956 the Soviet Union crushed a Hungarian revolt that some believe had been encouraged by the CIA-funded Radio Free Europe. In 1958, there was an unsuccessful covert action in Indonesia; and the next year, a long-lasting effort began in Tibet.

When the USSR exploded a nuclear device in 1949, collection of information about the Russians' capability to use their weapons against the West became one of the America's top intelligence targets. Efforts included: Recruitment and infiltration of agents into the Soviet Union (largely unsuccessful); U.S. and British air force flights along and even penetration of Russia's borders (this was one of the areas where the Cold War was closer to hot, as these "ferret" flights were subject to attack and losses of planes and crew occurred); and the release of unmanned high-altitude balloons equipped with cameras. None of these efforts produced sufficient information to improve the policymakers' comfort level. To provide better data from within the Soviet Union, the CIA and Lockheed Aircraft

Company developed the U-2 reconnaissance aircraft.[12] The aircraft was designed to fly at altitudes above Soviet interception capability, and its new generation of cameras provided remarkably detailed photographs. The U-2 flights over the Soviet Union began in 1956, and continued until Francis Gary Powers' plane was shot down in May 1960. Unaware of the espionage flights, many Americans found the U-2 incident disconcerting, especially when President Eisenhower initially sought to deny the plane's true mission. Cancellation of further flights by the President created an appearance of a significant loss of strategic intelligence on the Soviet military posture. However, except for the negative public relations associated with the shoot-down, there was less concern than might otherwise have been the case.

In early 1958, President Eisenhower had assigned the CIA responsibility for Project CORONA—to develop a photographic reconnaissance satellite employing a recoverable capsule system for the return of film to the earth. The first successful return of a film capsule occurred in August 1960. Coupled with the launch of a much smaller signals intelligence satellite (GRAB—for capturing Soviet radar emissions) a few months earlier, this was the beginning of the space age for American intelligence. Jeffrey T. Richelson views the photoreconnaissance satellite as "one of the most important military technological developments" of the twentieth century.[13] The success of CORONA and the existence of competing Air Force, Army, and Navy satellite systems led Eisenhower to establish a new member of the intelligence community—the National Reconnaissance Office (NRO). The NRO was created as a separate, national-level agency within the Department of Defense, but with the CIA continuing to have a substantial role in managing and developing space reconnaissance systems. Operational and budgetary control of the NRO remained a point of contention between the Defense Department and the CIA until the mid-1990s, when the CIA's role was considerably diminished. Today, the NRO remains responsible for designing, developing, procuring, and, once they are in orbit, operating all U.S. reconnaissance satellites. It spends the most money of all the intelligence agencies. The organization's existence was officially a secret until 1992.

President John F. Kennedy came to office in 1961 with a strong affinity for developing U.S. unconventional warfare capabilities as an alternative to conventional warfare in confronting communist insurgencies. Despite the failure of the CIA-funded invasion of Cuba by Cuban expatriates at the Bay of Pigs soon after he took office, Kennedy supported the CIA's large paramilitary operation in Laos, where tribesmen were recruited, trained, and armed for both guerrilla and conventional warfare. Control of U.S. paramilitary assistance to the South Vietnamese was passed from the CIA, working with the Army's Special Forces, to the Joint Chiefs of Staff in 1963 as the conflict moved toward a more conventional war.

In August 1961, Defense Secretary Robert McNamara added yet another new component to the U.S. Intelligence Community—the Defense Intelligence Agency (DIA). The goal was to consolidate the production of intelligence analysis by the military and to create a single source of intelligence support to the Secretary and the JCS. Like many reforms, this one did not turn out exactly as planned. A single DIA representative replaced the three services on the DCI's advisory board that coordinates intelligence activities; but the services retained substantial intelligence organizations, including their own analytical capabilities.

U.S. intelligence enjoyed a high point during the Cuban Missile Crisis in October 1962. Reconnaissance satellites and U-2 aircraft, together with the CIA's National Photographic Interpretation Center (NPIC), played crucial roles in supporting the Kennedy administration with the intelligence necessary to underpin a resolution of that tense moment in the Cold War. As the Vietnam War came to dominate Washington policy discussions, it was clear that intelligence agencies had differing views on the potential for achievement of U.S. goals in an endeavor that was increasingly splitting American public opinion. Analysis of how well the United States was doing in Vietnam became a hotly contested matter. CIA and INR analysts often tended to view the war less optimistically than the military services and the administration itself.

The post-Vietnam and Watergate period brought intense scrutiny from Congress, the media, and the public of a range of questionable activities by the intelligence agencies (from surveillance of and eavesdropping on U.S. citizens, to attempted assassinations of foreign leaders, to experimentation in mind-altering drugs). Although the CIA absorbed much of the attention at the time, the Congressional investigations of the mid-1970s were broader than a single agency; other intelligence components—Army Intelligence, the FBI, and NSA—were also subjected to close questioning. A committee chaired by Sen. Frank Church, an Idaho Democrat, conducted the best known of the investigations. The investigations led Congress to strengthen its oversight mechanisms for the Intelligence Community as a whole, but especially the CIA, by establishing both Senate and House intelligence committees.[14]

In the 1980s, President Ronald Reagan and his successor, George H.W. Bush, actively used the CIA to supply covert support to the indigenous groups confronting the Soviet forces in Afghanistan. During the Reagan administration, staff members of the National Security Council became directly involved in covert action operations of a type not previously engaged in by that body. These activities led to the Iran-Contra scandal. The CIA's close association with the Contra forces in Nicaragua in the face of Congressional opposition and its links to the secret arms sales to Iran subjected the agency to considerable criticism at the very time that the Cold War was drawing to a close.

Post-Cold War

When the red flag with gold hammer and sickle was replaced over the Kremlin with the white-blue-and-red tricolor flag of pre-Revolutionary Russia on December 26, 1991, the Soviet Union was no more; and the Cold War was truly over. The demise of the Soviet Union led some to question the need for continuing the large and expensive intelligence apparatus that had grown up in the preceding forty-six years. While the immediate post-Cold War period certainly saw a shift in public interest from international matters to domestic priorities, the hopes for a "peace dividend" did not last long. The 1991 Persian Gulf War convinced some top military leaders that the existing national-level intelligence-collection capabilities did not meet the military's war-fighting needs. This led to a greater focus on tactical and operational systems by the Defense Department, which continues to control the vast majority of U.S. intelligence resources.

At this time of intense questioning, the CIA and the FBI had their worst nightmares—both internally and with regard to public image—come true with a genuine counterintelligence debacle. Beginning with the arrest in 1994 of Aldrich Ames, a career CIA officer, and concluding with the uncovering in February 2001 of Robert Philip Hanssen, an FBI counterintelligence officer, at least four serving or retired employees of the two organizations were found to be spies for the old Soviet Union and the new Russia. Both Ames and Hanssen had been long-term Russian spies and had provided the types of intelligence that led to the arrest and execution of U.S. agents in Russia. As the lead agency for preventing and exposing the activities of foreign intelligence agencies in the United States, these were particularly galling times for the FBI.

In late 1993, the Defense Department announced the centralization of military human intelligence assets and activities in the new Defense HUMINT Service (DHS) within the Defense Intelligence Agency. By October 1995, the DHS had achieved "initial operational capacity," meaning that the transfer of functions, personnel, and resources previously spread among the armed services had been completed. Its mission is to conduct human intelligence operations worldwide. This is a clear challenge to the CIA's previous monopoly in the use of spies for collecting intelligence beyond military theaters of operation.

In 1996, the military's concerns about a lack of useful and timely satellite intelligence from the national agencies resulted in the creation of another new component of the Intelligence Community—the National Imagery and Mapping Agency (NIMA). In a contentious move, the new organization absorbed in whole or part eight defense and intelligence components, placing them under the control of the Defense Department. The CIA was stripped of its National Photographic Interpretation Center (NPIC), and the DIA lost its Directorate for Imagery Exploitation. Among the controversial aspects of this bureaucratic juggling act was the bringing together in a single administrative body of the disparate disciplines of mapmaking and photographic interpretation. In 2003, NIMA's name was officially changed to the National Geospatial-Intelligence Agency (NGA).

A Time of Change

The ongoing changes in the Intelligence Community were accelerated by the terrorist attacks on the American homeland on September 11, 2001 (9/11). Whether better coordination between the CIA and the FBI could have prevented the terrorists' acts will be debated well into the future. Nevertheless, a major revamping of U.S. intelligence has resulted from the recommendations of multiple groups that have reviewed both the 9/11 attacks and the intelligence about weapons of mass destruction (WMD) used by President George W. Bush in deciding to invade Iraq.

Barely more than a year after 9/11, Congress mandated the largest reorganization in the U.S. government since the Defense Department was created in 1947. The establishment of the Department of Homeland Security (DHS) in 2002 brought together in a single administrative structure some 170,000 employees from twenty-two agencies. DHS's Office of Intelligence and Analysis is a member of the Intelligence Community (IC), and is responsible for using intelligence collected by other IC components to identify and assess current and future threats to the U.S. homeland. One of its components—the U.S. Coast Guard—is a separate IC member, while the U.S. Secret Service, another agency swept into DHS, is not. The size and scope of this reorganization has presented enormous challenges to those charged with implementing it. The problems associated with the Hurricane Katrina disaster are the best known, but integration and coordination in other areas remain less than complete.

The challenges faced by the Homeland Security Secretary are in some ways mirrored by those confronting the other new kid on the block. The Director of

The Intelligence Community

There are sixteen members of the U.S. Intelligence Community (seventeen if you count the Office of the Director of National Intelligence):

There is one independent Executive Branch agency—the Central Intelligence Agency (CIA).

Eight members are Department of Defense departmental components—the Defense Intelligence Agency (DIA); the National Security Agency (NSA); the National Geospatial-Intelligence Agency (NGA); the National Reconnaissance Office (NRO); and Army, Navy, Air Force, and Marine Corps intelligence organizations.

Two members are part of the Department of Justice—the Federal Bureau of Investigation (FBI) and the Office of National Security Intelligence in the Drug Enforcement Administration (DEA).

Two members are Department of Homeland Security components—U.S. Coast Guard Intelligence and the Office of Intelligence and Analysis.

There is one member each from the Departments of State, Energy, and Treasury—Department of State, Bureau of Intelligence and Research (INR); Department of Energy, Office of Intelligence; and Department of Treasury, Office of Terrorism and Financial Intelligence.

National Intelligence (DNI) has the task of coordinating an Intelligence Community that historically has resisted being centrally managed. The Intelligence Reform and Terrorism Prevention Act of 2004 abolishes the position of Director of Central Intelligence (DCI), who was both head of the CIA and charged with coordination of the Intelligence Community, replacing it with two new jobs: a DNI separate from any one agency and a CIA Director. Substantial concerns continue to surround this arrangement. Some see the DNI as just another layer in the bureaucracy. (See sidebar "*The Intelligence Community*.") There is also doubt that the legislation has significantly altered the realities of an Intelligence Community, the greatest part of the personnel and budget of which remains in the control of the Defense Secretary.

While reorganizations of bureaucracies have been going on in Washington, the military services and intelligence agencies have been waging a war against terrorism. Ongoing activities include collecting intelligence about terrorist groups worldwide, assisting other countries in their counterterrorism efforts, and taking direct actions against al Qaeda operatives. The CIA's Northern Afghanistan Liaison Team deployed for Afghanistan on September 19, 2001, only eight days after the 9/11 attacks. Team members worked with tribal elements to support the actions of U.S. Special Operations Forces (SOF) and the use of airpower in removing the Taliban government and its client al Qaeda forces from power.[15]

In the search for additional weapons in this new kind of war, the Predator Unmanned Aerial Vehicle (UAV) has been modified from its original intelligence, surveillance, and reconnaissance (ISR) form into a "hunter-killer" by the inclusion of Hellfire missiles that can be remotely fired. In this configuration, the operator can be seated at a console somewhere in the United States while manipulating a UAV halfway around the world. In one acknowledged use of this new weapon, a missile launched from a CIA-controlled Predator killed a senior al Qaeda leader riding in a car in Yemen in November 2002. Such pinpoint targeting requires human intelligence from the scene in order to know that the individual was in that vehicle at that time.

Special Operations Forces (SOF) is another weapon the role of which is expanding in the war on terrorism. The Special Operations Command (SOCOM) reports to the Defense Secretary, and is not part of the Intelligence Community structure overseen by the DNI. The Defense Secretary's designation of SOCOM as the lead element in planning the war on terror has led to some friction within the national security apparatus. As special operators increasingly engage in the type of covert activities that for the CIA have required a specific Presidential mandate (called a "finding") and notification of Congress, the absence of a similar requirement for military-initiated activities has generated concern.

The last several years have been a time of upheaval and change for U.S. intelligence. Whether new agencies, reorganizations, and reallocation of responsibilities will produce a tighter managed and more effective Intelligence Community remains to be seen. Given the track record of America's past, further change seems likely. In any event, issues such as the ongoing war on terrorism, Iranian and North Korean pretensions to nuclear weapons, the prevention of even further proliferation of nuclear capabilities, unrest in many corners of the former Soviet Union, the growing role of China in world affairs, continuing conflict in the Middle East, and a host of others, some of which are at present unforeseen, argue that American intelligence activities will be needed as part of protecting the nation's national security well into the future.

Notes

1. See U.S. Central Intelligence Agency, *Intelligence in the War of Independence* (Washington, DC: 1976), https://www.cia.gov/cia/publications/warindep/index.html.

2. Edwin C. Fishel, *The Secret War for the Union: The Untold Story of Military Intelligence in the Civil War* (Boston, MA: Houghton Mifflin, 1996), 298–299.

3. See George J.A. O'Toole, *Honorable Treachery: A History of U.S. Intelligence, Espionage, and Covert Action from the American Revolution to the CIA* (New York: Atlantic Monthly Press, 1991), 188–200.

4. See Herbert O. Yardley, *The American Black Chamber* (Indianapolis, IN: Bobbs-Merrill, 1931), 283–317.

5. David Kahn, *The Codebreakers: The Comprehensive History of Secret Communication from Ancient Times to the Internet*, rev. ed. (New York: Scribner, 1996), 389.

6. James Bamford, *The Puzzle Palace: A Report on America's Most Secret Agency* (New York: Penguin, 1983), 58.

7. Anthony Cave Brown, ed., *The Secret War Report of the OSS* (New York: Berkley, 1976), 145.

8. William E. Colby, with Peter Forbath, *Honorable Men: My Life in the CIA* (New York: Simon & Schuster, 1978), 25.

9. Bradley F. Smith, *The Shadow Warriors: O.S.S. and the Origins of the C.I.A.* (New York: Basic Books, 1983), 223–224.

10. John Cecil Masterman, *The Double-Cross System in the War of 1939–1945* (New Haven & London: Yale University Press, 1972), 3. [Emphasis in original]

11. Edward J. Drea, *MacArthur's ULTRA: Codebreaking and the War against Japan, 1942–1945* (Lawrence, KS: University Press of Kansas, 1992), 226.

12. See Gregory W. Pedlow and Donald E. Welzenbach, *The CIA and the U2 Program, 1954–1974* (Washington, DC: History Staff, Center for the Study of Intelligence, Central Intelligence Agency, 1998), https://www.cia.gov/csi/books/U2/index.htm.

13. Jeffrey T. Richelson, *America's Secret Eyes in Space: The U.S. Keyhole Spy Satellite Program* (New York: HarperCollins, 1990), vi. See also Jeffrey T. Richelson, *The Wizards of Langley: Inside the CIA's Directorate of Science and Technology* (Boulder, CO: Westview, 2002).

14. See Loch K. Johnson, *A Season of Inquiry: The Senate Intelligence Investigation* (Lexington, KY: University Press of Kentucky, 1985).

15. See Gary Berntsen and Ralph Pezzullo, *Jawbreaker: The Attack on Bin Laden and Al Qaeda: A Personal Account by the CIA's Key Field Commander* (New York: Crown, 2005); and Gary C. Schroen, *First In: An Insider's Account of How the CIA Spearheaded the War on Terror in Afghanistan* (Novato, CA: Presidio, 2005).

CHAPTER 2

How Do We Get Intelligence?

Deciding What to Get

There is a tendency among Americans to equate intelligence with spies in much the same way as thriller writers do. This is because spying has an air of excitement that all the hard work of a team of cryptanalysts intent on breaking a hostile country's code cannot duplicate. Spy-versus-spy is "sexy," while the photo interpreter seated in a windowless room and pouring over the image of what might be a new nuclear-weapons production facility sounds dull. That is a mistake, not in terms of what makes enthralling fiction but in terms of describing the true nature of intelligence.

The multiple components of the U.S. Intelligence Community collect, process, analyze, and disseminate their products in many different ways for many different consumers. In doing so, however, they seek to be responsive to the needs of the users of their products. In the intelligence business, needs are expressed in terms of requirements and priorities. Priorities are necessary because, despite an Intelligence Community budget that is estimated at some $44 billion, neither the money nor the people are available to respond to all requests for information from every interested government or military official on every possible subject.

The interests of top-level policymakers can play a significant role in what resources are available to the intelligence agencies and how those resources are distributed and used. In the late 1970s, for example, National Security Adviser Zbigniew Brzezinski's emphasis on the importance of the Soviet constituent republics and nationalities, particularly those in the southern tier, led to an infusion of additional resources and a realignment of existing dollars to increase coverage of those areas. Given the breakup of the Soviet Union ten years later, such a reprioritization of requirements appears foresighted. But Brzezinski did not task individual agencies with collecting and analyzing specific pieces of intelligence; rather, the agencies presented their ideas of how they might respond to the requirement for more and better intelligence on the target area. Congress, then, appropriated new money for selected programs, not for specific items of information. However, the requirements process is rarely this simple.

There are, of course, many levels of requirements. The military services with their well-established chains of command handle the communication of intelligence needs upward and downward with greater facility than their civilian counterparts, especially at the tactical and operational levels. Because of the complexity of the national-level intelligence process, with each collection and production agency seeking a monopoly of its individual discipline, requirements serve the purpose of trying to get everyone on the same page. The tendency of agencies to want to control their process and product through the whole intelligence cycle has led to the main producers in the Intelligence Community being labeled "stovepipes." The image is appropriate. Nonetheless, the importance of requirements should not be underestimated, as they set the stage for the collection and analysis that will follow.

Michael Turner sees the main issues on the national security agenda as being established through "an interactive bargaining process among three environments: the policy world, the bureaucratic dynamics of the intelligence community, and the intelligence collectors and analysts."[1] Certainly, policymakers will on occasion step into the process and seek to redirect the focus of the intelligence agencies toward an area not in the headlines, as with Brzezinski and the Soviet nationalities issue. But the really big issues are usually clear to everyone in the needs-response chain. That the United States is deeply interested in the countries that may be seeking to acquire nuclear weapons and the capability to deliver them should not be a surprise. Policymakers make such top-level needs evident through speeches, press briefings, and other actions designed to alert the public more than the intelligence agencies to an area of concern. They can also take a more direct approach to aid in establishing priorities for the direction and division of resources. One example is Presidential Decision Directive 35 (PDD-35) on "Intelligence Requirements," signed by President Bill Clinton in 1995. As the President's press spokesman noted at the time, "How you structure the priorities of the intelligence community to reflect the new threats that are more urgent in the post-Cold War world is part of what . . . this directive [is] all about."[2]

One of the more controversial aspects of PDD-35 was the assigning of one of the highest priorities to support for military operations (usually referred to as SMO, but sometimes given a slightly different twist and called "support to the warfighter"). It is difficult to argue against getting the right information into the hands of deployed military personnel. However, concern was expressed at the time that such a reprioritization could lead to an overemphasis on military tactical requirements in the tasking of national systems. In a constrained resource environment, this would mean less support for users who were focused on more strategic issues, such as nuclear nonproliferation. This concern resurfaced after the 9/11 terrorist attacks.

The INTs

HUMINT—Human Intelligence can be derived by covert means (classical spying or espionage), semiopen observations (such as, by a military attaché), or completely overt activities (discussion with a foreign official).

IMINT—Imagery Intelligence comes from images made either from overhead (balloons, airplanes, or satellites) or on the ground. Since photography is today only one among several methods of imaging, use of the term IMINT has largely replaced the older term PHOTINT or photographic intelligence.

MASINT—Measurement and Signature Intelligence involves technical intelligence data other than imagery and signal intelligence. It uses nuclear, optical, radio frequency, acoustics, seismic, and materials sciences to locate, identify, or describe distinctive characteristics of targets.

OSINT—Open-Source Intelligence deals with information that is publicly available, such as newspapers, radio and television broadcasts, journals, the Internet, or commercial databases. It also includes videos, graphics and drawings, as well as other unclassified information that has limited public access or distribution (that is, you must ask for it).

SIGINT—Signals Intelligence is derived from either intercepted communications (COMINT), including the handling of written communications, such as letters written in invisible ink or that contain some form of encryption; or electromagnetic emanations (ELINT) that are not communications and are not from atomic detonations or a radioactive source, including emanations from radar systems, navigational radio beacons, and the signals (telemetry) sent by a test missile while in flight.

The Intelligence Community has tried a number of techniques for converting the broad guidance that comes from the top of the consumer chain into more specific directions. Whatever their name at any given time (such as, "Key Intelligence Topics/Questions," or "National Intelligence Topics"), the formal requirements documents are a product of an interagency process. The goal of that process is to identify and prioritize the central problems—and the elements within those problems—on which the agencies should focus their attention. However, the formal requirements also have been used to help an agency justify certain of its activities and budget.

At times, collectors and analysts are more on their own than the existence of policy guidance and a formal requirements system would suggest. Things happen that have not been—and perhaps could not have been—anticipated. Coordinated, formal requirements documents are simply more static than real life. Collectors of all types—whether human or technical—suddenly can be confronted with opportunities to acquire information that may be meaningful but appears on no list. They will rarely elect to pass up such chance moments. Similarly, analysts are expected to be the experts in their fields, and they must be prepared to ask and explore questions that have not been formalized by the requirements process. For a deployed soldier, the issue is sometimes even more current. An alert from a squad in the field that "we are taking fire" usually means that intelligence is needed now, and all available collectors need to be brought to bear to aid in a solution of the problem.

In many ways, formal requirements are like the kickoff to a football game: They help to get things started, they provide some structure to the game, but they rarely decide the contest. The players must play the game.

The game of intelligence collection is a multidisciplinary endeavor. There are many different kinds of information needed (or wanted), and there are quite a number of ways of trying to get at that information. The processes and techniques of gathering intelligence—the disciplines of intelligence collection (sometimes referred to as "*The INTs*," see sidebar)—include the identification, translation, and other processing of openly available information; old-fashioned spying; overhead imaging technology; the interception and processing of communications and other electronic emissions; and some exotic uses of technology to locate and identify objects by their distinctive emanations. Each of the disciplines can be more effective than the others depending on the type of information that is needed and where and how it is held.

There for the Taking, But You Have to Find It

Much of the information that represents input into the intelligence cycle comes from sources that are freely available, if you know where they are and have the resources to find, acquire, and process them. The handling of such information constitutes the intelligence discipline of open-source intelligence or OSINT. The terms open-source and intelligence may seem as though they do not belong together or that one contradicts the other. Certainly, Abram Shulsky in his classic work *Silent Warfare* defines intelligence in terms of discovering and protecting secrets. But he, too, accepts a role for open-source information, one of providing the "means to get around the barriers that obstruct direct access to the information being sought."[3] No matter how they are defined, open sources have been an integral part of intelligence collection since World War II (and sporadically even earlier, as in efforts by the Confederate Secret Service to acquire newspapers from the Union States). Whether open sources have received the respect that they are due is another matter. Although the importance of open-source collection to the U.S. intelligence effort has been given lip service over the years, its true significance often has been underestimated. Similarly, the complexity of collecting, handling, and disseminating open-source intelligence has not been fully appreciated by those more attuned to the secret side of intelligence.

OSINT collection consists of the acquisition and processing (that is, the review of the acquisitions for relevant materials and, as necessary, their translation) of publicly available information. Open sources cover a wide spectrum of potential data on political, military, economic, and scientific affairs. They include radio and television broadcasts, newspapers, technical and scholarly journals, popular and specialized magazines, published reports from governmental and nongovernmental entities, publications from and handouts at conferences, books, publicly accessible databases (either unrestricted or by subscription), and the Internet. In open societies, the flow of information can offer insights into a range of issues of relevance to U.S. policymakers. These might include the ascendance of a particular figure in a political party, a parliamentary debate about trade policy, a farmers' union protesting the import of foreign produce, a movement to declare a country's ports nuclear-free zones, or independent scientific advances.

In closed societies, such as the former Soviet bloc, Cuba, North Korea, Iran, or China, there are varying but often substantial amounts of information that may be extracted from an informed perusal of legally accessible media and documents. This is true even where all such materials present some level of regime propaganda and are tightly censored. For instance, when a dictatorship decides to change direction on a matter such as land use in the countryside, it needs to get the word out; and the media make it possible to do so in a manner that everyone hears the same thing. The leadership may not state precisely that there is a change, but their rhetoric—echoed over and over by those further down the hierarchy—is one way of getting everyone saying and eventually doing the same thing. Regional and local newspapers can provide a view into the effects on local conditions of national policy decisions. Scientific and technical journals from the former USSR were scrutinized carefully for hints of the kind of work being done at research institutions and the state of Soviet knowledge in particular fields. During the Cold War years, "[m]ost of the information on the USSR provided to policy officers by the intelligence community . . . came from open sources . . . . Once the open pieces [of the puzzle] were in place, finding the hidden ones was a task that fell to the clandestine collectors."[4]

Throughout the Cold War, one of the major players in the open-source business was the Air Force's Foreign Technology Division (FTD). The organization is now part of the Air Intelligence Agency's National Air and Space Intelligence Center (NASIC). FTD/NASIC's roots date back to 1917 when the Army Signal Corps established an aviation engineering and testing center in Dayton, Ohio. In World War I, the organization focused on acquiring aviation-related technical data by translating articles from European publications. FTD/NASIC's predecessor organizations translated and cataloged captured German and Japanese technical documents during World War II. From the late-1940s, the organization's attention swung to the technological threat posed by the Russians. In 1959, the Air Force delegated responsibility for collection of open-source intelligence to FTD; this involved primarily translations from commercial foreign-language publications. Then, in the late-1960s the Defense Department made FTD the executive agent for the military's entire program for collection and processing of science and technology literature. The end of the Cold War brought downsizing, reorganization, and a blending of the FTD mission with the general military intelligence program. Today, NASIC's large database, consisting heavily of open-source materials, is used to support a range of field-oriented activities. FTD had also been a leader in the development of machine translation, growing the capability of its system from word-for-word to sentence-by-sentence. The current translation branch uses human and machine capabilities to collect intelligence on and evaluate evolving technologies around the world.[5]

The Army's Asian Studies Detachment (ASD) has been engaged in the exploitation of open sources since 1947. Although it has been through a number of name changes and organizational affiliations (as is typical of many long-term military units), ASD today is located at Camp Zama, about twenty-five miles west of Tokyo, and is an element of the U.S. Army Intelligence and Security Command's (INSCOM) 500th Military Intelligence Brigade. The core work of reading, analyzing, and reporting on hundreds of publications received in paper or digital form and in dozens of languages is handled by Japanese nationals, who work for the U.S. Army under a contract with the Japanese government. ASD's primary mission is to support the tactical intelligence needs of U.S. Army Pacific (USARPAC); however, its products are disseminated widely, including to all military services, joint commands, DOD intelligence agencies, other non-DOD customers, and some nongovernmental strategic think tanks.[6]

When the CIA was formed in 1947, it was joined by an already existing organization—the Foreign Broadcast Information Service (FBIS). Begun by the Federal Communications Commission in 1941, the Foreign Broadcast Monitoring Service (as it was originally called) was responsible for recording, translating, and analyzing Japanese and German short-wave propaganda broadcasts. At the end of World War II, FBIS was transferred briefly to the War Department, then to the short-lived Central Intelligence Group, and finally to the newly formed CIA. Under the CIA, FBIS was a "service of common concern," covering foreign broadcasts for the whole of the Intelligence Community. During the Cold War years, the requirements for the open-source product, essentially translations of foreign radio and press agency transmissions from around the world, increased significantly. Its mission was further expanded in 1967 when it merged with the Foreign Documents Division, which had the charter for foreign press exploitation. Thus, FBIS became responsible for all the foreign mass media, both broadcast and print. In more recent times, new media dissemination technologies necessitated increased coverage of television and satellite broadcasts, government and commercial databases, "gray" literature (such as, symposia proceedings and academic studies), and the Internet.

FBIS has been a unique intelligence organization in several ways. First of all, its primary product—the *FBIS Daily Reports*—was available for sale to the public for over twenty years (1974–1996) through the Commerce Department's National Technical Information Service (NTIS). In 1997, dissemination to the public (largely, academics and journalists) of the FBIS materials was converted into an NTIS-run, online subscription service called "World News Connection."[7] Second, for most of its existence, FBIS has been an openly declared intelligence organization. At its peak, it had at least nineteen field collection sites worldwide. Those field activities were staffed by a combination of American and foreign national personnel. The host governments were fully aware of FBIS' status and had approved the organization's presence in their countries. Third, while much of the long-standing U.S.-British intelligence sharing agreement remains secret, FBIS maintains an openly acknowledged partnership with the Monitoring Service of the British Broadcasting Corporation (BBC). The two services have divided the world into radio and television monitoring areas with each responsible for a portion. And, fourth, FBIS engaged in outsourcing long before the term became a catchword for Washington-area consultants. Large volumes of foreign-language material from the print media are farmed out to independent contract translators all over the country.

Over the years, FBIS' collection activities not only supplied large volumes of background and reference material on most countries of the world but also served to alert the Intelligence Community and American leaders to major developing events. In this, it was part of the country's early warning system. During the Cuban Missile Crisis in 1962, the first word on the Russians' decision to remove their missiles came in an FBIS report from Radio Moscow about Premier Khrushchev's message to President Kennedy. The President responded immediately, even before the official text was delivered by the Soviets. In the 1956 Hungarian uprising and again in the 1968 Soviet invasion of Czechoslovakia, radio broadcasts were for some time the only source of information about what was happening in those countries. In fact, monitoring the broadcasts from local, low-power radio transmitters was the timeliest way to follow the progress of the Russians' advance into Czechoslovakia. Many of the Czech broadcasters stayed at their microphones until Soviet soldiers broke down their doors. In August 1991, FBIS monitored a report from the Soviet news agency TASS that Mikhail Gorbachev had been replaced by Gennadiy Yanayev. The report was, of course, incorrect, but it was the first indication of the failed coup attempt.

The 1990s were not kind to FBIS and open-source intelligence. Despite FBIS' responsibility as a service of common concern, in-house processing of open-source information had proliferated throughout other components of the Intelligence Community. In 1992, the DCI appointed an Open Source Coordinator with the goal of establishing interconnectivity to promote sharing open sources across the Community. That approach fizzled out when it was followed almost immediately by substantial budget cuts. By 1996, there was a growing fear among academics and freedom-of-information advocates (and, perhaps, by intelligence analysts as well) that FBIS was going to be abolished. The argument was that it was irrelevant in an era of twenty-four-hour cable news. The Federation of American Scientists was particularly active in trying to mount opposition to the elimination of the FBIS product. Editorials appeared in major newspapers decrying proposed reductions in FBIS activities. Concern was expressed in the House Permanent Select Committee on Intelligence about what was called the FBIS "re-engineering" plan. The worries even reached the British press with the *Sunday Telegraph*

(London) of November 24, 1996, running a story under the headline: "CIA Threatens to Pull Plug on World Service." FBIS survived at the time; but by 2001, it had been stripped of some 60 percent of its personnel.

Interest in open sources as an integral part of the intelligence process revived sufficiently after 9/11 that Congress, in the Intelligence Reform and Terrorism Prevention Act of 2004, encouraged the Director of National Intelligence (DNI) to establish an Intelligence Community center to coordinate the collection, analysis, production, and dissemination of open-source intelligence. That step was taken on November 8, 2005, when DNI John D. Negroponte announced the creation of the DNI Open Source Center (OSC). The OSC will be based at CIA and will be built around what was formerly FBIS.[8] Whether this move will result in strengthening the status of OSINT within the Intelligence Community remains to be seen. In any event, the need for paying attention to the open-source environment will continue. For example, there are reportedly some 5,000 Internet sites worldwide run by terrorists hostile to the United States. Some 1,500 of these are monitored regularly, and between twenty-five and a hundred are tracked daily by U.S. analysts. Despite these efforts, some terrorism experts see the United States falling even further behind in keeping up with the use of the Internet by radical jihadists.[9]

Old-Fashioned Spying

Michael Shaara opens his Civil War novel, *The Killer Angels*, with the Confederate spy "Harrison" discovering in June 1863 that the Union Army of the Potomac was marching northward. That information is conveyed, first, to Gen. James Longstreet and, then, to Gen. Robert E. Lee. Based on Harrison's intelligence, Lee turns the Confederate army East across the mountains toward the small Pennsylvania town of Gettysburg. The novelist brings drama to what could have been a rather prosaic scene: Longstreet's spy delivering his report. But the report really happened; and Lee did act on that intelligence, given that he had lost contact with his primary source for intelligence on the location of the Union army, Gen. Jeb Stuart's cavalry.[10] In a book not otherwise concerned with intelligence, the novelist has made a number of points about the nature of intelligence in general and, particularly, human intelligence (HUMINT) or spying. The generals' tone of distrust and even contempt for their spy is likely portrayed accurately. At a minimum, they found the whole process—and their dependence on it—distasteful. Such a reaction is not unusual. Americans both public and private have long been ambivalent about many aspects of the activities that fall under the heading of spying ("Gentlemen do not read each other's mail"). Nonetheless, Lee made a decision based on the intelligence then available to him—a situation often forced upon decision makers.

For a time in the 1980s and 1990s, it was possible for some writers on intelligence to argue that the application of modern technology to the collection of intelligence was beginning to make human spies less important. What they probably meant was that technical collection systems are less messy (they are things that can be programed, not people who have a tendency to do dumb things) and less prone to embarrass the government. There are certain kinds of secrets, however, that technical systems simply cannot provide.

Throughout much of the Cold War, a large number of Russian military and intelligence officers provided the United States and its allies with critical information from deep within the closed Soviet system. From 1953 until his arrest in 1959, Pyotr Popov, a lieutenant colonel in the GRU (Soviet military intelligence), supplied a steady stream of intelligence, ranging from information on GRU personnel and operations to important Soviet military documents. GRU Colonel Oleg Penkovsky spied for the United States and Britain from April 1961 until his arrest in October 1962. In that brief period, he provided an enormous quantity of intelligence on a wide range of subjects, including Soviet missile developments, nuclear planning, military structure and plans, and designs against Berlin. Penkovsky's information is credited with allowing President Kennedy to act with confidence when he had to face Soviet Premier Khrushchev's threats about Berlin and to deal with the discovery of Soviet offensive missiles in Cuba.[11] Both Popov and Penkovskiy paid for their actions with their lives, as did most of the American agents betrayed from the mid-1980s by the traitorous activities of CIA officer Aldrich Ames (arrested in 1994) and FBI officer Robert Hanssen (arrested in 2001). However, not all the stories of America's spies behind the Iron Curtain end without the individuals being able to experience the results of their work. From 1972 to 1981, Polish patriot and spy, Lt. Col. Ryszard Kuklinski, passed his CIA contacts "tens of thousands of pages of classified Soviet and Warsaw Pact documents. They included the Soviet war plans for Europe, information on new weapons systems, hidden Soviet wartime bunkers, and Soviet preparations to invade Poland."[12] Kuklinski and his family were exfiltrated from his homeland in 1981, and he lived to set foot (and spirit) back in a Poland freed from the oppression of both Soviet and Polish communists. Modern technical collection systems can accomplish amazing things, but they have inherent physical limitations (an imaging satellite cannot see inside a vault) and cannot deliver the kinds of detailed and authoritative materials represented by the mountain of documents and other intelligence supplied by the likes of Popov, Penkovsky, and Kuklinski. Access is what is required, and that comes through human intervention.

Access is, of course, the central issue in U.S. efforts to blunt the outbreak of radical Islamic terrorism exemplified by al Qaeda and Osama bin Laden. The terrorists' cell phones or their coded messages on the Internet can certainly be intercepted. And they just as easily can switch communications strategies, especially when such matters as whether throwaways can be traced becomes a public discussion item. To get at and stop a planned attack by individuals who accept that they will die in accomplishing their goal requires inside information. Yet, the terrorists are organized in small, self-contained cells, rather than in a top-down bureaucratic structure. Multiple attacks at multiple points by multiple groups possibly unaware of other participants would necessitate having someone in each of the execution cells. HUMINT collection requires either individuals who are willing to betray their group or an intelligence agency's ability to place a spy under its control in or near the group. The former remains a possibility, given the terminal nature of many terrorist acts—cold feet can bring on a change of heart. The latter is very difficult, if not impossible, in the short run.

Finding, evaluating, recruiting, and managing individuals who are willing to undertake the risk of spying on their own governments or organizations is a time-intensive, detail-oriented endeavor. It is often filled with frustration and dead-ends, and the potential for embarrassment to the American government is always present. For the United States, the primary collectors of foreign intelligence from human sources are the CIA's National Clandestine Service (NCS—formerly the Directorate of Operations), the Defense HUMINT Service (DHS), and, increasingly since 9/11, the FBI. These organizations have personnel stationed in countries around the world for the express purpose of conducting intelligence collection activities, including the recruitment of non-Americans to engage in espionage. In addition, the military services are active in seeking out all levels of intelligence in those areas where they are actively engaged or have forces stationed. To troops on the ground in hot spots, the gathering of intelligence has the immediacy of potentially life and death consequences.

Classic human intelligence operations involve the recruiting and handling of agents, and are managed by American citizens. In the intelligence profession, an agent is a non-American citizen—a foreign national—who has been recruited to commit treason and spy on his or her own country or group. Popular usage will also give the term "agent" to American citizens who are career employees of the U.S. government, as in "so-and-so was identified as a CIA agent." This is most often incorrect terminology. The American intelligence personnel about whom they are usually commenting are properly called operations officers or, specifically for CIA personnel, "case officers." While this is a more awkward formulation than agent, intelligence professionals tend to have little regard for commentators and other journalists who are either too lazy or unknowledgeable to use the correct language.

U.S. intelligence operations in foreign countries are normally conducted under some form of "cover." The term cover can be applied to an individual, organization, or installation. It refers to a publicly acknowledged occupation or identity meant to separate the person, organization, or place from its actual activities or sponsorship. An American facility based in another country might have a sign at the gate proclaiming it to be the "U.S. Atmospheric Research Center"; in fact, it could be a communications intelligence site downlinking data from reconnaissance satellites. This is "official cover"; there is no effort to hide that it is U.S. government installation, just what it is actually doing. Thus, an FBI officer collecting intelligence about Nazi plots in La Paz, Bolivia, before and during World War II might have held an officially acknowledged position as the legal attaché and worked out of an office in the U.S. Embassy. On the other hand, someone under "deep cover" or "nonofficial cover" in the same place might have worked ostensibly as a salesman for a farm equipment company or for a securities firm while collecting intelligence against the same target groups. The big difference in "official" and "nonofficial" cover is that the personnel under the former are protected against arrest and imprisonment in the host country, while the latter are not. In addition, nonofficial cover officers (NOCs) require different means of secure communications (which are readily available to officers stationed at U.S. facilities) and for secure storage of the incidentals of life and work that could identify them as working for an intelligence agency.

The officers in the Defense Attaché system also engage in HUMINT operations. Depending on the circumstances in the host country, attachés may undertake a range of direct and indirect collection activities. They will, for example, seek to identify and establish contact with foreign military officers who might be potential sources of information or who could become future leaders of the country. They personally observe and report on such events as military demonstrations and parades. For years, the Soviet May Day parade brought out almost the entire foreign military attaché corps in Moscow to see what new hardware would be on display. Attachés may also try to travel around the countryside of their host country (to the extent that travel restrictions allow) and observe and photograph installations or other military-associated activities.

Defectors are another important source of HUMINT. During the Cold War, defectors from the intelligence and security services of the communist countries were particularly prized. They could provide new or updated information on intelligence and counterintelligence operations and on the structure and leadership of the opposition services. Defector information can be particularly useful if it involves the identities of agents working for their previous service. When KGB archivist Vasili Mitrokhin defected to the British in 1992, he brought with him a treasure trove of notes and transcripts he had made from thousands of documents that had passed through his hands. A book based on Mitrokhin's materials, published by intelligence historian Christopher Andrew in 1999, created quite a stir when it named a number of British citizens as having spied for the Russian service.[13] (What would be really interesting to know is what was in the files that were not given to Andrew.) Even defectors who are not intelligence officers can still supply much useful information on the policies and leadership of the government components for which they were working.

One of the biggest problems faced with defectors is their bona fides, that is, their credentials or their reliability. In essence, are they real? It is especially difficult when one defector's story conflicts with information coming from another. The debate over the bona fides of Anatoli Golitsin and Yuri Nosenko in the early 1960s tied the CIA's Soviet and counterintelligence components in knots for years. And what do you do about the information supplied by a defector who three months later redefects to his home country? That is what happened with KGB officer Vitaly Yurchenko in 1985. Was Yurchenko in fact a defector who changed his mind or was he a plant sent over by the KGB to provide enough real information that some other piece might appear true? There remains no clear answer to this question.

Liaison arrangements with foreign intelligence services also play an important role in the collection of human and other forms of intelligence. The intelligence relationships forged in World War II with the United Kingdom, Australia, and Canada (until the 1980s, New Zealand was an integral part of the arrangement) have proved to be durable. This is particularly true regarding signals intelligence, where there are formal agreements on sharing both the work and the product (the UKUSA agreement of 1946); but the relationships extend to cooperation in HUMINT collection as well. Exchanges of intelligence with Israel date back at least to the 1960s. Bilateral relationships for intelligence cooperation in specific areas have also existed with a wide range of other countries. These include signals interception and nuclear detection stations in Norway; telemetry-monitoring sites in the People's Republic of China; Pakistan's close involvement with U.S. support to the Afghanistan mujahideen in the 1980s; and the ongoing effort in the war on terrorism to forge cooperative relationships with a wide range of countries and intelligence agencies, some of which were not too long ago regarded as unsuitable for such relations. One area in which the United States has at times been less forthcoming in some of its liaison relationships concerns imagery intelligence, where the tendency has been not to release widely the latest and best imagery available.

Pictures from on High

Visual observation from a high point has been a basic part of intelligence gathering from the first scout who, perched on a mountain ridge, watched the enemy army file through the pass below. The march of time brought new inventions for viewing and imaging: the telescope, binoculars, and the camera. Man also learned how to improve on his vantage point in relation to the ground, with balloons, airplanes, and satellites. And he developed better and faster ways to communicate, first, his observations and, later, the images themselves. Signal flags gave way to telegraph and telephone lines, then came the wireless radio, and today pictures transmitted as data streams. State-of-the-art imagery intelligence (IMINT) brings all three of these strands of human technological development together—clear views from high above available in the hands of the user virtually instantaneously.

World War I saw the marriage of the airplane and the camera for reconnaissance purposes. The union was somewhat awkward given the cumbersome nature of the photographic technology of the day; but it was a marriage that has lasted up to the present. By World War II, commanders had available photographic reconnaissance intelligence from both high-altitude bombers (B-17s and B-24s reconfigured for target identification and bomb-damage assessment) and high-speed interceptor aircraft (tactical intelligence support to ground forces). When the dropping of the "Iron Curtain" cut off direct access to Eastern Europe and the

Soviet Union, the U.S. Air Force began flying photographic and electronic intelligence reconnaissance missions along the Soviet and East European periphery. The target was Soviet order-of-battle information. However, the cameras in the airplanes could only look into Soviet territory for a limited number of miles.

When the Korean War started in 1950, President Truman began to authorize reconnaissance overflights of communist territory. Photographic missions were carried out over the Korean peninsula, Soviet territory around Vladivostok, and parts of Manchuria. President Eisenhower continued to approve overflights of Soviet territory after he took office in 1953. In May 1954, an RB-47 photographed Soviet Long Range Air Force airfields on a flight path that took it over Murmansk and Arkhangelsk. And between March and May 1956, 156 overflights mapped the entire Soviet northern frontier. These overflights and peripheral probings were, however, a dangerous business; and losses of lives occurred from planes being shot down.[14]

By the mid-1950s, the technology of cameras and film had advanced beyond the ceiling of existing aircraft. What was needed was something that could fly high enough to be well above the maximum altitude attainable by Soviet interceptor jets and surface-to-air missiles (SAMs). That airplane was the U-2, developed for the CIA by Lockheed Aircraft Company's Clarence ("Kelly") Johnson. It carried two cameras, "one a special long-focal length spotting camera able to resolve objects two to three feet across" from an altitude of 70,000 feet, and "the other a tracking camera that would produce a continuous strip of film of the whole flight path."[15] The U-2's first mission over the USSR was on July 1, 1956, and the last of over twenty missions was on May 1, 1960, when Francis Gary Powers was shot down over Sverdlovsk. During that time, the U-2 provided significant strategic photographic intelligence, including on the Soviet Union's bomber force (the "bomber gap" was a myth), missile forces, atomic energy programs, and air defense systems.

The loss of the U-2 and the capture of its pilot (Powers was exchanged for the Soviet spy Rudolf Abel in 1962) brought manned overflights of the USSR to an end. But that ended neither the collection of strategic photographic intelligence on the Soviet Union nor the use of the U-2 for intelligence gathering purposes. Flown by Taiwanese pilots, the U-2 was used for overflights of Chinese territory. The airplane played a crucial role in the Cuban Missile Crisis in 1962, bringing back photographs clearly showing that the Russians had indeed begun building strategic missile sites in Cuba. Over the years, the U-2 has continued to be used for both peripheral and overflight missions in other areas of the world. For much of its history, the U-2 was seen as primarily a "strategic" overhead platform. However, during the 1991 Gulf War and later in operations in the Balkans, it was credited with providing a substantial percentage of the imagery available for tactical ground surveillance and targeting. On the other hand, in both Afghanistan and Iraq, there has been an increasing use of unmanned aerial vehicles (UAVs) for some of the imaging functions previously handled by the U-2. The U.S. military's use of the U-2 is scheduled to be phased out by 2011.

Aware that Soviet countermeasures would eventually catch up with the slow-flying U-2, CIA management began working with Kelly Johnson on a whole new type of reconnaissance aircraft. The OXCART program resulted in the A-12, which could fly at extremely high speed (over 2,000 miles per hour) and at great altitude (over 90,000 feet) and which incorporated the best radar-absorbing (stealth) technology of the day. The OXCART had its first operational use in 1967, when the increased deployment of surface-to-air missiles around Hanoi led to the decision to substitute A-12s for the U-2s that were being used for photographic reconnaissance over North Vietnam. In addition to flying over North Vietnam, A-12 missions out of Kadena Air Force Base in Okinawa targeted North Korea following the seizure of the USS *Pueblo* in January 1968. By mid-1968, the SR-71—the Air Force's two-seated version of the A-12—had arrived in Okinawa, and the OXCART had flown its last operational mission. The cost of two similar programs and the Air Force's desire to control its own reconnaissance assets doomed the A-12.[16]

In addition to their service during the Vietnam War and continuing coverage of North Korea, SR-71s would be flown over the succeeding years to photograph "hot spots" around the globe. When tensions mounted somewhere in the world and quick photographic intelligence was needed, the SR-71s were used. They photographed the battlefields during the Yom Kippur War, overflew Cuba to monitor the presence of Soviet aircraft and troops, checked on the type of cargo being delivered to Nicaraguan ports, monitored the Iran-Iraq war, and provided bomb damage assessment after the U.S. air attack on Libya. In 1990, over the objections of many in Congress, the SR-71 was retired by the Air Force. It was returned to duty and used briefly during the conflict in the Balkans in the mid-1990s, but was permanently retired in 1998 after several years of debate about funding.

Stopped in May 1960 with the loss of the U-2, strategic photographic reconnaissance of the USSR resumed in mid-August with the first successful launch of an operational CORONA satellite. In February 1958, President Eisenhower had authorized the CIA to develop a satellite that would record its images on film and return the film to earth for analysis. The procedure developed had a film capsule being ejected from the spacecraft, de-orbited into the atmosphere, then parachuted, and caught in midair by an airplane equipped with a special device to snag the descending capsule. The backup was direct recovery from the ocean. The first pictures were not as good as those from the U-2, but they improved. The CORONA program would last fourteen years and change the face of America's strategic understanding of the Soviet Union. Beyond resolving concerns about a "missile gap," CORONA "located *all* Soviet ICBM [Intercontinental Ballistic Missile] sites, *all* intermediate-range ballistic missile (IRBM) sites, *all* antiballistic missile (ABM) sites, and *all* warship bases, submarine bases, and previously unknown military and industrial complexes."[17]

From an early ground resolution (that is, the smallest object that can be identified in an image) of perhaps thirty-five feet, the resolution on some succeeding imaging satellites would be measured in inches. Commercial satellite imagery is now available with a resolution of less than twenty inches. However, not all reconnaissance satellites are designed to do the same thing. The CORONA satellites produced "wide-area" coverage; but by 1964, the United States was also receiving pictures from a "close-look" satellite, codenamed GAMBIT. The latter was not a replacement for the former, since each type was needed depending on whether the requirement was for coverage of a broad area or for more detailed imagery of a much smaller target. For example, CORONA could survey whole regions of the Soviet Union looking for areas where ICBM sites might be under construction. GAMBIT could then be targeted to produce high-resolution photographs of suspected missile fields.

Development of new photographic reconnaissance satellites brought continuing improvements to the quality of the output—at ever increasing cost. After nearly getting cut for budgetary reasons in 1969, the first unit of the HEXAGON program blasted off in June 1971. The HEXAGON satellite is also referred as the KH-9, or the ninth in the KEYHOLE camera series. The press eventually started calling the satellite "Big Bird." The satellite's camera system doubled the previous wide-area swath to 80 by 360 miles and had a resolution of two feet compared to the existing close-look satellite's resolution of eighteen inches. The KH-9 carried four film capsules instead of two, giving it a longer useful life and more flexibility in choosing when to return film. And its sheer size (over 30,000 pounds) allowed it to carry other, nonphotographic sensors, such as antennae for collecting signals intelligence or for relaying covert communications to and from U.S. agents.

The next big technological breakthrough in imaging from space came with the launch of the KENNAN or KH-11 satellite in December 1976. Film-return satellites simply could not supply intelligence on fast-breaking situations. Logistics and weather meant that it took days and sometimes weeks for the film capsules to get from the orbiting spacecraft to the desks of the photointerpreters. An event of relatively brief duration could be over before the images depicting it were available for review. The KH-11's camera system converts visible light into electrical charges that, in turn, are transmitted as data to ground stations where they are transformed into pictures. The result is near-real-time imagery from space. (It is not real-time imagery because of the delays in transmission brought about by moving substantial volumes of data from the satellite to a data-relay satellite and on to the ground.) Because the images are digital, they can be further enhanced by additional processing after they are received.

A stream of digital images, even if for only parts of each day (the KH-11 cameras are not on and transmitting continuously), was as revolutionary to the photointerpreters as the satellite was technologically. From 1961 to 1996, the National Photographic Interpretation Center (NPIC), a "service of common concern" managed by the CIA and staffed with personnel from the CIA, DIA, and military intelligence units, was the focus of national-level interpretation activities. Although their former tools of the light table and magnification equipment were not discarded, the computer became a critical element in the work of photointerpreters. When the KH-11 came on line, NPIC's computers would "scan the stream of incoming imagery and store the billions of bits of information . . . for comparison with fresh intelligence. The torrent of digital imagery that began coming . . . would have been unmanageable" without the computers and their databases.[18] Today, the computers can recognize a vast range of standard items and also can compare previous images with new ones and alert an interpreter if a known item of interest or something new turns up in a fresh piece of imagery.

The capabilities of IMINT from satellites, planes, and UAVs have progressed well beyond simple photographs. Standard photography requires daylight to produce a picture and cannot show what is below heavy cloud cover. Additional imaging systems are deployed to compensate for these problems. Infrared sensors define objects by their differing temperatures and, therefore, can produce images even at night. Radar is used to provide yet another kind of image. Since it sends out radio waves that are bounced back to the emitter, radar can "see" both at night and through cloud cover. Other radar systems can detect underground sources of radiation and identify differences in density or composition.

The handling of the array of images produced by overhead reconnaissance platforms underwent significant change in 1996 with the reorganization of the U.S. IMINT community. Imagery exploitation was consolidated in a completely new organization within the Department of Defense—the National Imagery and Mapping Agency (NIMA), renamed in 2003 the National Geospatial-Intelligence Agency (NGA). NIMA/NGA combines the Defense Mapping Agency, CIA's NPIC, the Defense Department's Central Imagery Office, and parts of several other defense agencies. NGA is in the process of building a new "INT"—GEOINT or geospatial intelligence—through the merger of imagery, maps, charts, and environmental data.

A Big Ear or a Vacuum Cleaner?

David Kahn, generally recognized as the great historian of cryptography, traces the use of enciphered messages by the military back to the Spartans somewhere around the fifth century B.C.[19] Over the centuries, political and military leaders have regularly sought to communicate within their own community without outsiders having access to what was being said. That was true of handwritten letters, of telegrams sent by wire, of messages over radio links, and of today's multiple forms of communication. Secure communication is rightly seen as important to the success of many different kinds of ventures. The solution was codes and ciphers, and the countersolution was to break those codes and ciphers—to read the plain text that was being concealed.

The value of signals intelligence (SIGINT) to national security is etched in collective memory by the successes of the American MAGIC and the British ULTRA in World War II. More recently, the VENONA program, with its decrypted KGB messages confirming the high level of Soviet espionage in the United States during the 1940s, was made public in 1995. These successes are associated with an important part of SIGINT—communications intelligence (COMINT) and specifically the breaking of codes. But the intelligence discipline of SIGINT includes a much wider range of activities. Before work can begin on what might be an important encrypted message, that message must be intercepted and identified as potentially significant from the midst of millions of other pieces of information. Even if the message has been sent without encryption, it still must be found, identified, either transcribed (if in English) or translated (if in a non-English language), and put into context, as few communications are so unambiguous as to have instant meaning by themselves.

In the United States, the National Security Agency (NSA) has primary responsibility for collecting and processing SIGINT. However, other agencies may at times engage in some specialized forms of SIGINT collection that are specific to their missions. For example, the CIA may monitor local police radio bands when a surveillance team is on the street in a hostile country. In addition, deployed military units often have with them the capability to monitor an enemy's radio communications. Nonetheless, it is NSA's job to eavesdrop on the diplomatic and military communications of the countries of the world and to try to find in a sea of words those that belong to terrorists who mean harm to the United States.

NSA was created by Executive Order in 1952 and placed in the Defense Department under the Secretary of Defense. Over the years, several attempts have been made to find a visual image that might succinctly describe NSA. One image is of a big ear, hearing everything. Another is of a vacuum cleaner, sucking in all the words around it. Either of these will do in a pinch, but neither is really accurate nor does full justice to NSA's contribution to U.S. national security. As an organization, NSA brought together the SIGINT and communications security (COMSEC—now most often referred to as information security or INFOSEC) activities of the armed services within a single agency outside the direct line of military command. The goal was to a provide unified management of two vital and highly sensitive functions and, thereby, eliminate the kind of interservice competition and bickering that had flourished since before World War II.

The two main components of NSA's signals intelligence mission are communications intelligence (COMINT) and electronic intelligence (ELINT). The intelligence produced by the interception of Japanese and German encrypted messages—and the breaking of the encryption systems through which those communications were sent—is classic COMINT. As the name makes clear, COMINT involves the interception, processing, and analysis of the communications of foreign governments or other groups, such as terrorists or narcotics traffickers. On the other hand, ELINT focuses on electromagnetic emanations that are not communications but are not from atomic detonations or a radioactive source. Radar systems of potentially hostile countries are a prime target of ELINT collection. By identifying radar locations and collecting such specifications as frequencies, pulse lengths and rates, and signal strengths, plans can be made to circumvent or neutralize these systems.

As was the case with all of the U.S. intelligence agencies, the three top target areas of NSA's activities from 1952 until the early 1990s were the Soviet Union, the Eastern Bloc countries, and China. In keeping with its vacuum cleaner image, however, there was also plenty of intercept activities targeted on the diplomatic and military communications of other countries. Occasionally, specific areas would be raised to the top of the requirements list during times of upheaval, such as wars in the Middle East, the Vietnam War, or the hostage crisis in Iran. Nevertheless, much of NSA's network of multiple collection capabilities was keyed to watching the Soviet Union.

Over the years, NSA has used every natural medium for intelligence collection—air, sea, land, and space. During the 1950s and 1960s, the U.S. airborne fleet for ELINT collection included the RB-47. Loaded with specialized antennas and an array of monitoring equipment, it flew what was known as ferret missions. The same program under which U.S. overflights photographed much of northern Russia in 1956 also had an ELINT collection component focused on Soviet radars, air bases, and missile installations. Other flights along the USSR's periphery constantly probed the Soviet air-defense radar system. The idea was to get the Russians to react by turning on their tracking equipment, the signals from which could then be intercepted and analyzed. The dangers of these activities were quite real, both in terms of the potential repercussions if the Soviets mistook a probe for an attack and of the loss of life that came when aircraft were shot down. On September 2, 1997, a National Vigilance Park was established at Ft. George G. Meade, Maryland, to honor "those 'silent warriors' who risked, and often lost, their lives performing airborne signals intelligence missions during the Cold War."[20]

That the United States continues to fly ELINT missions and that danger is still associated with this activity is illustrated by the collision between a Navy EP-3e and a trailing Chinese fighter jet on April 1, 2001. The EP-3e is used for maritime surveillance and can also intercept electronic signals from military units on land. The damaged Navy plane was forced to land on China's Hainan Island, and the crew was held for ten days until the United States said it was sorry for the loss of the Chinese pilot and for intruding into Chinese airspace. The disassembled plane was returned to the United States in July. U.S. reconnaissance flights off the coast of China had resumed in May, when an Air Force RC-135 from Kadena Air Base in Okinawa flew a mission in international airspace off China's northeastern coast and returned to base without interference from Chinese interceptors.

In the early 1960s, NSA began converting some old World War II ships into floating intercept facilities. The idea was that ships could go to places too far away for regular airborne reconnaissance and where land-based stations could not be built. Such ships are loaded with antennas, racks of receivers and tape recorders, and teletype machines. COMINT collection operators work alongside ELINT specialists who are searching for radar emissions. Positioned correctly, a ship also can loiter and pick up the narrow, straight-line emissions of microwave transmitters, which are difficult for airborne ferret flights to intercept since they fly through the beam too quickly. The operators are usually Navy personnel, but NSA civilians will spend time on board during crisis times or for special assignments.

As with ferret flights, intelligence collection from ships is also hazardous duty. In 1967, in the midst of the Six-Day War, Israeli fighter planes and torpedo boats attacked the SIGINT ship USS *Liberty*. The toll was 34 dead and 171 wounded. The blame for the attack—whether it was deliberate or an accident—continues to be debated to this day. Then, in January 1968, the Navy SIGINT ship USS *Pueblo* was attacked and captured by the North Koreans. The crew (one sailor died in the attack) was held in North Korea for eleven months. The *Pueblo* remains in North Korea, serving as a tourist attraction and a propaganda piece.

During the Cold War, the Navy and NSA also had intercept operators on submarines. They watched Soviet nuclear tests from as close to the sites as they could get. The operators in the submarines would also record shore-based transmitters and collect Soviet fleet communications. In 1975, a covert submarine operation codenamed "IVY BELLS" succeeded in tapping a Russian communications cable running from the Kamchatka Peninsula to Vladivostok in the Sea of Okhotsk. The submarine eventually attached a pod with monitoring equipment, from which it could periodically pick up the recorded communications rather than have to sit on the sea bottom and record them directly. The operation lasted until a former NSA employee compromised it around 1980. It is likely that similar activities continue today. For example, the submarine USS *Memphis* was eavesdropping on a naval exercise in the Barents Sea on August 12, 2000, when the Russian submarine Kursk suffered a fatal internal explosion and sank, killing all aboard. The disaster was electronically recorded by the *Memphis*.[21] The use of submarines as platforms for electronic and other spying missions continues. The *Seawolf*-class submarine USS *Jimmy Carter* (SSN-23), commissioned in January 2005, is designed as a multimission vessel, with unique reconnaissance and special warfare capabilities.

By the late 1980s, NSA and its service affiliates also had established permanent listening posts literally all over the world, including stations about as far North as you can go. Jeffrey T. Richelson identified some sixty stations in twenty countries, but noted that there were also forty-five joint NSA-CIA special collection activities in various U.S. embassies and consulates. Some of the permanent facilities are large, manned stations and others are unmanned locations from which the collected signals are remoted to other sites and back to NSA headquarters.[22] In the late 1990s and early 2000s, a number of stations located on U.S. military facilities fell victim to the budget cutting that accompanied the collective sigh of relief at the end of the Cold War. These included such stations as Adak in Alaska and Vint Hill Farms in Virginia, which were closed in 1997, and Bad Aibling in Germany, which closed in 2002. It was reported that substantial numbers of the NSA staff at Bad Aibling transferred to the NSA facility on the Royal Air Force base at Menwith Hill in the United Kingdom.

SIGINT collection was part of the dawn of America's space age. Throughout the 1960s, the United States deployed low-earth orbiting satellites targeted on radar emissions. The satellites retransmitted the intercepted signals to ground stations from where they were dispatched on tape back to the United States for analysis. By the early 1970s, a much more sophisticated SIGINT satellite, initially codenamed RHYOLITE, was flying in geosynchronous ("stationary" above the equator) orbit at 22,300 miles above the earth. From that vantage point, a constellation of satellites can intercept microwave transmissions, telemetry from rocket launches, and telephone communications over the VHF and UHF frequency bands. For areas that cannot be monitored from geosynchronous orbit, other satellites (originally launched under the codename of JUMPSEAT) are placed in highly elliptical orbits designed to give them more sustained periods of time over their primary areas of interest. The follow-on system to RHYOLITE—codenamed MAGNUM—was first launched in 1985. In recent years, design of the next generation of SIGINT satellites has been delayed (perhaps for as much as a decade) by disagreements over what these expensive pieces of technology need to be doing in the modern world of communications.

The interconnectedness and ease of communication in the world in which we live can be both a blessing and a curse. At a minimum, such communications have immeasurably complicated the job of trying to intercept and understand the communications of the "bad guys." The Internet, circuit encryption, fiber optics, and digital cellular telephones are all part of the accelerated pace of change in public and private communications. In particular, a shift away from microwave and satellite communications to buried fiber optic cable presents significant challenges in the continued collection of COMINT.

Under the UKUSA Communications Intelligence Agreement of 1946, much of the SIGINT collection effort is shared among NSA, the United Kingdom's Government Communications Headquarters (GCHQ), Canada's Communications Security Establishment (CSE), and Australia's Defence Signals Directorate (DSD). (The role of New Zealand in the partnership has been clouded ever since the country declared itself a nuclearfree zone.) The partnership has endured for a long time, and has been useful to all parties, as the sharing of responsibilities has helped reduce the pressure on any one country. However, its importance was reemphasized on January 24, 2000, when NSA's computers crashed. Collection was not affected, but processing intercepts had to be shifted to GCHQ for the better part of four days.

NSA's ability to break into and read the enciphered message traffic that flows freely around the world is not a subject about which there is much known publicly. That is, of course, as it should be. If you tell someone you are reading their codes, they will change those codes and seek better ones. That NSA regards the current encryption environment as challenging is documented in the agency's prolonged effort through the 1990s to outlaw the export from the United States of powerful encryption software. The futility of that attempt—and the penalty it exacted from American companies—eventually was recognized, and the effort has been virtually abandoned.

As the SIGINT world continues to face difficulties in adjusting to twenty-first century communications challenges, some have raised the question of its continuing relevance. The simple answer is that interception and processing (including breaking and reading encrypted materials) of the communications and other electronic emissions of such nation-based threats as North Korea and Iran is likely to remain a high-priority item. Tactical interception of an enemy's communications in the field will certainly continue to be necessary. However, there may be targets—such as the communications of the terrorist network of al Qaeda—that remain a puzzle for which at any given moment there are too few pieces available to create a workable picture.

Measuring the Unseeable

There are some rather exotic and highly classified technical collection activities that have been drawn together and given the lengthy name of measurement and signature intelligence or MASINT. It is a relatively new addition to the INTs. Official recognition by the Intelligence Community came in 1986. A MASINT office was established in the Department of Defense in 1992 and upgraded in 1999 to a DIA directorate. Earlier, the Central MASINT Organization and, now, the Directorate for MASINT and Technical Collection coordinates MASINT activities across the other intelligence disciplines. Although MASINT has some independent collection systems, including at the tactical level, coordination is needed because much data comes from sensors associated with signals and imagery intelligence. Primary responsibility for exploitation of collected data rests with the Air Force's National Air and Space Intelligence Center (NASIC).

As an intelligence collection discipline, MASINT utilizes a range of technologies to detect, locate, identify, and describe objects through their basic physical properties. Measuring the physical characteristics of objects allows the creation of unique "signatures" for potential targets. The types of measurements used include size, shape, sound, heat, vibration, unintentional radiation, density, and chemical and biological composition. For example, spectral sensors measure the way objects reflect and emit electro-optical energy. This allows identification through an object's surface composition (ranging from type of metal to the nature of vegetation). Spectral analysis, thus, can readily distinguish the use of camouflage. Seismic and acoustic sensors measure the sound or vibration created by moving objects (a tank or a submarine). MASINT infrared sensors on satellites have been used to identify rocket launches for decades. And today's "smart weapons" use MASINT signatures for the internal guidance systems that direct them to their targets. Computerized databases containing many thousands of "signatures" allow measurements and signatures to be compared with known data for rapid identification of a newly detected object. Insuring the operationally timely processing and transmission of this intelligence to the point where it is needed is the real challenge for the future of MASINT.[23]

Notes

1. Michael A. Turner, *Why Secret Intelligence Fails* (Dulles, VA: Potomac Books, 2005), 73.

2. The White House, Office of the Press Secretary, "Press Briefing," March 10, 1995, http://www.fas.org/irp/offdocs/pdd35.htm.

3. Abram N. Shulsky, *Silent Warfare: Understanding the World of Intelligence* (New York: Brassey's, 1991), 175. [Footnote omitted]

4. Loch K. Johnson, *Secret Agencies: U.S. Intelligence in a Hostile World* (New Haven, CT: Yale University Press, 1996), 193.

5. Air Force Historical Studies Office, "A Brief History of Air Force Scientific and Technical Intelligence," https://www.airforcehistory.hq.af.mil/PopTopics/histechintel.htm.

6. David A. Reese, "50 Years of Excellence: ASD Forges Ahead As the Army's Premier OSINT Unit in the Pacific," *Military Intelligence* 31(4) (October-December, 2005): 27–29.

7. At http://wnc.fedworld.gov/.

8. U.S. Central Intelligence Agency, Public Affairs Staff, "DNI and D/CIA Announce Establishment of the DNI Open Source Center," November 8, 2005, https://www.cia.gov/cia/public_affairs/press_release/2005/pr11082005.html.

9. "White House Week: Measuring Hatred, One Site at a Time," *U.S. News & World Report* (May 15, 2006): 18.

10. Michael Shaara, *The Killer Angels* (New York: Crown, 1974), 3–15.

11. On Popov, see William Hood, *Mole* (New York: Norton, 1982). On Popov and Penkovskiy, see Clarence Ashley, *CIA SpyMaster* (Gretna, LA: Pelican, 2004), 81–234; and John Limond Hart, *The CIA's Russians* (Annapolis, MD: Naval Institute Press, 2003), 18–127. On Penkovsky, see Jerrold L. Schecter and Peter S. Deriabin, *The Spy Who Saved the World: How a Soviet Colonel Changed the Course of the Cold War* (New York: Scribner's, 1992).

12. Benjamin Weiser, *A Secret Life: The Polish Officer, His Covert Mission, and the Price He Paid to Save His Country* (New York: PublicAffairs, 2004), ix.

13. Christopher Andrew and Vasili Mitrokhin, *The Sword and the Shield: The Mitrokhin Archive and the Secret History of the KGB* (New York: Basic Books, 1999).

14. Larry Tart and Robert Keefe, *The Price of Vigilance: Attacks on American Surveillance Flights* (New York: Ballantine, 2001), 130–137.

15. Ben R. Rich and Leo Janos, *Skunk Works: A Personal Memoir of My Years at Lockheed* (Boston, MA: Little, Brown & Co., 1994), 126.

16. Thomas P. McIninch, "The OXCART Story: Record of a Pioneering Achievement," *Studies in Intelligence* 15(1) (Winter 1971): 1–34, https://www.cia.gov/csi/kent_csi/docs/v15i1a01p_0001.htm.

17. Dwayne A. Day, John M. Logsdon, and Brian Latell, eds., *Eye in the Sky: The Story of the Corona Spy Satellites* (Washington, DC: Smithsonian Institution Press, 1998), 7.

18. William E. Burrows, *Deep Black: Space Espionage and National Security* (London: Bantam Press, 1988), 218.

19. David Kahn, *The Codebreakers: The Comprehensive History of Secret Communication from Ancient Times to the Internet*, rev. ed. (New York: Scribner, 1996), 82.

20. "National Vigilance Park," http://www.nsa.gov/vigilance/index.cfm.

21. James Bamford, *Body of Secrets: Anatomy of the Ultra-Secret National Security Agency from the Cold War through the Dawn of a New Century* (New York: Doubleday, 2001), 173–174.

22. Jeffrey T. Richelson, *The U.S. Intelligence Community*, 2nd ed. (New York: HarperCollins, 1989), 181, 187.

23. See John Macartney, " 'John, How Should We Explain MASINT?' " *Intelligencer* 12(1) (Summer 2001): 28–34; John L. Morris, "The Nature and Applications of Measurement and Signature Intelligence," *American Intelligence Journal* 19(3 & 4) (1999–2000): 81–84; and "The MASINT Association," http://www.masint.org/index.htm.

CHAPTER 3

What Does It Mean?

Putting the Pieces Together

After information or "raw" intelligence is collected, it needs to be given meaning. Single pieces of data can be important—they may, in fact, give warning of something that might be prevented—but they rarely provide answers to complex questions. As unambiguous and significant as it was, the Zimmermann Telegram of 1917 represented only the final item in a lengthy decision chain that led the United States into World War I. It was, in fact, over a month from when the British supplied the text of the telegram until President Wilson went to Congress for a declaration of war. For neither Pearl Harbor nor September 11 (9/11) was there a single source, image, intercept, or open announcement that indicated the enemy was going to strike when and where they did. The accepted belief is that there was, to use the current terminology, a failure "to connect the dots." This conclusion is essentially an argument that in each case sufficient individual pieces of intelligence existed, which if understood in their proper relationship and acted upon would have prevented the event. That viewpoint will undoubtedly be revisited many times over in the coming years. Nonetheless, the underlying point is generally accurate—disparate items of information need to be brought together before a picture (sometimes fuzzy, sometimes clear) can emerge.

It is the function of the intelligence analysis process to derive meaning from the flood of individual pieces of information produced by multiple intelligence collection systems. Giving data meaning involves, first of all, placing it into context. This context can involve geographic, religious, political, or military matters; it may deal with the past, present, or future; or it can be all of these and more in a complicated matrix of time, place, and circumstance. It is from this process that a piece of "finished" intelligence emerges. That product must then be shared in a timely fashion with the points in the government that need this particular expansion of knowledge for action or informational purposes.

Military and political recipients of intelligence have always performed some level of what can be called analysis of the information presented to them. George Washington basically incorporated the whole intelligence cycle in his own person. He handled his own spies, heard reports directly from his other intelligence sources (such as, scouts and cavalry), and took action based on his evaluation of the available information. Former intelligence officer and Civil War historian Edwin W. Fischel credits Col. George H. Sharpe's Bureau of Military Information with providing Gen. Joseph Hooker and the Army of the Potomac the kind of synthesized product from multiple collectors that we today call all-source intelligence.[1] However, the modern structure and concept of all-source intelligence analysis is rooted in the Research and Analysis Branch (R&A) formed, first, in the Office of the Coordinator of Information and, then, part of the Office of Strategic Services (OSS). Gen. William J. Donovan brought scholars and specialists from many intellectual disciplines into the Branch. R&A's staff would eventually encompass historians, political scientists, economists, geographers, psychologists, and others. They were organized into regional sections (Europe-Africa, Far East, USSR, and Latin America) with functional subsections (economic, political, and geographic), and produced daily, weekly, and longer-term publications.

Combining these disparate and sometimes-competing fields of study and harnessing them in the name of intelligence was an innovative approach; and multidisciplinary research and analysis remains central to the way the job is done today. R&A Branch "operated in an intelligence area previously little developed by the United States—the complex field of economic, political and geographic relationships. The collection of great stores of source material and the analytic employment of such material furnished a rounded background of intelligence."[2] The eminent historian William L. Langer headed R&A throughout most of the war years, and many well-known scholars of the day and others who would become well known worked there. These included Herbert Marcuse, Walt W. Rostow, and Arthur Schlesinger, Jr. Also getting their start in intelligence work at R&A Branch were some of the individuals who would be part of the founding of analysis at the Central Intelligence Agency (CIA) after 1947, including Ray Cline, Sherman Kent, and R. Jack Smith.

Not all intelligence output is subjected to the extensive degree of handling applied by all-source analysts before it is forwarded to potential users. Electronic dissemination systems now ensure that the main decision-makers (or at least their offices) receive much of the raw intelligence product as rapidly as do those charged with analyzing it. This is, of course, just one of the challenges faced by today's intelligence analysts. In addition, the main foreign policy, defense, and intelligence departments and agencies maintain twenty-four-hour "watch offices" or "operations centers" (such as, the White House Situation Room or the CIA Operations Center). These offices review incoming intelligence reports for matters of immediate interest or that are responsive to their organizations' particular needs. Some information is so time-sensitive that it must be put in the hands of the person who needs to take action on it as quickly as possible. For instance, knowledge of the location of a potential threat that is supplied to a soldier in the field an hour after the target has moved has little value or meaning. Therefore, upon acquiring information, intelligence collectors make an initial evaluation (an "on-the-fly" analysis) of the nature and sensitivity of that information. Based on that evaluation, the information can be reported in a number of ways, including everything from a telephone call to a formal, stylized message ("fill-in-the-blanks") sent over a data line. Whatever the chosen mode, the information usually will go forward over some form of controlled communications channel, with appropriate instructions for its secure handling. The largest exception to this is the publicly available, online subscription service managed by the Commerce Department's National Technical Information Service. The "World News Connection" carries the open-source material collected and processed by the Open Source Center (the former Foreign Broadcast Information Service).

The distribution list for the information from the collectors includes both direct consumers of the raw intelligence and the Intelligence Community agencies that are responsible for performing more formal intelligence analysis. Some organizations have intelligence units that are relatively small and specialize in specific kinds of information (such as, Treasury's Office of Terrorism and Financial Intelligence and the Office of National Security Intelligence in the Drug Enforcement Administration). Others are home to all-source intelligence analysts, such as those at the CIA, the Defense Intelligence Agency (DIA), and the State Department's Bureau of Intelligence and Research (INR). It is these all-source analysts who perform in-depth assessments of newly collected information and integrate it into the materials that have been obtained from other collectors and sources—both classified and unclassified.

Today's intelligence analysts communicate their findings in many different ways to many different potential users. Some of their work is pointed at the topmost national leaders. Other products are directed toward the analysts' peers in similar (and often competing) units in Intelligence Community components. Some are even done to please their bosses ("I haven't seen anything from you recently"). Some of the day-to-day work is done to maintain the knowledge base against which new events or developments within a country or region can be evaluated (see sidebar, "*Basic Intelligence*"). Some analytic products are focused on the most recent developments (current intelligence). Others seek to reach farther into the future (estimative intelligence). And there are multiple points in this basic-current-estimative spectrum where there are both ongoing and niche publications. Although the Intelligence Reform and Terrorism Prevention Act of 2004 has produced several new wrinkles in the way the U.S. analytic community is organized, the basic categories of intelligence products can be expected to remain largely the same. Names of publications, formats, presentational means, and even emphasis may change; but the demands of the primary users of intelligence are likely to parallel closely the well established ways of doing business.

Basic Intelligence

One of the legacies of the war in the Pacific and OSS's Research and Analysis Branch was the government's recognition of the need to collect, collate, and store as source material some very basic information about foreign places and countries. This included the requirement for an enhanced knowledge base on geography, demographics, climate, infrastructure, natural resources, and the like. From 1943 to 1947, coordinated basic intelligence was produced in a combined Army-Navy-OSS effort and published as the *Joint Army Navy Intelligence Studies*. From 1948, such information was compiled by the Intelligence Community and published under the *National Intelligence Survey* (NIS) program. These were book-sized compilations for every country in the world. By the late 1960s, it was becoming obvious that much of this kind of information was publicly available; and the NIS program was ended in 1973, with an exception. That exception continues as the CIA-produced (but with multiple contributors) *World Factbook*, a veritable storehouse of information about the countries of the world. *The World Factbook* is available in printed form from the Government Printing Office and as a searchable database at https://www.cia.gov/cia/publications/factbook/index.html.

What Has Happened Today?

Standing requirements, ongoing projects, an understanding of their coverage areas, and the ever-present "inbox" are the staples of an intelligence analyst's world. Inboxes are a driver; sometimes, they feel almost like a force of nature. They seem never to be empty, perhaps because the world refuses to stand still while the analyst reads the material that has accumulated since the last time the incoming mail was opened. Inboxes used to be physical things that would fill with reams of paper. Today, they are most often electronic mail boxes. Opening the inbox accesses screen after screen of material that meets the parameters an analyst has established for receiving reports from the intelligence collectors. There may be cables from State Department officers, National Security Agency (NSA) intercepts, imagery readouts, reports from CIA clandestine service officers, and translations from the open media pertinent to the analyst's area of responsibility. Some sort of decision needs to be made on each item of information. This piece needs to be digested fully; that one deserves only a scan; this one gets a glance at the subject line and no more. Much will be saved to the analyst's "library," in either electronic or old-fashioned paper form. Some items may automatically fit into a piece of analysis that the analyst has underway. The first question, however, is the same wherever the analyst works. This question is whether there are developments that need to be written up for dissemination in the ongoing flow of current intelligence products.

The concept of "current intelligence" is almost self-explanatory. It deals with the latest news, events, and developments from around the world. It is what is happening. But it is more than just news. Current intelligence goes beyond simple reportage into the realm of what these things mean for now and tomorrow. It draws upon the kinds of sources (imagery, intercepts, or a spy's report from inside) that are not available to the cable news reporters who have flocked to the scene of the latest crisis. It is created by people who are experts—or at least specialists—in their subject matter, whether it is a specific country or a particular topic. It is usually relatively brief, making it more likely that the busiest consumers will read it. What may be most important, it is an expected part of what intelligence units do. As Professor Arthur S. Hulnick has noted, "[t]he delivery of a daily report about current events is one of the most traditional of intelligence activities and is replicated at many levels from the highest offices of government in Washington down to field units in the various agencies involved in foreign and security affairs."[3] Inside Washington's Beltway, the "big three" producers of current intelligence are the CIA, the DIA, and INR. From 1950 to 1977, the CIA's Directorate of Intelligence even had an Office of Current Intelligence that focused specifically on shorter-term issues. Since that time, the CIA's current intelligence requirements have been met from within the regional and topical offices that comprise the Directorate of Intelligence or, in some cases, a staff element that handles special assignments.

The most prestigious of the current intelligence publications is the *President's Daily Brief* (PDB). Presenting the President with a daily intelligence summary dates back to Harry Truman's time. Copies of the PDB are also hand-delivered to a limited number of other top-level officials, as designated by each President. Recipients usually have included the secretaries of State and Defense, the chairman of the Joint Chiefs of Staff, and the national security adviser. Others are added to the distribution list as the President directs. The preparation and presentation of the PDB is one of the functions that has been significantly impacted by the downgrading of the former position of Director of Central Intelligence (DCI) to Director of the Central Intelligence Agency (DCIA) and the creation of the position of Director of National Intelligence (DNI) by the Intelligence Reform and Terrorism Prevention Act of 2004. Nevertheless, the process remains much the same even though the players have changed.

Until the Senate's confirmation of John D. Negroponte as the first DNI on April 21, 2005, it had been the responsibility of the DCI (in the words of the National Security Act of 1947) to "serve as head of the United States intelligence community" and "act as the principal adviser to the President for intelligence matters related to the national security." In response to that mandate, a CIA analytic component was responsible for preparing and presenting the PDB to the President. The document's all-source intelligence analysis was highly classified, since the supporting information was drawn from the country's most sensitive sources. It was designed to be read in approximately fifteen minutes, and usually was presented early in the day (unless the President preferred a briefing at the close of business, as Lyndon Johnson did). It focused on what had happened over the preceding twenty-four hours, and sought to provide context and meaning for events. Like almost everything else about the PDB, the length varied depending on who was sitting in the Oval Office. President Jimmy Carter, for example, wanted a less lengthy PDB than had been supplied to President Gerald Ford. In the past, the PDB was usually hand-carried to the White House (if the President was out of town, it would be forwarded by secure fax) by a briefing officer from the CIA staff in charge of preparing the publication. In some administrations, the CIA briefing officer (and, at times, the DCI) might sit with the President and, at times, the national security adviser while the PDB was being read. At other times, such as with Presidents Carter and Clinton, the President may choose to read the material without the briefer being present. The oral briefings resumed under President George W. Bush, and included the participation of the DCI and later the DNI. When they are included in a reading session with the President, briefing officers must be prepared to respond to questions on the material. The best answer to a question to which the officer does not know the answer is, "I don't know, but I will find out."

Whether Presidents have been well served by this process has been the subject of controversy throughout the extended debate over intelligence reform precipitated by the events of 9/11. For example, in the transmittal letter for its report to the President on March 31, 2005, the Commission on the Intelligence Capabilities of the United States Regarding Weapons of Mass Destruction (the Silberman-Robb or WMD Commission) recommended that the President "rethink" the PDB. The letter expressed the Commission's belief that "[t]he daily intelligence briefings given to you before the Iraq war were flawed. Through attention-grabbing headlines and repetition of questionable data, these briefings overstated the case that Iraq was rebuilding its WMD programs." The letter added, "There are many other aspects of the daily brief that deserve to be reconsidered as well, but we are reluctant to make categorical recommendations on a process that in the end must meet your needs, not our theories." The blue-ribbon presidential panel then stated, "[W]e do not believe that the DNI ought to prepare, deliver, or even attend every briefing. For if the DNI is consumed by current intelligence, the long-term needs of the Intelligence Community will suffer."[4] President George W. Bush's view of whether he gets the support he needs from the PDB process has essentially been supplied by the steps he has taken to continue receiving such briefings, but through a revamped procedure.

In words similar to but expanding on those of the 1947 Act, the Intelligence Reform and Terrorism Prevention Act of 2004 states that the DNI shall "serve as head of the intelligence community" and "act as the principal adviser to the President, to the National Security Council, and the Homeland Security Council for intelligence matters related to the national security." Well before Negroponte had been confirmed and sworn in, the White House indicated that the new DNI would be responsible for producing the intelligence material to be given to President Bush at his morning national security briefing. Consequently, just days after he took office, Negroponte presented the daily briefing to the President. In choosing not to heed immediately the WMD Commission's admonition against involving the DNI in the daily briefings, the President may have been sending a signal to the rest of the intelligence community that the "new kid on the block" was someone to be taken seriously in terms of access to the President, an all-important commodity in Washington. Organizationally, the Deputy Director of National Intelligence for Analysis (who also chairs the National Intelligence Council) has been given the responsibility for managing the production of the PDB. The media have reported that Negroponte has instructed that the PDB be broadened to include more contributions from agencies other than the CIA, although some level of coordination with DIA, INR, and NSA was already the norm. In addition, the PDB now includes a previously separate daily terrorist threat assessment.

An interesting aspect associated with high-level analytical products and associated briefings has been the willingness of sitting Presidents to make these available to the presidential candidates in election years. President Truman initiated the practice in 1952 for candidates Dwight Eisenhower and Adlai Stevenson, and it has continued since. After the elections, the CIA also has traditionally provided preinaugural intelligence support to the presidents-elect. In recent years, all the candidates have received the PDB; and some have requested and received additional information and publications. At times, the CIA has even found it necessary to devise a "second" PDB for the President-elect. This could happen when he or his staff does not like the format of the existing PDB, a situation not too surprising as the regular version is tailored to reflect the desires of the outgoing President. In the case of President-elect Richard Nixon, the PDB forwarded to his headquarters, while substantive the same, was longer, and provided more background details than President Johnson's version.[5] It will be interesting to observe whether the DNI replaces the CIA in this effort that recognizes both the significance of the democratic electoral process and the importance of continuity in our political system.

Not a great deal is known publicly about the PDB's substantive content. All the Presidents from Truman forward have resisted the declassification and release of the Daily Briefs on the grounds of both national security and Executive Privilege. Ten redacted and excerpted PDBs from the 1965–1968 period of Lyndon Johnson's presidency have been released in response to Freedom of Information Act (FOIA) requests. For example, the PDB for August 7, 1965 (declassified on July 15, 1993), contains six items: Vietnam (Soviet cargo ship en route to Haiphong), South Vietnam (fighting in Pleiku Province), Communist China (Nationalist and Communist patrol boats clash), Indonesia (Sukarno still sick), Greece (political crisis), and Dominican Republic (OAS talking to both rebels and government). Under pressure to make public what the intelligence community had been telling him about the terrorist threat prior to 9/11, George W. Bush became the first president to release even a portion of a near contemporaneous PDB. In April 2004, he declassified a page-and-a-half section of the PDB from August 6, 2001, headlined "Bin Ladin Determined to Strike in US." (See sidebar, "*The PDB of August 6, 2001*.") Both the White House and the CIA have argued that this action should not be regarded as establishing a precedent for the release of material from past, present, or future Daily Briefs.

The PDB of August 6, 2001

The following is an excerpt from the *President's Daily Brief* of August 6, 2001, declassified and released on April 10, 2004 (italics in original):

"*Clandestine, foreign government, and media reports indicate bin Laden since 1997 has wanted to conduct terrorist attacks in the US.* Bin Laden implied in US television interviews in 1997 and 1998 that his followers would follow the example of World Trade Center bomber Ramzi Yousef and 'bring the fighting to America.'

"After U.S. missile strikes on his base in Afghanistan in 1998, bin Laden told followers he wanted to retaliate in Washington, according to a [redacted] service.

"An Egyptian Islamic Jihad (EIJ) operative told [redacted] service at the same time that bin Laden was planning to exploit the operative's access to the US to mount a terrorist strike.

"*The millennium plotting in Canada in 1999 may have been part of bin Laden's first serious attempt to implement a terrorist strike in the US.* Convicted plotter Ahmed Ressam has told the FBI that he conceived the idea to attack Los Angeles International Airport himself, but that in [redacted], Laden lieutenant Abu Zubaydah encouraged him and helped facilitate the operation. Ressam also said that in 1998 Abu Zubaydah was planning his own U.S. attack." Text of this item from the PDB is available at: http://www.gwu.edu/~nsarchiv/NSAEBB/NSAEBB116/index.htm.

There are a number of other all-source, current intelligence publications that circulate at various levels of the foreign policy and defense bureaucracy. The State Department's INR, formed originally from some of the remnants from the breakup of Office of Strategic Services' Research and Analysis Branch, has for years produced a morning document that is read with interest well beyond the bounds of Foggy Bottom. How much American Presidents actually read is dependent on the individual occupying the office, but INR's daily summary is certainly read by many of the people, including the national security adviser and staffers on the National Security Council, who may interact with the President on any given day. This is both because the top decision makers hate to discover that one of their peers knows something they do not and because the INR product is held in high regard in terms of its relevance to policy. Similarly, the Defense Department's DIA produces a number of current intelligence publications on both a daily and weekly basis. The DIA's output, as might be expected, focuses on military-related matters; but the DIA analysts are not shy about entering into discussion of political and other issues as well. For many years, the DIA products have been considered to have the best graphics, especially photographs of military equipment, of all the current publications.

Even when it was still in charge of producing the PDB, the CIA had another, more widely disseminated current publication, which continues to be produced. The *Senior Executive Intelligence Brief* (SEIB—previously the *National Intelligence*

Daily) is usually longer than the PDB, and may omit some material based on the most sensitive sources. It does, however, routinely include reporting based on imagery and signals intelligence, and therefore its classification will be Top Secret along with several codeword designators that signify further restrictions on its dissemination. The circulation of the SEIB is officially in the hundreds, but it is likely that each office receiving the publication has more than one reader. Many items from the SEIB are sent to major U.S. military commands; and a version is forwarded overseas to a limited number of U.S. ambassadors and CIA station chiefs. Other intelligence components with a departmental focus also produce daily summaries of major developments affecting their areas of interest. The availability of the classified version of the Internet has probably given some of these more limited analytic efforts wider dissemination than they had in earlier years.

Looking at the Longer Term

Intelligence analysts expend a significant amount of their time, thought, and energy keeping up with the current intelligence on an ever-changing world. One reason for this focus on what is happening now is rooted in the wants and needs of the top-level users of the intelligence products. Decision makers in the policy and intelligence communities are much more likely to expect updated information on fast-breaking developments or looming crises than they are to pay attention to or want to read about something that might be. Another reason is that, for the analyst, current intelligence can be more fun. Much of the analysts' written product goes out under the imprimatur of their offices or agencies, not with their names attached. Therefore, the opportunity to be even a small part of the U.S. response to an international crisis can be exciting and personally satisfying. The feeling that, "I was part of that," is hard to beat. However, even with this emphasis on current intelligence, analysts are also engaged in a production process that yields multiple types of analysis. These can include various intelligence assessments, memoranda, staff reports, and oral briefings to a range of consumers. Oral briefings to members of Congress and Congressional staff have, in fact, become increasingly a mainstay of the analytical function in recent years.

The best known of the products focused on the longer term are the National Intelligence Estimates (NIEs) and Special National Intelligence Estimates (SNIEs). The series of documents generated under the NIE label represent an effort to produce forward-looking assessments, that is, to look at political, military, and economic trends in terms of likely future developments and to project or estimate the potential implications of those trends. The goal is to produce a thoroughly coordinated document on a particular geographic region or functional topic by incorporating the best analysis that can be brought to bear by the Intelligence Community. Over time, there have been changes in the way the NIEs are produced, with the latest change coming with the creation of the DNI's office by the Intelligence Reform and Terrorism Prevention Act of 2004. Because of the central role that the NIEs (and SNIEs, which follow the same process but usually are generated in response to some unanticipated development in the international scene) play in the intelligence-policymaking interface, the manner in which they have developed organizationally is particularly significant.

From 1950 to 1973, the CIA's Office of National Estimates (ONE) and that office's Board of National Estimates were responsible for managing the drafting of NIEs. Initially, it was expected that NIEs would be written in reaction to specific requests from the National Security Council. Over time, however, the subject matter of many NIEs became routine, with planned production times and a standardized numbering system. After the drafting process was completed, an interagency advisory board—headed by the DCI or the Deputy DCI—would review and approve the drafts. This review focused on ensuring, one, that the quality of the analysis was at the level it needed to be; two, that the analysis represented the positions of all participating agencies; and, three, that dissent to the conclusions or any part of the NIE was taken into account. The completed NIE would then be disseminated over the signature of the DCI as representing the best judgment of the Intelligence Community.

For the first two years of their existence, ONE and the Board of National Estimates were led by noted Harvard historian William L. Langer, who during World War II had headed OSS's Research and Analysis (R&A) Branch. When Langer returned to academic life in 1952, he was succeeded by Sherman Kent, who had also served in R&A and had been ONE's deputy chief. Kent would head ONE for the next fifteen years, and is regarded as a seminal figure (some regard him as the intellectual father) in the development of intelligence analysis. Under Kent's leadership until his retirement in 1967, ONE

> emerged as a body with the authority to issue even unwelcome substantive intelligence judgments, while remaining tolerant of dissent from within the ranks of the "departmental" [State Department and military] intelligence organizations.... [However, its] reputation for intellectual integrity... left it isolated in the intensely political environment of the Washington defense and foreign policy establishment.... [Through the 1960s, ONE] was increasingly under fire.... Finally faced with the overt hostility of the Nixon administration, it was unable to defend itself effectively and in 1973 was reorganized out of existence.[6]

In 1973, DCI William Colby replaced ONE with a system of National Intelligence Officers (NIOs). Like their predecessors in ONE, the NIOs are substantive experts in regional and topical matters as they relate to national security issues. These experts were given a collective existence in 1979 with the creation of the National Intelligence Council (NIC). Until 2004, the NIC reported to the DCI as head of the Intelligence Community; and its primary product—the NIEs—represented the DCI's statement of the coordinated views of the Community as a whole. Although its first director came from within the CIA, individuals recruited from the academic community, who had little or no previous intelligence experience, have also headed the NIC. Over the years, there has been an on-again-off-again debate over whether the NIC should continue to be housed at CIA Headquarters. The NIOs technically were not part of the CIA but, rather, belonged to the DCI's community structure. There have been complaints at times from other analytic offices that the NIC or individual NIOs were "captives" of the CIA because their offices were alongside those of Agency officers. That argument is in the process of being resolved. In accordance with the Intelligence Reform and Terrorism Prevention Act of 2004, the NIC has been transferred to the Office of the Director of National Intelligence. A new headquarters building is projected for the DNI, which will include the NIC and its personnel, thus completing the removal of both function and people from the CIA Headquarters.

Although the NIOs' work will henceforth go forward over the DNI's signature, the NIC's role remains one of being the Intelligence Community's authoritative voice on substantive issues concerning national security. The 2004 Act makes clear that within their areas of expertise and under the DNI's direction, "the members of the National Intelligence Council shall constitute the senior intelligence advisers of the intelligence community for purposes of representing the views of the intelligence community" within the U.S. Government.[7] The Deputy Director of National Intelligence for Analysis serves as Chairman of the NIC and oversees production of the PDB. In mid-2007, there were thirteen NIOs with areas of responsibility for Africa, East Asia, Economics and Global Issues, Europe, Military Issues, Near East, Russia and Eurasia, Science and Technology, South Asia, Transnational Threats, Warning, Weapons of Mass Destruction and Proliferation, and Western Hemisphere. The NIOs also serve as contact points for supporting the needs of senior consumers of intelligence and work with experts outside the government to broaden the range of viewpoints being brought to bear on a given issue.

Both the estimating process and individual NIEs have been and are likely to remain controversial. Part of the problem is associated with the very nature of the exercise. The NIEs are exactly what their name says—they are estimates. They do not "predict" the future; they "estimate" where a certain set of circumstances may lead, based on the available intelligence. To call them "best guesses" would be to denigrate the combined intellectual effort that goes into them, but they do cross the line between the certain and the unknown and engage in speculation as to what might, could, or is likely to be. A second cause for tension in the NIE process is the existence of competing interests among the participants necessary to produce a coordinated document. Disputes within the Intelligence Community's various departments and agencies are not uncommon and may, in fact, be even more marked on the more important matters. Throughout the Cold War, there were a number of instances where differences of opinion arose among State's INR, the Defense Department's DIA, the individual service intelligence arms, and the CIA. Different constellations of supporters and opponents of a particular viewpoint would emerge depending on the issue being considered. One such dispute led to what was then heralded as a unique approach to addressing the differences.

The NIEs of the late 1950s and early 1960s overestimated potential Soviet Intercontinental Ballistic Missile (ICBM) deployments. The Air Force believed that the Russians would go all-out in producing its first-generation ICBM. The Army and Navy argued that initial deployment would be minimal, since the Soviet military leaders would choose to wait for the second and third-generation missiles. The CIA's projection for missile deployments was between those of the services, and that position was adopted in the NIEs of the period. Even the compromise number was too high, leading to the famous "missile gap" dispute of the 1960 U.S. election. Over the next decade, the opposite occurred—the estimates were too low. In this argument, the three military services were united in projecting a high rate of Soviet deployment of strategic missiles. INR's analysts foresaw a much lower rate of deployment. Again, the CIA's position fell between the two extremes. NIEs throughout the 1960s tended to project a rate of growth in Soviet strategic weapons between the extremes of the Air Force and the State Department, while the Air Force's higher figures would have been closer to the actual deployment rate.

Criticism surrounding these problems led DCI George H. W. Bush to approve in 1976 the so-called Team A/Team B exercise as part of creating an NIE entitled "Soviet Forces for Intercontinental Conflict through the Mid-1980s." The effort was designed to explore whether "competitive analysis" would improve the quality of the judgments included in the NIE. The competitive aspect involved the use of two teams of analysts—"Team A" of intelligence insiders and "Team B" with individuals from outside the intelligence agencies—to consider the same issue with the same data available to both teams. There were three sets of two teams, with each set considering a different aspect of the Soviet strategic military posture—air defenses, missile accuracy, and intentions. After the teams had completed their work on their topics, the conclusions from each team were compared and an effort was made to reconcile the differences. Much of the discussion in the years since this experiment has centered on one of the B Teams' more hawkish assessment of Soviet preparations for war. Although some modifications in the production of Estimates followed the Team A/Team B exercise, the changes were not so much driven by the exercise as by the dynamic within the analytic community that had brought about the exercise in the first place.

A fair analysis of the Team A/Team B exercise suggests that the most significant outcome may have been the decision to move dissenting views from their previous presentation as footnotes to a more prominent place as an explanation directly in the narrative text. Interestingly, the existing process of fully coordinating Estimates—and, in fact, the very existence of multiple analytic organizations in the Intelligence Community—means that "competitive analysis" is a routine part of the intelligence analysts' work. In addition, other efforts to give greater structure to competitive analysis on particularly contentious issues will at times involve the designation of a "Red Team" to review the available intelligence and the conclusions being projected for a particular NIE. Clearly, Congress intends competitive analysis to remain an important feature in the U.S. analytic effort, directing the DNI to "to ensure that the elements of the intelligence community regularly conduct competitive analysis of analytic products, whether such products are produced by or disseminated to such elements."[8]

And does any of this matter? There have been questions raised for years about whether anyone of importance reads such intelligence products as the NIEs. It is easy to doubt that busy policymakers personally sit down and read documents sometimes running up to a hundred pages. What is more likely is that a staff person briefs them on the major conclusions of those reports in which they have shown the greatest interest. Nonetheless, the impact of NIEs gone wrong has been reaffirmed by events surrounding President Bush's decision to invade Iraq. In early October 2002, the U.S. Intelligence Community completed a highly classified, ninety-page NIE ("Iraq's Continuing Programs for Weapons of Mass Destruction") that concluded Saddam Hussein had weapons of mass destruction (WMD). [See sidebar, "*Key Judgments" from October 2002 NIE* (Excerpts)."] Events have proved that conclusion to be completely wrong. Because the Bush administration used the document in its interactions with Congress and the American public in the debate prior to launching the war, it has been the centerpiece of much of the criticism directed toward the Intelligence Community generally but the CIA in particular. In hindsight, the evidence was too weak to justify the "High Confidence" attached to the critical judgment that Saddam Hussein had ongoing chemical, biological, nuclear, and missile programs. The Senate Select Committee

"*Key Judgments" from October 2002 NIE* (Excerpts)

"Iraq's Continuing Programs for Weapons of Mass Destruction
We judge that Iraq has continued its weapons of mass destruction (WMD) programs in defiance of UN resolutions and restrictions. Baghdad has chemical and biological weapons as well as missiles with ranges in excess of UN restrictions; if left unchecked, it probably will have a nuclear weapon during this decade. (See INR alternative view at the end of these Key Judgments.) . . .

"State/INR Alternative View of Iraq's Nuclear Program
The Assistant Secretary of State for Intelligence and Research (INR) believes that Saddam continues to want nuclear weapons and that available evidence indicates that Baghdad is pursuing at least a limited effort to maintain and acquire nuclear weapons-related capabilities. The activities we have detected do not, however, add up to a compelling case that Iraq is currently pursuing what INR would consider to be an integrated and comprehensive approach to acquire nuclear weapons."
These excerpts were declassified on July 18, 2003, and released at a White House background briefing. The Key Judgments as released are available at: http://www.fas.org/irp/cia/product/iraq-wmd.html.

on Intelligence's report on pre-Iraq war intelligence, released on July 9, 2004, stated the matter thusly: "The U.S. intelligence community gave lawmakers debating whether to wage war on Iraq a deeply flawed and exaggerated assessment of Saddam Hussein's weapons of mass destruction."[9]

On September 24, 2006, another classified analysis made an unwanted appearance in the headlines. An NIE, entitled "Trends in Global Terrorism: Implications for the United States," was leaked to the media (by whom is a matter of debate) in the midst of the run-up to the November mid-term elections. The analytical value of the Estimate was immediately overtaken by a political furor. NIE 2006-02D, completed in April 2006, was portrayed as contradicting President Bush's public assessments of the impact of America's continuing involvement in Iraq on terrorism in general and the threat to the United States.[10] To counteract such conclusions, the President ordered the "Key Judgments" portion of the NIE declassified. Although it certainly presents a stark evaluation of the state of the worldwide jihadist movement, what some people chose to read into the NIE is more startling than its actual conclusions. (See sidebar, *"Key Judgments" from NIE 2006-02D.*") What has occurred in this instance is a form of politicization of intelligence and the intelligence product. It is probably inevitable that intelligence appraisals will

***"Key Judgments" from NIE 2006-02D, "Trends in Global Terrorism: Implications for the United States," dated April 2006* (Excerpts)**

"United States-led counterterrorism efforts have seriously damaged the leadership of al-Qa'ida and disrupted its operations; however, we judge that al-Qa'ida will continue to pose the greatest threat to the Homeland and US interests abroad by a single terrorist organization. We also assess that the global jihadist movement . . . is spreading and adapting to counterterrorism efforts.

- Although we cannot measure the extent of the spread with precision, a large body of all-source reporting indicates that activists identifying themselves as jihadists . . . are increasing in both number and geographic dispersion . . . .
- The Iraq conflict has become the "cause celebre" for jihadists, breeding a deep resentment of US involvement in the Muslim world and cultivating supporters for the global jihadist movement. Should jihadists leaving Iraq perceive themselves, and be perceived, to have failed, we judge fewer fighters will be inspired to carry on the fight . . . .
- We judge that groups of all stripes will increasingly use the Internet to communicate, propagandize, recruit, train, and obtain logistical and financial support."

Text of the "Key Judgments," declassified on September 26, 2006, is available at: http://www.dni.gov/press_releases/Declassified_NIE_Key_Judgments.pdf.

on occasion be used for partisan political purposes. However, the estimative process, already reeling under the impact of the miscall on Iraqi WMD and the new organizational structures brought about by the move from under the DCI to the DNI, has again been presented to the American people as a participant in domestic political matters. It is not a healthy situation for the President, the DNI, the analysts, or the American people to have the credibility of the intelligence process undermined in this fashion.

Of course, it is not the goal of the producers of the NIEs for their estimates to end up being parsed in the day's headlines. It certainly is not often that NIEs end up at the center of Congressional investigations, and not many of them play a significant role in ongoing public policy disputes. Thankfully, few are as wrong as the NIE on Iraq's WMD capabilities. Asked about the quality and usefulness of NIEs and similar intelligence products, consumers and intelligence watchers will provide about as many answers as the number of people queried. Robert L. Suettinger, whose government career encompassed roles as both producer and consumer of Estimates, provides one judicious judgment:

> If they are written at the specific request of a policy principal, or focused on an ongoing crisis, Estimates are likely to be read avidly and be an important factor in crisis management and decisionmaking. If they are highly technical and involve weapons of mass destruction, they will be read carefully and be factored into long-range planning processes, particularly by military consumers. If they are more general overviews of internal politics, economic development, or even foreign policy, they are less likely to be read by key policymakers, but they may be highly useful in educating middle-level officials and other members of the Intelligence Community on general policy issues and potential problems just over the (invariably short) horizon of the policy players.[11]

A substantial number of NIEs and other analytic documents from the Cold War period have now been declassified and released to the public, either individually or as compilations. The compilations are particularly useful in getting a feel for what the Intelligence Community was saying to U.S. policymakers over time on some significant topics. These include: Vietnam, 1948–1975; China, 1948–1976; Soviet Union, 1947–1991; Soviet Union and East Europe, 1989–1991; the early Cold War years; and Soviet strategic forces, 1950–1983.[12] A contemporary, unclassified version of the NIC's view of how developments in the world could evolve in the future—*Mapping the Global Future: Report of the National Intelligence Council's 2020 Project* (2004)—is accessible at: http://www.dni.gov/nic/NIC_2020_project.html. This site also offers access to the interactive International Futures Web site and a computer simulation that allows users to develop their own scenarios of the future.

Anticipating the Next Crisis

The shambles of Pearl Harbor and the surprise at the onset of the Korean War gave rise to a form of intelligence analysis that reached its peak during some of the Cold War's tensest moments, when conventional or even nuclear war seemed to loom on the horizon. The discipline of indications and warning (I&W) intelligence (most often referred to simply as warning intelligence) was originally predicated on the logic that countries tend to engage in certain types of behaviors and activities preparatory to launching an attack. If such behaviors and activities (indications) can be identified and observed on the part of a potential adversary, they can trigger a warning to the national decision makers that some type of response may be necessary. If warning is given early enough, diplomatic, political, and economic countermeasures may be possible.

During the Cold War, the focus of much I&W work was the Soviet Union and the entire range of its armed forces. Substantial "watch" lists were developed and refined to form the theoretical base for identifying anomalous activities that might warn of a developing crisis or imminent hostilities. And mechanisms (the Watch Committee, the NIO for Warning, and, later, the National Warning Committee) were established for integrating departmental views on the significance of observed indicators into a national-level analysis. In essence, warning intelligence was initially about watching for the kinds of activities—short of total mobilization—that a country must take to get ready to wage war. Over time, the methodologies of I&W were extended beyond the bounds of simply guarding against a "sneak" attack to seeking to identify the potential for events around the world that might have an unexpected or negative effect on U.S. foreign policy concerns generally. Such events could be the buildup toward a Middle East war, substantial indications of a coup in an allied or otherwise strategic country, or intelligence that a previously nonnuclear nation may be developing a nuclear weapon. As before, the goal was to provide timely warning of the potential event, so U.S. decision makers could engage in efforts to avert its actual occurrence.

During the 1990s, the cutbacks in budgets and personnel that came with the illusory "peace dividend"—together with an attitude on the part of some intelligence managers that a methodology honed in the past had no place in the post-Cold War era—impacted the warning staffs at almost all of the Intelligence Community agencies. Previously dedicated warning staffs at the CIA, INR, NSA, and DIA were reduced, some reportedly to a single officer. Nevertheless, the position of NIO for Warning has continued, and that position serves today as the principal adviser on warning matters to the DNI and the Intelligence Community as a whole. The NSA continues to maintain the worldwide CRITIC system that provides for the rapid and near-simultaneous alerting of American officials of situations with the potential to affect U.S. security. In addition, at the Pentagon, DIA manages the Defense Indications and Warning System that seeks to supply timely warning of developing threats (including possible terrorist attacks) to the military interests of the United States and its Allies. The military's Combatant Commands also maintain I&W centers that are part of this system.

One of the problems surrounding warning intelligence is that warning by itself is only half of the equation in preventing surprise. The other half is the responsibility of the decision makers—that is, acting on the warning. Iraq's invasion of Kuwait in 1990 is often cited as an instance where U.S. officials were "surprised" by events and, therefore, is regarded as an "intelligence failure." Charles E. Allen, a highly regarded senior intelligence officer who was NIO for Warning from 1988 to 1994, takes issue with that view. Allen notes that, based on appropriate indicators, both an early "warning of war" (initiation by Iraq of preparations for war) and a timely "warning of attack" (action is imminent) were issued by the National Warning Staff, given wide circulation at senior government levels, and briefed to responsible military and civilian leaders. Rather than warning not being given, the warnings given were not heeded by either senior intelligence officials or the top-level military and civilian decision makers. It appears that the warnings were dismissed because "senior US officials talked with, and accepted the judgment of[,] a number of leaders in the Middle East as well as the Soviet Union, all of whom were of the opinion that Saddam did not intend to attack."[13]

The events of 9/11 have again put the spotlight on the warning aspect of intelligence analysis. And the most talked about target—the terrorist threat—is not one to which the indications and methodologies used for nations are likely to apply. Nations are very stationary objects with defined borders, interests, and goals; al Qaeda, on the other hand, is amorphous and diffuse. The exact role that the discipline of warning intelligence will play in America's continuing response to terrorism is as yet less than fully defined. New and refined analytical techniques and thought processes will be required to develop the indicators necessary to create warning of future terrorist attacks. A perceived need for warning may have played a role in the controversial decision to have NSA (with the assistance of some of the telephone companies) gather domestic U.S. telephone records into a huge database. By sifting through ("mining") such data, using a process termed "link analysis," it is theoretically possible to establish patterns of telephone activity that could be associated with an upcoming terrorist attack. With that information, such an attack might be forestalled. Beyond the terrorist threat, however, there is no doubt that the warning community remains engaged in watching and evaluating on a continuing basis such potential trouble spots as North Korea, Iran, and China, as well other regions of the world that can become flashpoints for developments harmful to U.S. interests.

Analytic Issues

Intelligence in general is a very difficult profession. Even if it does most things right most of the time, intelligence is still accountable for the things that go wrong—which seem to occur more frequently on the toughest issues. Intelligence analysis shares the difficulties of the profession as a whole, and introduces some aspects that are unique to the effort of trying to determine what others are going to do. That the future is unknowable is a truism. Yet, we employ analysts of various sorts—a stock broker, for instance—to assist us in looking forward to what might or is most likely to be. Intelligence analysts typically must work with incomplete and ambiguous data. The analyst who is working on the most critical issue—that is, the one about which least is known—is often in the position of trying to put together a jigsaw puzzle for which there is no picture and no border pieces. To the extent that the collectors can supply more and better information, the easier it is for the picture to begin to take on coherence. In the absence of detailed intelligence—or, worse, when the available information is inaccurate or has been deliberately falsified by the other side—analysts must rely on their knowledge of the subject area and their intellectual skills in seeking to create the most accurate picture of the unknown as possible. That they will at times fail should not be surprising. Nonetheless, the very humanness of analysts (and of the decision makers who use or misuse intelligence) also introduces patterns of behavior that can exacerbate the incidence of error in the analytic process.

Writing about chairing a working group in the mid-1970s to review Intelligence Community processes for warning of impending attack or major international crisis, long-time senior CIA officer Cord Meyer identified several aspects of the challenges that bedevil analysts:

> In reading the history and Agency-conducted postmortems of past international crises . . . , I was struck by one common denominator running through the incidents. . . . [T]here were in each case bits and pieces of information collected in advance that should have alerted the intelligence analysts and policymakers to what was coming. But to find these germs of wheat in the abundant chaff and to understand their significance in time to affect decision making was no easy job in the face of a preponderance of evidence pointing the other way. More important, these intelligence gems usually contradicted the prevailing optimistic assumptions of the policymakers . . . , and these preconceptions were to some extent shared by the intelligence analysts. There was a persistent tendency to assume that our opponents . . . would act in a logical and rational manner, like Western statesmen, and intelligence that went against this preconception tended in some cases to be discounted.[14]

In a perfect world, it is the function and even duty of intelligence analysts to provide support to those who make policy, not to support particular policies. Analysts do not, however, live in a perfect world. Whatever their personal beliefs, the environment in which analysts work is suffused with the ideological and political leanings of their elected and appointed bosses. The top-level decision makers tend to judge the value of intelligence by its congruence with their views. That is to say, they want to receive intelligence that supports the political positions they have taken. Thus, there is pressure throughout the intelligence process, but particularly on the analytical side, to produce "intelligence to please." This phenomenon is sometimes referred to as "cooking the books" or the "politicization" of intelligence.

As previously noted, it was until recently the DCI whose job it was to present the President with the Intelligence Community's most vital intelligence on the major issues of the day. Henceforth, that role will rest with the DNI. DCIs who were out of synch with their Presidents on policy issues tended to resign or be fired. John McCone (1961–1965), Richard Helms (1966–1973), and William Colby (1973–1976) fall into this category. On the other hand, William Casey (1981–1987), Robert Gates (1991–1993), and, most recently, George Tenet (1997–2004) have all been accused of politicizing the intelligence they were providing their Presidents. Although theory holds that there should be a bright line between policymaking and intelligence, practice has shown that such is almost impossible to maintain at the top of the system. Therefore, it should not be surprising that there is a tension in a job that straddles informing and supporting, two separate but overlapping activities. DCIs/DNIs are appointed officials, and as such are part of the President's "team." This was true even when the DCI had a background as a professional intelligence officer (the last professional to hold the position was Robert Gates and the last before that was William Colby). Whether in the past some DCIs have gotten too close to the policymaking process and whether in the present and future the DNI should be a Cabinet member are questions that will continue to elicit varying responses, with no clear, always-right answer.

The issue remains, however, as to the effect that the political environment has on the production of objective intelligence by the analysts who work much further down in the bureaucratic hierarchy. Can, for example, a DIA desk analyst go forward with an assessment that a shooting war—whether Vietnam or Iraq—is going badly? Is the Air Force analyst going to contradict the Chief of Staff's opinion that additional bombing will have the desired effect on a particular target set? When the Secretary of State has gone on the public record that further talks are necessary, will an INR analyst project that talking will only exacerbate the situation? Do telephone calls from the Vice President or other senior officials directly to CIA analysts or their supervisors constitute pressure on them to alter their judgments in order to conform to prevailing policy prescriptions? Will analysts sometimes give in to such pressure out of fear for their jobs or skew their conclusions in order to advance their own interests? We would like to think that the analysts can and will hold firm in their well-considered judgments, but the record is not clear on whether such pressure is a frequent matter or how much effect it has on the objectivity of intelligence. To the extent that it exists, the pressure to "be a team player" and alter a judgment tends to be indirect and subtle, and often may originate within the analyst rather than from outside.

Beyond the political realities of life that can impact on analysis, aspects of the human thought process also influence the quality of the intelligence product. Manifestations of these potential problems include mirror-imaging, the power of preconceptions, and cognitive biases.

Mirror-imaging occurs when people analogize from the familiar in an effort to understand the unfamiliar or to fill in the unknown. In this fashion, analysts will seek to address that which they do not know about the potential acts of another country or leader by assuming that they will act in a particular way since that is what we would do in a similar position. Absent any other information, it may be necessary for an analyst to use what we would do to guide a conclusion about what someone else will do; but judgments based on such reasoning need to be explained carefully and should not be given with a high degree of confidence. People from different cultures do not think alike, nor do they perceive their interests (national or personal) as we do. After his formal review of the Intelligence Community's failure in 1998 to warn that India was going to test a nuclear weapon, Adm. David E. Jeremiah suggested as his bottom-line assessment that

> both the intelligence and the policy communities had an underlying mindset going into these tests that the BJP [Bharatiya Janata Party] would behave as we behave. For instance, there [was] an assumption that the BJP platform would mirror Western political platforms. In other words, a politician is going to say something in his political platform leading up to the elections, but not necessarily follow through on the platform once he takes office and is exposed to the immensity of his problem . . . . So, first of all, we had a mindset that said everybody else is going to work like we work . . . . [W]e don't think like the other nation thinks.[15]

As individuals, our preconceived ideas about things that we believe we know and understand tend to shape how we receive new information. The same is true for analysts. Actions by a nation viewed as friendly will be interpreted differently than similar actions by a nation regarded as hostile. This phenomenon is referred to as the power of preconceptions. Long-time CIA analyst and intelligence theoretician Jack Davis suggests that preconceptions can play a useful role in helping analysts to process and organize newly available but incomplete and ambiguous information. However, preconceptions also can distort how analysts interpret new information. For the most part, analysts "will see more vividly and pay more attention to information that is consonant with what they expect [or, we can add, want] to see . . . . This makes the estimative process vulnerable in anticipating unusual events."[16] Thus, even accurate information that conflicts with an analyst's preconceptions—or that would increase uncertainty if accepted—may well be dismissed, rather than being incorporated into a new, changed understanding. This tendency can be reinforced by the view analysts have of themselves as "the experts" in their areas. That is, they may not be psychologically prepared to tear apart the edifice of explanation that they have constructed so painstakingly over time.

Richards J. Heuer, Jr., has written extensively on the human thought process as it applies to intelligence analysis. He projects that we process information through building mental models of how things ought to be. At the same time, by constructing (even if the act is unconscious) these models, we introduce bias into our evaluation of new information. This is known as cognitive bias, and it manifests itself in the manner in which analysts reach many types of judgments. Because humans have a need for order in their environment, there is a tendency to seek causes for what may be no more than accidental or random phenomena—and to believe that the causes have been found. Analysts often look for and project that other countries will pursue "a coherent, coordinated, rational plan." By taking this approach, they will "overestimate their own ability to predict future events in those nations." In addition, when inferring the causes of behavior, analysts may give "too much weight . . . to personal qualities and dispositions of the actor and not enough to situational determinants of the actor's behavior."[17]

As intelligence analysis moves forward under the Intelligence Community's present organizational arrangement, it remains to be seen whether the DNI can bring greater coordination and cohesion to that community's fragmented and competing analytic components. Many of the personnel resources and program dollars remain entrenched in the Defense Department, with lesser numbers and amounts tucked away in other parts of the governmental structure. There is a strong likelihood that the DNI will find it necessary to continue to build up that office's own analytic resources (a process already well underway), thus further isolating the previously dominant CIA intelligence directorate. Whether a DNI analytic arm will represent a unifying element rather than just another competing element in an already crowded field will be interesting to watch. Whatever the organizational outcome, many of the problems associated with intelligence analysis will remain, as they are rooted in the strongly human aspect of the process.

Notes

1. Edwin C. Fishel, *The Secret War for the Union: The Untold Story of Military Intelligence in the Civil War* (Boston, MA: Houghton Mifflin, 1996), 298–300.
2. Anthony Cave Brown, ed., *The Secret War Report of the OSS* (New York: Berkley, 1976), 78.
3. Arthur S. Hulnick, *Fixing the Spy Machine: Preparing American Intelligence for the Twenty-First Century* (Westport, CT: Praeger, 1999), 45.
4. Commission on the Intelligence Capabilities of the United States Regarding Weapons of Mass Destruction, "Transmittal Letter," *Report to the President of the United States*, March 31, 2005, http://www.wmd.gov/report/index.html.
5. John Helgerson, *Getting to Know the President: CIA Briefings of Presidential Candidates, 1952–1992* (Washington, DC: Center for the Study of Intelligence, Central Intelligence Agency, 1995), 1, 3, 86, https://www.cia.gov/csi/books/briefing/index.htm.
6. Donald P. Steury, ed., "Introduction," *Sherman Kent and the Board of National Estimates: Collected Essays* (Washington, DC: History Staff, Center for the Study of Intelligence, Central Intelligence Agency, 1994), xii–xiii (footnote omitted), https://www.cia.gov/csi/books/shermankent/toc.html.

7. U.S. Congress, *Intelligence Reform and Terrorism Prevention Act of 2004* (Pub. Law No. 108–458), §103B(d), http://frwebgate.access.gpo.gov/cgi-bin/getdoc.cgi?dbname=108_cong_public_laws&docid=f:publ458.108.

8. Ibid., §102(h)(1)(C).

9. Dana Priest and Dafna Linzer, "Panel Condemns Iraq Prewar Intelligence," *Washington Post* (July 10, 2004): A1.

10. See Karen DeYoung, "Spy Agencies Say Iraq War Hurting U.S. Terror Fight," *Washington Post* (September 24, 2006): A1; Mark Mazzetti, "Spy Agencies Say Iraq War Worsens Terror Threat," *New York Times* (September 24, 2006), http://www.nytimes.com; and Greg Miller, "Spy Agencies Say Iraq War Fuels Terror," *Los Angeles Times* (September 24, 2006), http://www.latimes.com.

11. Robert L. Suettinger, "Introduction," in *Tracking the Dragon: National Intelligence Estimates on China during the Era of Mao, 1948–1976,* National Intelligence Council, eds., John K. Allen, Jr., John Carver, and Tom Elmore (Washington, DC: NIC 2004–05, October 2004), xi, http://www.dni.gov/nic/NIC_foia_china.html.

12. National Intelligence Council, *Estimative Products on Vietnam, 1948–1975* (Washington, DC: NIC 2005-03, April 2005, http://www.dni.gov/nic/NIC_foia_vietnam.html; Gerald K. Haines and Robert E. Leggett, eds., *CIA's Analysis of the Soviet Union, 1947–1991* (Washington, DC: Center for the Study of Intelligence, 2001), https://www.cia.gov/csi/books/princeton/index.html; Benjamin B. Fischer, ed., *At Cold War's End: US Intelligence on the Soviet Union and Eastern Europe, 1989–1991* (Washington, DC: Center for the Study of Intelligence, 1999), https://www.cia.gov/csi/books/19335/art-1.html; Woodrow J. Kuhns, ed., *Assessing the Soviet Threat: The Early Cold War Years* (Washington, DC: Center for the Study of Intelligence, 1997), https://www.cia.gov/csi/books/coldwaryrs/index.html; Donald P. Steury, ed., *Intentions and Capabilities: Estimates on Soviet Strategic Forces, 1950–1983* (Washington, DC: Center for the Study of Intelligence, 1996), https://www.cia.gov/csi/pubs.html.

13. Charles E. Allen, "Warning and Iraq's Invasion of Kuwait: A Retrospective Look," *Defense Intelligence Journal* 7(2) (Fall 1998): 43.

14. Cord Meyer, *Facing Reality: From World Federalism to the CIA,* 2nd ed. (Washington, DC: University Press of America, 1982), 227.

15. Jeremiah News Conference, June 2, 1998, http://www.fas.org/irp/cia/product/jeremiah.html.

16. Jack Davis, "Combating Mind-Set," *Studies in Intelligence* 36(5) (1992): 34, https://www.cia.gov/csi/studies.html.

17. Richards J. Heuer, Jr., *Psychology of Intelligence Analysis* (Washington, DC: Center for the Study of Intelligence, Central Intelligence Agency, 1999), 127, https://www.cia.gov/csi/books/19104/index.html.

CHAPTER 4

How Do We Protect Ourselves?

Defining Our Subject

Just as the U.S. government seeks to collect information about foreign activities that may require its attention, so other countries want to gain access to similar knowledge about the United States. Preventing and neutralizing the efforts of others to steal our secrets—and sometimes using our knowledge of their activities to our advantage—is the function of counterintelligence (CI). Some writings about intelligence offer a definition that separates counterintelligence (information) from counterespionage (action). Other writers use the two terms interchangeably. We will follow the lead of Executive Order 12333, signed by President Reagan in December 1981, which defines counterintelligence as both the "information gathered and [the] activities conducted to protect against espionage, other intelligence activities, sabotage, or assassinations conducted for or on behalf of foreign powers, organizations or persons, or international terrorist activities."[1] At the same time, there are other, defensive actions taken to protect certain people, places, and things from prying eyes or unwelcome intrusions. Not all such activities necessarily constitute CI. Nonetheless, they are part of a protective continuum that ranges from reminding defense industry workers not to talk too much (World War II's slogan of "loose lips sink ships") to rooting out a spy in our midst. These actions buttress the practice of CI in its function of protecting America's secrets. They include document, communications/information, physical, and personnel security programs.

People, Places, and Things

Document Security

One of the ways to protect information that you do not want to be widely known is to control access to it. The government's basic means for limiting access to information involves the classification of documents. Its system is based on a hierarchy (from least to most restrictive) of Confidential, Secret, and Top Secret. (See sidebar, "*Classification System*.") Although Confidential is rarely used these days, the idea is to define progressively more restrictive levels of sensitivity of the information and to grant access to documents at each classification only to individuals who have been authorized to handle information at that level. In addition, access by individuals to specific items of information is further restricted—in theory, at least—by the "need-to-know" principle. That is, whatever their clearance level, individuals are supposed to see only the classified material necessary for them to do their jobs. Even given the murky differentiation between the classification levels and the potentially idiosyncratic views of classifiers, this system sounds relatively simple. However, actual practice makes the classification system much more complicated than it first appears.

Classification System

The U.S. Government classifies information at one of three levels:

Confidential is "applied to information, the unauthorized disclosure of which reasonably could be *expected to cause damage* to the national security that the original classification authority is able to identify or describe."

Secret is "applied to information, the unauthorized disclosure of which reasonably could be *expected to cause serious damage* to the national security . . . "

Top Secret is "applied to information, the unauthorized disclosure of which reasonably could be *expected to cause exceptionally grave damage* to the national security. . . ."[2]

Beyond the standard system is a set of restrictions designed for what is known as Sensitive Compartmented Information (SCI). Information from and about imaging and signals intelligence satellites falls into the SCI category, as does the information from special reconnaissance aircraft and intelligence-collection submarines. Each of these types of materials has additional classification markings (code words), and access requires clearances in addition to the standard level. The idea is to create "compartments" for particular types of information, which require specific clearance before access is granted. This code-word system for "special intelligence" dates from the U.S. and British practices in World War II when various code words (the best known are MAGIC and ULTRA) were used to guard the knowledge that important Japanese and German communications were being intercepted and broken. There are even different code words for various levels of sensitivity within the special handling categories. In the past, the National Security Agency (NSA) has applied individual code-name restrictions to specific operations or methods of intercept. The same is true for the military services (particularly their investigative arms), as well as for the CIA's clandestine operations where there are numerous special compartments for reporting from specific human sources. Thus, the U.S. classification system involves layers upon layers.

Outside the formal classification system, there is a growing body of agency-by-agency controls on what is known as "sensitive but unclassified" information. There are dozens of different kinds of access controls being placed on unclassified information. These take such formulations as For Official Use Only, Law Enforcement Sensitive, or Limited Official Use. Because they are generated and defined by individual agencies, these controls lack the broad compatibility of the formal system. Today, information sharing is being promoted across federal agencies and among different levels of government, such as state and local authorities involved in homeland security. The additional restrictions on the dissemination of even unclassified information complicate an already difficult information-sharing environment.

There is general agreement that classifying documents and other materials relating to national security is an appropriate means for protecting information. However, beyond its overly complex structure and the tendency of individual agencies to add their own layers to the system, the system has been criticized for the manner in which it is implemented. Complaints about overclassification of information, in terms of both amount and levels, have come from inside the system, congressional committees, and nongovernmental organizations. In addition, freedom-of-information groups continue to voice concerns about slowness in compliance with declassification mandates. The major argument regarding overclassification involves the expectation under the American political system that the public will be part of the debate on national security policy. The unnecessary—even arbitrary—withholding of information short-circuits that critical role in the country's governance. Other critics claim that government officials often classify documents to shield themselves from public accountability or to avoid being embarrassed by the exposure of their mistakes.

It is likely that there is a tendency to overclassify national security materials. Protecting the men and women in the services and guarding the sources and methods of the intelligence business are deeply ingrained habits for military and intelligence personnel. In addition, policy and intelligence analysts are inclined to classify their written products as highly as they can. This is done on the supposition that their readers are more likely to read a document stamped "Top Secret" than they are one stamped "Unclassified." That presupposes officials who select what they read based on classification rather than subject matter. This is an interesting, if somewhat insulting, proposition. In general, however, based on the report of the Information Security Oversight Office (ISOO), which gives the total number of classification decisions in the Executive Branch in 2005 as 14,206,773,[3] we can conclude that—overclassification or not—a lot of documents are being protected from people the government believes should not be seeing them.

Communications/Information Security

Intelligence is of little value unless those who need it are able to receive and understand it. Consequently, at any given moment, there are large volumes of classified information flowing over various communications systems and being handled in military and civilian communications centers around the world. Protecting that flow against unauthorized access is the function of communications security (COMSEC). The arrival of the electric typewriter followed by the computer has required that the umbrella of protection be extended beyond what may be printed on a piece of paper or sent over the airwaves. The term information security (INFOSEC) covers both communications and computer security (COMPUSEC). Thus, the practice of INFOSEC seeks to protect telecommunications and automated information systems, and the information they process. More recently, the term information assurance (IA) is being used to underscore the point that it is not just the messages that require protection but the whole information infrastructure. A substantial part of the communications of the national security agencies does not take place over dedicated, government-controlled lines but, rather, over public telephone and fax lines. The geometric increase in computer connectivity, which represents a revolution in the way the government (and everyone else) communicates, has certainly brought benefits; but it has also increased the level of risk to U.S. information technology systems and the critical operations they support.

A committee of the National Security Council (NSC) makes U.S. information security policy. NSA then implements that policy, establishing the procedures that the agencies must follow. As the older term COMSEC implies, the main focus is on protecting the government's electronic communications. Information security policies include maintaining the security of related materials and information against unauthorized access. In this regard, the NSA Director has the authority to determine the classification of all information security equipment and documentation. INFOSEC policies also seek to prevent the detection and interception of emissions from electronic typewriters and computer systems, protect against interception of transmissions, and safeguard the flow of information with robust cryptographic systems.

All electrical equipment emits electromagnetic waves. If these "emanations" can be intercepted, it is theoretically possible to analyze them and deduce the characteristics of the device that created them. In this way, the text of a message that is being typed on an electric typewriter or a computer keyboard can be reconstructed. For example, during the Cuban Missile Crisis of 1962, NSA was unable to read the enciphered communications the Soviet forces were sending from their sites in Cuba. The agency placed special equipment on a U.S. signals intelligence ship stationed off the Cuban coast. The target was the radiation emitted by the machines enciphering messages to Moscow at a Soviet communications station. Although the ship normally stayed about eight miles offshore, collecting the deciphered information contained in these emanations was potentially so valuable that the ship would move in as close as four miles from the Cuban coastline.[4] As a countermeasure against such potentially compromising events, NSA oversees the government's "Tempest" program, under which only properly shielded equipment can be used in classified environments.

Almost any transmission over radio or wire can be intercepted either directly or, in the case of commercial lines, at a switching point. A good example of how ingenuity can provide access where it is least expected is the success in 1975 of a U.S. submarine in placing a recording tap on a Russian communications cable in the Sea of Okhotsk, as detailed in Chapter 2. (The growing use of fiber-optic cables by the telephone companies is a double-edged sword for NSA. Because it is difficult if not impossible to tap, fiber-optic cable adds a built-in element of additional security to the use of telephone lines. On the other side is the fact that such lines will be just as difficult for NSA to monitor.) The effort in transmission security is focused on protecting against traffic analysis (a steady stream of data prevents assumptions about the cause of a peak in activity), imitative deception (authentication procedures are a necessity), and disruption (alternate communication routes for the critical circuits are most important in times of crisis).

The ultimate line of defense in communicating national security information is cryptographic security, an area in which NSA has wide-ranging responsibilities. NSA is not only this nation's codebreaking organization, but it is also responsible for America's codemaking. An NSA component designs and produces or procures the cryptographic equipment and associated materials for the U.S. military services and national security agencies. This is not a simple task. Cryptographic equipment is not a one-size-fits-all commodity. Requirements across a range of consumers necessitate the creation of multiple enciphering systems. The needs of an embassy are quite different from those of the pilot of an Air Force stealth bomber. NSA prescribes how cryptographic systems are to be used, promulgating the national cryptographic security doctrine and overseeing its execution. Its role includes development of secure data and voice transmission links through such systems as the Defense Satellite Communications System (DSCS). The agency also has been at the forefront of the development of "scrambler" telephones, to allow secure voice communication between and among the main national security individuals and organizations.

Physical Security

The manifestations of physical security are all around us, whether or not we ever handle classified information. Many of the obstacles that people may encounter when they want to enter some facility—fences, gates, guards, identification badges, swipe-card locks, retina scans—are physical security measures. Such measures seek to "build a wall" around America's secrets (or a private company's proprietary information), and are linked with and provide support for CI efforts.

The national security agencies take elaborate precautions to guard their classified materials and activities from targeted or inadvertent disclosures. Using the CIA compound outside Washington, DC, as an example, we can see that physical security is usually applied in layers. (The same general types of defensive measures can be found at the Pentagon, military installations, and the State Department, but with individual modifications to fit different circumstances. The Pentagon, for instance, contains an underground metro station.) The CIA "campus" is surrounded by a substantial fence and is monitored by security cameras. Entrance is through guarded gates, where positive identification is required before passing through. Visitors must have had their presence authorized prior to arrival, or they cannot proceed. Guards and electronic devices also control access to the individual buildings. Visitors require a "cleared" escort to proceed beyond the entryway, and must be accompanied by that escort or another person to whom custody has been passed in writing.

Inside the buildings, just as classification and code words provide compartmentation of access to documents, physical barriers segregate specific areas away from the general traffic flow. Regular CIA employees have Top Secret clearances, but there are vaulted offices with special access controls where individuals who do not work there must stop, request entry, and identify themselves. At the Pentagon, as another example, additional access clearances are required to enter the area that contains the National Military Command Center. Inside all offices, even vaulted areas, code-worded documents are signed in and placed in approved storage containers, usually safes with combination locks. At the end of the day, desks are cleared and all classified materials are put in safes that are locked and, then, checked by another individual. As employees are leaving the buildings, briefcases are subject to being checked. The introduction of electronic storage devices has made the threat of a briefcase check largely an empty gesture in terms of stopping someone who is determined to remove classified material from the building. However, that is basically true of most physical security measures. A trusted employee who is working for the other side has many ways of doing damage. That is one of the reasons why the national security organizations place considerable emphasis on personnel security practices.

Personnel Security

National security agencies seek to employ people who are loyal, reliable, and stable. Applicants must first clear the hurdle of getting a security clearance. A Top Secret clearance requires what is known as a full field investigation. The FBI usually conducts this background investigation, but some agencies do their own fieldwork. The investigation is based on the personal and professional information that applicants supply on a detailed, multipaged form, and is partially at least a check on how honest the applicant has been. A full field investigation may take months if the applicant has lived overseas or moved around in a number of jobs. Almost everyone with whom an applicant has come into contact is a potential target for an interview—neighbors, schoolteachers, classmates, college roommates, employers, and anyone in-between. In addition, school, police, and credit histories are checked.

For some agencies, the background check is accompanied by a polygraph examination. While hooked up to a machine that measures physical responses—respiration, heart rate, blood pressure, and perspiration—the applicant is asked a series of questions. At this point, the questions focus largely on lifestyle and loyalty issues. With the polygraph, long mislabeled the "lie detector," a trained operator is supposed to be able to identify reactions that could be indications of falsehoods or deception. Use of the polygraph is not universal among the national security agencies. In fact, it remains controversial; and doubts about its reliability are raised on a continuing basis. Nonetheless, the CIA, Defense Intelligence Agency (DIA), National Reconnaissance Office (NRO), and NSA have the polygraph as part of the employment process. The State Department does not require a polygraph examination, arguing that the use of a suspect device is essentially demeaning to its personnel. Following much the same reasoning, the Federal Bureau of Investigation (FBI) had refused to use the polygraph until 2001, when veteran agent Robert Philip Hanssen was arrested for spying for the Soviet Union/Russia for over fifteen years.

The results of the background investigation and of the polygraph examination, if used, go to the security offices of the employing agency, and a decision is made there as to the applicant's suitability for employment. Even after being hired, individuals remain subject to periodic background reinvestigations, including new polygraph examinations at the agencies where the device is used. For current employees, the target of the polygraph is primarily security and counterintelligence issues. Questions will normally concern such matters as contacts with foreign nationals or the media and whether the employee has engaged in any compromising or illegal behavior. These reinvestigations are theoretically on a cycle of every five years, although there are indications that for various reasons (including too few polygraph operators) these timelines are not always met. Even given the various agencies' continued commitment to its use, it is clear that CIA officer Aldrich Hazen Ames, who spied for the Soviet Union and Russia for nine years, was able to "beat" the polygraph (that is, avoid implicating himself in traitorous activities) on more than one occasion. The merits of the polygraph will probably continue to be debated as long as it is used. Its effectiveness may be more psychological than scientific, especially if it intimidates most people into revealing more than they might otherwise.

The question remains, however, whether all the efforts put into classification, information security, physical security, and the vetting of personnel prevent American secrets from getting into the hands of those who wish us ill. The answer is obviously that they do not provide perfect security for America's secrets. The presence of too many spy cases from among the national security agencies makes that very clear.

Finding Their Spies

Counterintelligence through World War II

The need to guard against penetration by an enemy's spies is not something new to Americans. During the Revolutionary War, British spies were an ongoing problem, given the substantial percentage of the population who remained loyal to the Crown. In the best-known spy episode, American forces captured British intelligence officer Maj. John André in September 1780 on his way back from a clandestine meeting with Benedict Arnold. General Arnold had been selling military information to the British for some time, but the meeting with André was to negotiate the surrender of his command at West Point, New York. Arnold was able to escape, in effect defecting to the British; André was hanged as a spy.

In the years between the Revolution and the end of World War II, the interest of Americans and their government in counterintelligence has swung from action to inaction, depending on the country's perception of the threat. In the Civil War, President Lincoln suspended *habeas corpus*, allowing the government to hold suspected Confederate spies (among others) indefinitely without formal charges. It is also in the Civil War that we find an early example of the mixing of counterintelligence with efforts to stamp out subversion, sabotage, and other such activities. Working for the War Department, Lafayette Baker ran the government's counterintelligence activities, and succeeded in catching such Confederate spies as Belle Boyd. However, legend has it that Baker went beyond his spy-catching duties, throwing into jail (and perhaps not treating very well) Southern sympathizers, military deserters, war profiteers, and even regular criminals—without providing them the benefit of due process. Just where such actions by the government cross over into arbitrariness and the suppression of dissent remains a topic that deservedly generates considerable debate.

Before the United States entered World War I, American counterintelligence was brought back to life to neutralize massive German subversion and sabotage operations. In 1916, Congress gave the Justice Department's Bureau of Investigation (FBI after 1935) authority to conduct CI investigations. The Bureau worked with the Secret Service, the Military Intelligence Division (MID), and the Office of Naval Intelligence (ONI) in an effort to stem the violence associated with the German covert campaign. After the war, the Army's involvement in investigating domestic political and labor groups produced a public backlash against military CI. Similarly, the FBI seemed much more interested in chasing radical political groups than spies. As World War II loomed, the focus shifted back toward the activities of foreign intelligence services. In 1939, President Roosevelt placed coordination of counterespionage activities with a committee consisting of the heads of the FBI, MID, and ONI, in recognition of the military's CI responsibility for service personnel and military bases.

Thanks to able counterintelligence work, the United States avoided the disruptive level of subversion and sabotage encountered prior to World War I. This was due largely to the assistance of a German-American double agent, William G.

Sebold. While pretending to work for German military intelligence, Sebold provided the FBI with the information needed to neutralize Germany's espionage network in the United States by June 1940. Although the Germans tried to reestablish a clandestine network, the FBI and local authorities kept picking up their agents. Concerns about the possibility of Japanese subversion led President Roosevelt to the drastic (and, history argues, wholly unnecessary) act of ordering in early 1942 the internment of over 100,000 Japanese-Americans living on the West Coast. In retrospect, this move seems to have been more for political than CI reasons, as by all accounts FBI Director J. Edgar Hoover advised against the evacuation and internment order.

World War II saw the success of one of the greatest CI operations of all time. The German espionage network in Britain was rolled up early in the war, and some of the captured agents put to work for the British domestic intelligence service (MI5). These double agents were used to feed a mixture of true and false intelligence to German military intelligence. This was the famous Double-Cross (XX) System. It worked with precision because ULTRA—the intelligence product from reading German military communications—allowed them to confirm that German intelligence believed and was acting on the agents' information. Using the Double-Cross System, an elaborate deception plan (Bodyguard) was devised to hide the date, time, and place of the Allied landing in France. Even after the landings had taken place in Normandy, the German High Command continued to look for the main invasion force well away from the actual landing sites.

Cold War Counterintelligence

American counterintelligence emerged from World War II with some successes to its credit but as fragmented as it had been earlier. The National Security Act of 1947, which created the National Security Council, the Defense Department, a separate Air Force, and the CIA, did not change the situation. The 1947 Act and follow-on directives gave the CIA primary responsibility for CI in foreign countries. It had no responsibility for domestic CI, and no law enforcement authority. The FBI's responsibility was only for domestic CI, and its law enforcement authority was limited to the United States. The military services and field commanders could conduct CI operations both overseas and in the United States. In addition, the services had some enforcement authority at home and abroad for military personnel and installations. Thus, the United States moved through the Cold War years with CI spread among multiple (and not always cooperating) agencies. As Professor Roy Godson points out, "[n]one of the specific programs, modi operandi, or organizational arrangements of [the CI] agencies was managed by a single government entity."[5] Essentially, the CIA, FBI, and military services were "doing their own thing," and coordinating with the others when the thought occurred or it seemed expedient to do so. Such a disposition, of course, matched the general decentralization of intelligence in the U.S. government.

Success and failure in counterintelligence go hand in hand; in fact, they are frequently the same thing. A flurry of arrests of spies often brings on a response from the media, the public, and sometimes Congress of, "How could this happen?" That is, the uncovering of spies can mean that they have been successful in their spying efforts, and they are just now getting caught. The revelations beginning in the late-1940s about Soviet espionage in the United States are an example of a success that illuminates a failure. Despite years of debate, there can be no doubt today that the Soviet Union ran massive and very successful intelligence-collection operations in the United States in the 1930s and 1940s, and that these operations were assisted and participated in by members of the Communist Party of the United States (CPUSA).

Although the FBI had moved decisively against Nazi and other fascist subversive elements in the country even before World War II began, the efforts directed toward communist espionage efforts were more halting. In some ways, this reflected the realities of political and strategic considerations about how to handle the Soviet Union and its leader, Josef Stalin. What ongoing efforts there were came to a standstill following the German invasion of Russia in June 1941, although the FBI continued to keep a watch on some CPUSA activists. The main Soviet intelligence organizations—the GRU (military intelligence) and the KGB (the later, better-known name for the USSR's foreign intelligence organization)—were each running separate "legal" and "illegal" espionage networks. "Legal" operations were managed under some type of recognized organization, such as the Soviet Embassy, consulates, the Amtorg Trading Company, or the Tass news agency. Intelligence officers with no obvious connection to the regular organizations and usually working under an assumed name managed the "illegal" networks. Both the GRU and the KGB were able to infiltrate multiple layers of the Washington bureaucracy, including Congress, the White House staff, OSS, and the State, Justice, and Treasury departments. Soviet intelligence also was able to walk away with America's greatest secret—how to make an atomic bomb.

Two parallel streams of counterintelligence work—one human and the other cryptanalytic—converged in the mid-1940s to expose the extent of Soviet spying in America. The best way into what another intelligence service is doing is to recruit a spy in that service. Lacking that, defectors can play a key role in revealing the workings of other intelligence organizations. That is what opened the door in the 1940s for the FBI to begin to slow down Soviet operations in the United States. Defection of former Communist agents Whitaker Chambers and Elizabeth Bentley, coupled with the defection in Canada of Soviet code clerk Igor Gouzenko, gave the FBI the names of a number of Russian spies. Gouzenko also provided information about Soviet penetration of the Manhattan Project, the joint U.S.-U.K. program to construct an atomic weapon. Also in the mid-1940s, another stream of intelligence on Soviet spying began to produce results.

For communicating operational details of their espionage efforts to Moscow (longer items were sent via courier or diplomatic pouch), the GRU and KGB used commercial telegraph lines. Their messages were first encoded and then enciphered using a "one-time pad." Created and used properly, a one-time pad should be unbreakable, as enciphering by random numbers with only two copies of the cipher in existence (the user with one and the receiver with the other) is not amenable to cryptanalytic attack. However, a manufacturing mistake created duplicate pages in the Soviet one-time pads. The U.S. Army began intercepting and collecting the then-unreadable cables in the late 1930s. The duplicate pages began showing up in 1942, and their use continued for several years. Utilizing the discovery of the printing mistake and a lot of hard work, Army cryptanalysts broke this particular Soviet code. From 1946 until the project ended in 1980, they were able to read significant portions of almost 3,000 Soviet messages sent between 1942 and 1948. This particular cryptanalytic breakthrough was given the codename of VENONA, and it would remain a closely held government secret until 1995.[6]

The intersection of the two streams of intelligence had multiple effects on America at mid-twentieth century. For one, they created the leads that eventually produced arrests or otherwise ended the careers of a large number of Soviet spies. Second, the attendant trials, congressional hearings, and media publicity created an atmosphere in the country often referred to as "the Red scare" or associated with the name of Senator Joseph McCarthy who sought to ride people's suspicions and fears to political gain. The arguments went on for decades about the "persecution" of Alger Hiss and the "innocence" of Julius and Ethel Rosenberg. One of the victims of all the animosity was the FBI, as its involvement in the cases raised concerns about it being a "political police." Because the VENONA materials remained hidden from public knowledge for so many years, the evidence contained in the Soviet messages could not be used to argue against accusations of repression of political dissent.

In its domestic CI role, the FBI initially focused on penetrating and neutralizing American communists. In the mid-1950s, it began an operation called COINTELPRO ("counterintelligence program") against the CPUSA. The idea was to disrupt Party activities by sowing dissention in its ranks. COINTELPRO was so successful that the Bureau transferred the tactic to dealing, first, with the Ku Klux Klan and, later, with civil rights groups and the antiwar movement. The techniques utilized included planting agents in the target groups, wiretaps and other electronic surveillance, surreptitious break-ins (so-called "black bag" jobs) to gather information about a group's activities, and covert operations designed to denigrate and undermine those in leadership positions (such as divisive rumors, anonymous accusations of improprieties, even false reports that an individual was reporting to the FBI). When it became known that Martin Luther King had been the target of many of these kinds of "dirty tricks," the image of the FBI and of domestic counterintelligence was smudged for years to come. The release in 2000 of the FBI's files (including British MI5 materials) on John Lennon did not improve the FBI's image.

Other intelligence components were also engaged in CI operations targeted on Americans. By the late 1960s, Army intelligence was heavily involved in clandestine collection against groups and individuals engaged in antiwar activities. The fear was that the antiwar activists were being supported and manipulated by the Soviet Union. From the mid-1940s to the mid-1970s, private communications companies provided NSA access to all international telegrams sent by Americans; and these were read on the basis of an NSA watch list of suspicious groups or individuals (Operation SHAMROCK). Over the same timeframe, the CIA was photographing and opening mail from the United States to overseas addresses (Operation HTLingual). All of these activities—some legal, some illegal, and all shocking with their tale of government spying on American citizens—became public knowledge in the mid-1970s when open hearings were held by the Senate Select Committee to Study Governmental Operations with Respect to Intelligence Activities (otherwise known as the Church Committee, after its chairman, Democratic Sen. Frank Church of Idaho). While generally inaccurate, the image of an out-of-control intelligence and law enforcement apparatus was difficult to defend against. However, in one form or another, these activities continued under four U.S. Presidents, from Eisenhower, to Kennedy, to Johnson, to Nixon. Rightly or wrongly, each of these Presidents believed that there was a domestic threat to U.S. security; and each expected the intelligence agencies to help contain that threat.

The Year of the Spy

When it began, 1985 seemed like any other year; by the time it ended, it had its own name—"the year of the spy." During that year, seventeen individuals were charged with espionage-related activity, a former CIA officer defected to the Soviet Union, and a KGB officer defected to the United States and then changed his mind and returned to Moscow. Some of those arrested were engaged in relatively low-level efforts. An airman is caught trying to sell documents to the Russians. A Navy quartermaster is found to have classified material at his home, intending to sell it to a foreign service. A CIA clerical employee is charged with giving classified information to her Ghanaian boyfriend who passed it to Ghanaian intelligence. A Navy petty officer steals cryptographic materials and involves his brother, nephew, and another person in a scheme to sell them to the Soviet Union or blackmail the U.S. government into paying to get them back.[7] Such are terribly misguided, even stupid, acts; and they happen more frequently than we like to think.

The other cases were more serious. In May 1985, thanks to information from his former wife, John A. Walker was arrested after seventeen years of spying for the Soviet Union. Walker had "volunteered" his services for pay while in the U.S. Navy. After he retired in 1976, he managed an espionage network that, at the time of his arrest, consisted of his son (a Navy petty officer), his brother (a defense contractor), and Jerry Whitworth (a retired Naval communications specialist). Walker and Whitworth had provided the KGB with a large volume of cryptographic information. Among other materials, they passed along cipher keys (the specifications for setting a cipher machine so it can convert cipher into readable text). They also provided information about the design of cryptographic equipment. In the event of a U.S.-Soviet war during the time when the ring's cryptographic information was current, the Russians would have been able to read a substantial portion of U.S. Naval communications, a situation fraught with potentially disastrous results. Walker and his coconspirators were tried, convicted, and sentenced to lengthy prison terms.

When KGB defector Vitaly Yurchenko walked out of a Washington restaurant in early November 1985 and did not return, the CIA knew it had a problem. Its full extent became clear two days later, when Yurchenko appeared at a news conference at the Soviet embassy and claimed that the CIA had drugged and kidnapped him. Two days later, the KGB officer, who had defected in Rome barely three months earlier, was headed back to Moscow. What happened? Was he homesick? Did his rejection by his Canadian girlfriend turn him around? Had the CIA mishandled him so badly that fleeing back seemed the only option? Was he a genuine defector or had the Russians sent him over to sow doubts in U.S. counterintelligence? The general feeling today is that Yurchenko did defect and then, perhaps because of the instability that led him to defect initially, decided to go back. That conclusion is supported by the value of the information he supplied while still in the CIA's hands.[8]

Beyond providing details about the workings of specific KGB departments, Yurchenko knew of two former intelligence community employees who had passed classified information to the Russians. He did not know names, but his hints allowed counterintelligence officers to zero in on a former CIA officer and a former NSA employee. The CIA had fired Edward Lee Howard following a polygraph examination that turned up, among other items, continued drug use. At the time of his firing, Howard had been preparing for assignment to the CIA's Moscow station. After his employment ended, he sold the KGB information about CIA agents in the Soviet Union, ending their work for the United States and, in at least one case, an agent's life. Howard slipped FBI surveillance and fled the country, eventually turning up in Moscow where he was granted "political asylum." The other spy fingered by Yurchenko became the third in a flurry of espionage cases that broke into public view in a five-day period between November 21 and 25, 1985. After declaring personal bankruptcy and leaving his NSA job in 1979, Ronald William Pelton began to sell what he knew to the KGB. Given his earlier access to a wide range of highly classified projects, the Russians were happy to pay him even for information that was not completely current. Among the operations he exposed was the NSA-Navy IVY BELLS project to tap the Soviet communications cable in the Sea of Okhotsk. Convicted of espionage, Pelton was sentenced to life in prison.

Four days before Pelton was arrested, Jonathan Jay Pollard and his wife were picked up in front of the Israeli Embassy. They had been turned away in an attempt to find shelter from the U.S. authorities. A civilian counterintelligence analyst for the Naval Investigative Service, Pollard had been selling classified information to the Israeli Defense Ministry's scientific intelligence unit. Observations by fellow employees of his excessive copying of documents and habit of taking classified materials home are credited with his exposure. The Israeli unit that had been running Pollard apparently failed to provide him with an escape plan. The norm would have been, at a minimum, emergency telephone numbers where his handler or a substitute could be reached twenty-four hours a day. Negotiated guilty pleas netted Pollard a life sentence and his wife a five-year sentence. Despite Israel's apologies and assertions that Pollard's recruitment was a rogue operation, the case serves as a vivid reminder that it is not just a country's enemies that must be guarded against.

On November 22, 1985, the day after the Pollards' found nowhere to run, Larry Wu-tai Chin was arrested and charged with spying for the People's Republic of China for over thirty years. Chin had retired from the CIA in 1981. Born in Beijing, he was a true "mole," in that he was already a Chinese agent when he successfully penetrated U.S. intelligence. Such a major feat of spying legerdemain is rarely accomplished. After working for the U.S. military in the Far East in the late 1940s and early 1950s, Chin was employed by the CIA's Foreign Broadcast Information Service (FBIS) as a Chinese-language translator at its overseas installation in Okinawa. He later resigned and immigrated to the United States. After obtaining his U.S. citizenship, Chin was rehired by FBIS as a staff employee. As a CIA employee, he held a Top Secret clearance; and his job gave him access to many of the Intelligence Community's classified reports on China and the Far East. While these reports were undoubtedly of great interest to the Chinese government in terms of providing insight into what the United States knew and was thinking about the PRC, Chin's treachery is unlikely to have supplied China with the kinds of high-level operational secrets that the espionage of Walker, Howard, and Pelton gave the Soviet Union. His espionage activities may have been uncovered through information from a CIA source in Chinese intelligence. A jury found Chin guilty of espionage, conspiracy, and tax fraud in February 1986. He committed suicide while in jail awaiting sentencing.

Post-Cold War

Espionage directed against the United States did not go away after 1985, but the years 1986–1993 saw mostly a depressing string of what might be called "people behaving stupidly." Numerous retired, former civilian, and even active members or employees of the military, usually with some sort of money difficulties or a grievance against the services, attempted to commit espionage and managed only to get caught in "stings" run by the FBI or one of the service investigative agencies. In addition, employees and contractors of the CIA, DIA, FBI, and the State and Defense departments were also arrested in connection with espionage-related charges. In instances where classified information was actually passed to a foreign entity, the recipients included China, East Germany, Ecuador, Greece,

Hungary, Japan, Jordan, Liberia, the Philippines, South Africa, the Soviet Union, and Taiwan.

Two cases in the late 1980s stand out. Clayton Lonetree, a Marine Corps security guard at the U.S. Embassy in Moscow, was arrested in 1986 for passing classified information to his Russian girlfriend and her KGB control officer. There was concern that this "honey trap" had given Soviet intelligence physical access to the building. Later reports concluded, however, that such was not the case. Sent to prison for thirty years, Lonetree's sentence was later reduced; and he was released in 1996. In the other case, the West Germans arrested retired Army Sergeant Clyde Lee Conrad in 1988. His spy ring had provided Hungarian and Czechoslovak intelligence with information that included the North Atlantic Treaty Organization's plans for defending Western Europe, detailed descriptions of Allied nuclear weapons, and communications manuals. Conrad's espionage ring operated for over ten years and was so wide-ranging that when all the participants had finally been identified, the courts in four countries—West Germany, Austria, Sweden, and the United States—had been involved. The last known agent, a former Army clerk, was finally arrested in 1997. Sentenced to life in prison by a West German court, Conrad died in 1998.

All this was prelude to the arrest in February 1994 of CIA intelligence officer Aldrich Hazen Ames and his wife. A veteran of more than thirty years with the CIA, Ames had volunteered to spy (a "walk-in") for pay for the KGB in 1985. Positioned in the Counterintelligence Branch of the CIA's Soviet East European Division and later in the Counterintelligence Center (among other Washington and overseas assignments), Ames was able to provide the KGB and its successor service, the SVR, with the identities of CIA and FBI agents recruited among Russians at home and in the United States. A number of those agents were executed. In addition, he is reported to have passed along information on U.S. counterintelligence operations, the identities of CIA and other intelligence personnel, technical collection activities, and reams of intelligence reports. The Russians paid Ames well (an estimated $2.5 million), and the Ames family lived well. In the end, the high living (such as paying cash for a $540,000 home) helped focus attention on Ames when a serious investigation got underway to determine how the KGB was able to roll up virtually all U.S. intelligence agents in Russia. Following guilty pleas in April 1994, Ames was sentenced to life in prison without the possibility of parole; his wife received five years and three months.

A river of ink has flowed about the Ames case, much of it focused on what went wrong (see sidebar, "*The Ames Library*"). The answer is many things. For one, the CIA ignored the vagaries of a mediocre officer with a drinking problem and lackadaisical work habits. It was more convenient to move him around than to deal with the matter. Handling personnel problems in this manner is not unusual in large bureaucracies, but it is scarcely the way to manage matters of national security when lives are at risk. Then, there is the on-again-off-again attention paid by the FBI and the CIA to the devastation of U.S. human intelligence assets in the Soviet Union in the mid-1980s. Neither agency seemed able to focus on what had happened with these operations. The after-the-fact investigation by the CIA Inspector General "concluded that the intelligence losses of 1985–86 were not pursued to the fullest extent of the capabilities of the CIA."[9] A separate report by the FBI's Inspector General reached a similar conclusion: "FBI management devoted inadequate attention to determining the cause of the sudden, unprecedented, and catastrophic losses suffered by both the FBI and the CIA in their Soviet intelligence programs."[10] A third problem area concerns a negative attitude in the CIA's clandestine service toward CI generally. The fact that an employee with Ames' work record and known problems would be pushed off into the CIA's main CI component represents a level of disrespect that is difficult to defend. The attitude seems to run deeper than just being a reaction to the earlier excesses of James Angleton, the head of CIA counterintelligence until his forced retirement in 1974.

The Ames Library

There have been five full-length treatments of the Ames spy case:

James Adams, *Sellout: Aldrich Ames and the Corruption of the CIA* (New York: Viking, 1995).

Pete Earley, *Confessions of a Spy: The Real Story of Aldrich Ames* (New York: Putnam's, 1997).

Peter Maas, *Killer Spy: The Inside Story of the FBI's Pursuit and Capture of Aldrich Ames, America's Deadliest Spy* (New York: Warner, 1995).

Tim Weiner, David Johnston, and Neil A. Lewis, *Betrayal: The Story of Aldrich Ames, An American Spy* (New York: Random House, 1995).

David Wise, *Nightmover: How Aldrich Ames Sold the CIA to the KGB for $4.6 Million* (New York: HarperCollins, 1995).

In addition, a KGB officer has published a memoir in which his handling of the Ames case and that of FBI spy Robert Hanssen is discussed:

Victor Cherkashin, with Gregory Feifer, *Spy Handler—Memoir of a KGB Officer: The True Story of the Man Who Recruited Robert Hanssen and Aldrich Ames* (New York: Basic Books, 2004).

One of the conclusions drawn from the Ames debacle was that lack of coordination (or, even, cooperation) between the CIA and FBI made it possible for Ames to spy for as long as he did. This forced changes in the CIA's counterintelligence practices. A senior FBI officer was named to head the Agency's Counterintelligence Center (CIC). The idea was to put the FBI in a position to fully coordinate joint CI efforts. At least one additional FBI Special Agent also was assigned full-time to the CIC. Congress got into the act with a requirement that the CIA notify the FBI whenever there are indications that classified information may have been disclosed without authorization to a foreign country. Essentially, Congress mandated that the CIA would no longer handle the early stages of a CI investigation on its own. Internally, the CIA created the position of Associate Deputy Director of Operations/Counterintelligence to provide a management focal point for its CI effort and to ensure senior-level coordination with the FBI. In addition, the FBI used its jurisdiction over transnational crimes and the CIA's diminished stature in the CI arena to begin to expand its overseas operations. Over the next few years, dozens of new FBI legal attaché offices were opened around the world.

Despite the shock to the system of the Ames case and the changes that followed it, a string of embarrassing spy cases would continue to bedevil the CIA and FBI, casting doubt on the capability of either organization to manage the CI function. In November 1996, the other shoe dropped for the CIA, when Harold James Nicholson became the highest-ranking (GS-15) CIA officer ever charged with espionage. This time, the CIA and FBI stressed that a high level of coordination had been instrumental in limiting Nicholson's spying for Russia to two and half years. Nicholson is reported to have received about $120,000 for providing the SVR with a range of classified information, including biographic data on every CIA case officer trained between 1994 and 1996. Suspicions began in late 1995 when he failed a series of polygraph examinations. Nicholson pleaded guilty to spying for Russia, and was sentenced to twenty-three years and seven months in prison. The FBI had little time to celebrate Nicholson's arrest, since a month later one of the Bureau's own was arrested for spying for Russia from 1987 to 1992. Edwin Earl Pitts was uncovered as a spy when his SVR handler became an FBI double agent. Among the information Pitts passed to the SVR was a list of FBI assets who were providing intelligence on Russia. He pleaded guilty and was sentenced to twenty-seven years in prison. An even more painful experience for the FBI was yet to come.

In February 2001, veteran FBI Special Agent Robert Philip Hanssen was arrested in the act of loading a "dead drop"—leaving a bag containing classified documents in a covert location in a Virginia park. Hanssen had spent most of his twenty-five years in the FBI working in counterintelligence, and he spied for the Soviet Union and Russia for over twenty of those years. He was a volunteer spy, who was paid well for his efforts—by some accounts, close to $1.4 million. Hanssen began his spying as early as 1979 with the GRU and continued it intermittently with the KGB/SVR until his arrest. The information that led to his identification apparently came from a source within the SVR. Hanssen was accused of compromising U.S. human sources (at least three of whom were executed), important technical operations, investigative techniques, and thousands of pages of classified documents. In retrospect, it is clear that many of the FBI and CIA assets and operations that were wiped out in the mid-1980s resulted from Hanssen's treachery. Hanssen pleaded guilty in exchange for a life sentence. As with Ames, there have been multiple retellings of Hanssen's career as a spy for the Soviet Union and Russia (see sidebar, "*The Hanssen Library*").

The Hanssen Library

In addition to Victor Cherkashin's *Spy Handler* (New York: Basic Books, 2004), which mentions both Aldrich Ames and Hanssen, there have been five full-length treatments of Hanssen's life and career:

Adrian Havill, *The Spy Who Stayed Out in the Cold: The Secret Life of FBI Double Agent Robert Hanssen* (New York: St. Martin's, 2002).

Lawrence Schiller and Norman Mailer, *Into the Mirror: The Life of Master Spy Robert P. Hanssen* (New York: HarperCollins, 2002).

Elaine Shannon and Ann Blackman, *The Spy Next Door: The Extraordinary Secret Life of Robert Philip Hanssen, the Most Damaging FBI Agent in U.S. History* (New York: Little, Brown, 2002).

David A. Vise, *The Bureau and the Mole: The Unmasking of Robert Philip Hanssen, The Most Dangerous Double Agent in FBI History* (New York: Atlantic Monthly Press, 2002).

David Wise, *Spy: The Inside Story of How the FBI's Robert Hanssen Betrayed America* (New York: Random House, 2002).

The FBI Inspector General's review of the Hanssen case was scathing. The report found that the FBI suffered from "longstanding systemic problems" in its CI program and "a deeply flawed" internal security program. The Bureau's security procedures were "not in compliance with Executive Orders, Justice Department regulations, and Intelligence Community standards." Internal security in the FBI was based on trusting that employees were and would remain loyal. There were none of the safeguards used by other Intelligence Community components, such as requirements for "regular counterintelligence polygraph examinations, financial disclosures, and meaningful background reinvestigations, and utilizing audit functions regarding computer usage." The laxness in internal security led to an "absence of effective deterrence to espionage at the FBI and undermined the FBI's ability to detect an FBI mole . . . . In sum, the absence of adequate security controls at the FBI made espionage too easy for Hanssen to commit."[11]

In the aftermath of Hanssen's exposure, the FBI took a number of steps to improve its internal security. The Bureau now claims to have a counterintelligence-focused polygraph examination program. This includes a polygraph examination as part of the standard five-year background reinvestigation, unscheduled and random examinations, and polygraphs for employees with access to the most sensitive information or who are going to or returning from an overseas assignment. Success in this part of the FBI's security program will revolve around a willingness to enforce such steps and applying the resources to make the system work. The FBI has also developed a financial disclosure program. Given its experience in dealing with white-collar crime, this could be a serious investigative tool. Again, however, success will depend on the FBI's commitment to enforcement. The FBI will need to be rigorous in requiring its employees to answer the kinds of questions that it has been loath to ask in the past. In an effort to put management's stamp on the importance of security, the FBI created a new Security Division, headed by an Assistant Director who reports directly to the FBI Director. This step centralizes such previously fragmented functions as personnel, physical, and information security. The first head of the new division was an experienced former CIA security officer. To insure closer liaison, senior CIA officers are detailed to work with the FBI's counterintelligence teams.

Post-9/11 Developments

At the same time that it was just beginning to assess the CI, psychological, and other damage wrought by Hanssen's treachery, the FBI came under heavy criticism for its role in failing to prevent the terrorist attacks of September 11, 2001. These criticisms hastened potentially even more revolutionary change. The focus of the *Report* of the National Commission on Terrorist Attacks Upon the United States (the 9/11 Commission) was, of course, on the FBI's failures in the realm of counterterrorism (the so-called failure "to connect the dots"). Nevertheless, both the recommendations of the 9/11 Commission and the requirements of the subsequently enacted Intelligence Reform and Terrorism Prevention Act of 2004 deal with the counterterrorism problem in a fashion that directly impacts the CI discipline as well. The basic thrust was that, in dealing with terrorism, the FBI needed to move its focus of its activities from meticulously collecting the kinds of forensic evidence required for a grand jury to expeditiously gathering, analyzing, and acting on intelligence information that could prevent future events like the 9/11 attacks. In June 2005, President Bush ordered the creation in the FBI of a new career field, the National Security Service, and the formation of a new organizational component, the National Security Branch (NSB). The move brings together the Bureau's intelligence, counterterrorism, and CI activities under a single manager, essentially creating a new intelligence agency. The NSB operates within the FBI but is theoretically under the overall direction of the Director of National Intelligence (DNI) and reports both to the DNI and the FBI Director. The Presidential memorandum establishing the service did not define the ground rules on how this split-responsibility is supposed to work. That is a matter that will require the cooperation of the DNI and the FBI Director. The creation of the National Security Service and its accompanying organizational change was precipitated by the existence of proposals that would have relieved the FBI of its intelligence and CI activities, leaving it to focus solely on its law enforcement functions. Under such a scenario, the FBI's intelligence-related responsibilities would have been assumed by a separate domestic intelligence agency, similar to the British Security Service (MI5).

Despite its ongoing efforts to reinvent itself, the FBI still has some serious problems that could impede success. These include the failure, even after spending millions of dollars, to develop a secure and efficient information technology system to replace the much-maligned Automated Case Support (ACS) system. In fact, the proposed replacement system, the Virtual Case File (VCF), had to be scrapped. This leaves the FBI among the least wired of the national security agencies until a follow-on system is brought on line. The Bureau continues to be able to get legal approval for more CI and counterterrorism wiretaps than it can process. The shortage in translators in target languages will not be solved in the near future. In the area of establishing an integrated intelligence program, a Congressional Research Service report released in August 2005 was not very positive. It concluded: "*While areas of promise exist, field research indicates that the FBI's ability to formally harness intelligence collection . . . to analytically identified intelligence gaps, remains nascent.*"[12]

Law Enforcement and Intelligence

William H. Webster, the only person to serve as both FBI Director and DCI, headed a Justice Department commission to review FBI security programs in the wake of the Hanssen disaster. That group's report, issued in March 2003, was echoed in many ways by the FBI Inspector General's review a few months later; but the Webster Commission was clearer on the central issue confronting the FBI in trying to remake itself—a cultural divide between the two separate worlds of law enforcement and intelligence. The Webster Commission noted that until the events of 9/11, the FBI's focus was on "detecting and prosecuting traditional crime." Consequently, the Bureau's internal culture reflected the priorities of its criminal components. Its culture "was based on cooperation and the free flow of information inside the Bureau." This is "a work ethic wholly at odds with the compartmentation characteristic of intelligence investigations." For those conducting criminal investigations, rules restricting the information flow "are perceived as cumbersome, inefficient, and a bar to success." Thus, "[a] law-enforcement culture grounded in shared information is radically different from an intelligence culture grounded in secrecy." Whether the law enforcement and intelligence cultures "can co-exist in one organization is a difficult question, but they will never do so in the FBI, unless the Bureau gives its intelligence programs the same resources and respect it gives criminal investigations."[13]

An institutional culture is not automatically a negative thing. It provides, among other positive attributes, a sense of shared purpose among those involved. However, it is also not something that is readily open to change. The dichotomy between law enforcement and intelligence has sometimes been framed as the difference between "cops" and "spies"; that is, cops want to arrest the bad guys, while spies want to recruit them. It is really not that simple, but there is some truth in the characterization. Good law enforcement is about building a case based on solid, usable evidence. The collection of that evidence must fall within legal parameters, and the evidence itself will need to be revealed in court. Intelligence officers live in a much more ambiguous environment. This is especially true with regard to human sources who, if brought into open court, lose future usefulness. In essence, the ways that law enforcement and intelligence officers think and act are fundamentally different. Further clouding the counterintelligence horizon, given that the FBI remains the country's lead CI agency, is the situation where CI is second on the Bureau's priority list (see sidebar, "*FBI's Priorities*") to counterterrorism. That is not necessarily a bad idea. It does, however, raise questions about whether, given its law enforcement heritage and the effort to remake itself as an intelligence agency focused on counterterrorism, the FBI will neglect its CI role. The vision of the FBI as an intelligence agency is also dimmed by an internal viewpoint (clearly a holdover from its law enforcement culture) that divides its personnel into two categories—special agents and support staff, with the latter including its intelligence analysts.[14] Two questions are pertinent here: Can the FBI be a domestic intelligence organization? And should it be?

FBI's Priorities

1. Protect the United States from terrorist attack
2. Protect the United States against foreign intelligence operations and espionage
3. Protect the United States against cyber-based attacks and high-technology crimes
4. Combat public corruption at all levels
5. Protect civil rights
6. Combat transnational/national criminal organizations and enterprises
7. Combat major white-collar crime
8. Combat significant violent crime
9. Support federal, state, local and international partners
10. Upgrade technology to successfully perform the FBI's mission[15]

The Civil Liberties Wall

Certain aspects of CI work have proved to be quite controversial at various stages in American history. This has occurred because it is in counterintelligence that the realms of intelligence and law enforcement meet. Although as a nation we have traditionally sought to keep the two government-dominated disciplines of intelligence and law enforcement separate, there have been occasions when that has not happened and difficulties have followed. Counterintelligence brings intelligence into the domestic arena, as it must operate both abroad and at home. Thereby, of all the intelligence disciplines, CI raises the strongest issues of civil liberties. This is particularly the case since the terrorist attacks of September 11, 2001, as many of the practices of counterintelligence have been extended to encompass counterterrorism activities within the United States itself.

Constitutional bounds have been overstepped in the past. This has most often occurred when dissent came to be treated as subversion. Such incidents include the so-called "Palmer Raids" of 1919–1920, the extension of the surveillance and covert action activities of COINTELPRO to civil rights and antiwar groups in the 1960s and 1970s, and the violation of the rights of members of the Committee in Solidarity with the People of El Salvador (CISPES) in the 1980s. Since 2000, the FBI has heard criticism of its Carnivore e-mail surveillance tool, the use of secret (without court approval) wiretaps and searches, intelligence-gathering operations against environmental and animal rights groups, and searches conducted for radioactive materials at private locations. In addition, the decision to create the National Security Branch within the FBI and have it report to both the DNI and the FBI Director has raised concerns about the linking of law enforcement and intelligence activities. Timothy Edgar, American Civil Liberties Union (ACLU) Policy Counsel for National Security, has argued:

> Spies and cops have different roles and operate under different rules for a very important reason: to ensure that our law enforcement agencies stay within the Constitution. This proposal could erode the FBI's law enforcement ethic and put parts of the FBI under the effective control of a spymaster who reports to the president—not the attorney general.[16]

The longer and deeper the United States goes into the war on terrorism, the greater the likelihood that the government's sophisticated surveillance techniques will fuel serious discussions about their impact on individual privacy and civil liberties. There have already been disputes about NSA's warrantless eavesdropping on telephone and Internet communications into and out of the United States and a CIA-Treasury Department program to examine financial records from an international database. They will not be the last difficulties encountered as intelligence and counterintelligence methodologies are applied domestically to search for and neutralize the terrorists. Finding the point of balance on the civil liberties wall, with chaos on one side and repression on the other, is a challenging task. Yet, the goal remains to protect both the security of the nation as a whole and our laws and culture that stress personal liberties.

Notes

1. Ronald Reagan, "Executive Order 12333: United States Intelligence Activities," §3.4(a), December 4, 1981, http://www.fas.org/irp/offdocs/eo12333.htm.
2. George W. Bush, "Executive Order 13292: Classified National Security Information" (amending Executive Order 12958, as amended), §1.2(a) (1)-(3), March 25, 2003 (emphasis added), http://www.fas.org/sgp/bush/eoamend.html.
3. Information Security Oversight Office, "Report to the President," May 25, 2006, http://www.fas.org/sgp/isoo/index.html.
4. James Bamford, *Body of Secrets: Anatomy of the Ultra-Secret National Security Agency from the Cold War through the Dawn of a New Century* (New York: Doubleday, 2001), 110.
5. Roy Godson, *Dirty Tricks or Trump Cards: U.S. Covert Action and Counterintelligence* (Washington, DC: Transaction, 2001), 67.

6. See Robert Louis Benson, *The VENONA Story* (Ft. George G. Meade, MD: National Security Agency, Center for Cryptologic History, [n.d.]), http://www.nsa.gov/publications/publi00039.cfm; and John Earl Haynes and Harvey Klehr, *Venona: Decoding Soviet Espionage in America* (New Haven, CT: Yale University Press, 1999).

7. See U.S. Department of Defense, *Espionage Cases, 1975–2004: Summaries and Sources* (Monterey, CA: Defense Personnel Security Research Center, 2004), http://www.dss.mil/training/espionage/.

8. See Ronald Kessler, *Escape from the CIA: How the CIA Won and Lost the Most Important KGB Spy Ever to Defect to the U.S.* (New York: Pocket Books, 1991).

9. U.S. Central Intelligence Agency, Office of the Inspector General, "Preface to the Report," *Unclassified Abstract of the CIA Inspector General's Report on the Aldrich Ames Case*, October 21, 1994, http://www.loyola.edu/dept/politics/hula/hitzrept.html.

10. U.S. Federal Bureau of Investigation, Office of the Inspector General, "Unclassified Executive Summary," *A Review of the FBI's Performance in Uncovering the Espionage Activities of Aldrich Hazen Ames*, April 21, 1997, http://www.usdoj.gov/oig/special/9704.htm.

11. U.S. Federal Bureau of Investigation, Office of the Inspector General, "Unclassified Executive Summary," *A Review of the FBI's Performance in Deterring, Detecting, and Investigating the Espionage Activities of Robert Philip Hanssen*, August 14, 2003, http://www.fas.org/irp/agency/doj/oig/hanssen.html.

12. Alfred Cumming and Todd Masse, *Intelligence Reform Implementation at the Federal Bureau of Investigation: Issues and Options for Congress* (Washington, DC: Congressional Research Service, Library of Congress, August 16, 2005) [italics in original], http://www.fas.org/sgp/crs/intel/RL33033.pdf.

13. U.S. Department of Justice, Commission for Review of FBI Security Programs, *A Review of FBI Security Programs* (Washington, DC: U.S. Department of Justice, March 2002) [The Webster Commission], http://www.fas.org/irp/agency/doj/fbi/websterreport.html.

14. From "Our People," at http://www.fbi.gov/quickfacts.htm, accessed July 1, 2006.

15. From "Our Priorities," at http://www.fbi.gov/quickfacts.htm, accessed July 1, 2006.

16. American Civil Liberties Union, "ACLU Slams Plan to Place Parts of the FBI Under Control of Intelligence Agencies, Warns of Further Mixing of Law Enforcement with Intelligence Operations," Press Release, June 29, 2005, http://www.aclu.org/safefree/general/17621prs20050629.html.

CHAPTER 5

What If We Don't Want to Be Seen?

Who, Us?

Classic intelligence work is a support function for policy; it is not a policymaking or action-taking activity. However, there is one area within the U.S. intelligence structure that is instrumental—action-oriented—in nature. That area involves the use of what is known as covert action (CA), arguably the most controversial of all intelligence functions. At its most basic, covert action represents the effort to exert in some way an influence on the internal affairs of other countries or groups (occasionally an individual), while seeking to avoid the attribution of such acts to

> ***Official Definition of Covert Action***
>
> The Intelligence Authorization Act of 1991, Pub. L. 102-88, 105 Stat. 429 (Aug. 14, 1991), Section 503 (c) (4) (e), defines covert action as "an activity or activities of the United States Government to influence political, economic, or military conditions abroad, where it is intended that the role of the United States Government will not be apparent or acknowledged publicly, but does not include: (1) activities the primary purpose of which is to acquire intelligence, traditional counterintelligence activities, traditional activities to improve or maintain the operational security of United States Government programs, or administrative activities; (2) traditional diplomatic or military activities or routine support to such activities; (3) traditional law enforcement activities conducted by United States Government law enforcement agencies or routine support to such activities; or (4) activities to provide routine support to the overt activities (other than the activities described in paragraph (1), (2), or (3)) of other United States Government agencies abroad.
>
> "(f) No covert action may be conducted which is intended to influence United States political processes, public opinion, policies, or media."

the government. The goal is to do things that appear to be overt and indigenous to the target area in a manner that the hand of the actual instigator is not obvious and, in fact, can be denied. (See sidebar, "*Official Definition of Covert Action.*") While covert operations are not intelligence in the informational sense, they have in modern times largely been carried out by intelligence organizations. This is because these agencies are the governmental entities that can operate primarily in secret and are most likely to have the capabilities and practices needed to conduct such activities.

Types of Covert Action

The practice has been around a long time, but covert action as a term is modern in usage and American in origin. Few other countries use the term, although they engage in the same kinds of activities. The British speak of "special political action," and the Russians refer to "active measures." Covert action is also a generic term applied to a number of activities by which policy is carried out in secret. From the instigator's point of view, it can range along a spectrum from relatively low-risk and low-profile activities founded on persuasion to high-risk and high-profile activities involving the use of force. Given its great flexibility, covert action is often seen as providing decisionmakers additional options between talking (diplomacy) or fighting (war) in the effort to protect national interests. It is often referred to as the "third option" or the "quiet option." Traditionally, covert action has been seen as taking one of three basic forms—propaganda, political action, or paramilitary activity—although all three can exist in the same operation. The techniques of "information warfare" represent a new tool—or, perhaps, a fourth type—that has been added in recent years to the options available for covert action. Like the broader area of covert action, information warfare has a range of uses that cover from the minimally invasive to the highly invasive and highly disruptive.

Propaganda

Propaganda sits at the minimally invasive end of the covert action spectrum. A propaganda campaign may appear as simple as paying a journalist in the target country to write articles supporting U.S.-backed policies. Things are rarely that simple. Even a low-end propaganda campaign requires purpose, guidance to insure that it follows the policy it is supposed to be supporting, and preparation. It may be the main thrust of an effort or an ancillary part of a broader operation. Most of all, it requires the people ("assets") both capable of understanding what needs to be done and able to do it. Propaganda campaigns are not spur-of-the-moment happenings. The contacts necessary to make them work need to be in place (and tested) before they are undertaken. This is part of the "infrastructure" of any covert operation, which must be built up over time whether or not it is immediately needed. The need for preparation and in-place infrastructure is just as valid for a propaganda campaign built around leaflets, wall posters, or clandestine radio broadcasts. One of the hopes for a newspaper placement is that it will be repeated by other news media, especially foreign wire services. This creates the potential for "blowback," where U.S. media report the planted information for U.S. audiences. Although U.S. intelligence services are prohibited from propagandizing the American public, "blowback" assuredly happens. In fact, the more important the issue involved in the planting of a story, the greater the likelihood that it can show up on a major U.S. news service.

There are other forms of propaganda generally referred to as "black" propaganda. This material presents itself as truth (but may be entirely false) and as originating with some group or person (but in reality has been produced by someone else entirely). The Soviet form of black propaganda, called *dezinformatsiya* or disinformation, was an effective weapon for that side during the Cold War. Several of the false stories of that era continue to circulate with some credibility in certain parts of the world (for example, that AIDS was created in a U.S. government laboratory). Deception (such as, the effort to mislead the Germans on where the Allies would land) is a similar activity that shows up primarily in military operations.

Political Action

The types of activities that fall within the political action category go beyond propaganda in terms of aggressiveness, but stop short of the use of force. There are multiple ways, some more invasive than others, in which political action is used. They may involve, for example, providing funding and advice for political campaigns, supporting cultural and other kinds of civic groups, funding labor strikes and other kinds of demonstrations, creating adverse economic conditions, and aiding in the preparation of coups to remove a sitting government. Assisting other governments or groups to improve their intelligence capabilities is another form of political action. Intelligence assistance includes providing specialized training for local police, paramilitary, and intelligence personnel; or supplying technical equipment (such as, creating a signals intelligence capability for a foreign service) or other material. Many political action activities involve making funding and advice available to groups or individuals to assist them in doing something (such as, winning an election) that they want to do but lack the resources to accomplish. The key is that what they are trying to accomplish is viewed as in the interest of the supplier of the assistance. Many political action operations are also buttressed with propaganda campaigns designed to reinforce the effects of other activities.

Paramilitary

At the opposite end of the covert action spectrum from propaganda are paramilitary (PM) operations—military-type actions using nonmilitary personnel. Discussions immediately following World War II centered on such activities as support to underground resistance movements, guerrilla liberation groups, and indigenous anticommunist movements. Intelligence assistance can begin to creep into the paramilitary realm, as training to resist an insurgency gives way to helping plan or participating in operations. In fact, the larger a paramilitary operation grows, the less likely that it can really be called covert. At most, large-scale paramilitary activities might be "officially unacknowledged."

From Independence to Cold War

Revolution to World War II

Covert action did not just appear on the U.S. political scene at the beginning of the Cold War. Such activities were, in fact, an integral part of the Founders' waging of the War of Independence. Among early covert operations was the Continental Congress's effort to procure gunpowder and arms from France and Spain, neither of which wanted to be seen as supporting the revolutionaries. Covert political and propaganda activities sought to induce Canada into joining the colonies, funded a pro-American newspaper in Quebec, planted favorable reports in overseas newspapers, and fabricated documents encouraging the Hessian mercenaries to desert. Plans (none successful) were devised for kidnapping the traitorous Benedict Arnold. Another proposal (not carried out) involved capturing the son of King George III, Prince William Henry (the future William IV), during a visit to New York. There is also one known instance where American representatives commissioned sabotage work in England. Although the perpetrator was caught and hanged, the fires set at British ports created a substantial uproar at the time.[1]

Few Presidents who followed President Washington had his grasp of the essentials of intelligence. Nonetheless, most found it useful to couple overt diplomacy with a less open backup plan. In many instances, the use of covert measures allowed the new and vulnerable nation to grow without facing the high-risk option of open warfare. Thomas Jefferson negotiated with the Barbary States on just such a dual level. The President positioned himself so he could deny involvement in the attempt to overthrow the Tripoli government when that effort was abandoned. James Madison supported covert operations in acquiring Florida from Spain, and did not hesitate to leave his surrogates hanging when circumstances changed. John Tyler and Secretary of State Daniel Webster used money from the President's Contingency Fund to build public support in Maine for settlement of a boundary dispute with Canada. James K. Polk was party to a deal that allowed the exiled General Santa Anna to return to Mexico for his agreement to resolve the ongoing territorial dispute. Santa Anna instead rallied Mexican forces to continue the war. In the Civil War, the United States and the Confederacy initiated propaganda campaigns in Canada and Europe. Benjamin Harrison's administration encouraged and assisted insurrectionists in overthrowing the Hawaiian monarchy in January 1893. Grover Cleveland replaced Harrison in March 1893 and repudiated the proposed annexation treaty because of the circumstances surrounding the revolt. Annexation was completed after the outbreak of the Spanish-American

War. Ten years after the Hawaiian revolt, Theodore Roosevelt used a similar strategy, when Colombian intransigence blocked his acquisition of the land needed to build the Panama Canal. He encouraged a separatist movement in the Isthmus of Panama and provided U.S. warships to protect a "revolution" that created an independent state. The new Republic of Panama then ceded the rights to build, run, and defend the Canal to the United States.[2]

World War II

Prior to World War II, Presidents' use of covert actions tended to be one-of-a-kind operations run at their instigation or with their knowledge but often managed at least one step below the President for deniability purposes. Franklin Roosevelt's naming of William J. Donovan as head of the Office of Strategic Services (OSS) began the institutionalization of covert action in the U.S. government. OSS combined in a single entity human intelligence gathering, analysis, counterintelligence, and covert action. This organizational pattern would eventually be duplicated in the CIA. OSS's Special Operations Branch (SO) worked with the British Special Operations Executive (SOE) on guerrilla warfare and sabotage operations on the European continent. In these activities, U.S. and British personnel teamed with indigenous groups ("partisans") to provide communications links back to Britain, coordinate airdrops of arms and supplies, and participate in hit-and-run and sabotage attacks against the German forces. Similarly, OSS operatives in Burma recruited and led a small army of Kachin natives in intelligence gathering, sabotage, and psychological operations against the Japanese. OSS's Morale Branch (MO) worked with its British counterpart, the Political Warfare Executive (PWE), in "black" propaganda operations. Designed to look as though it came from disgruntled Germans or Japanese, "black" propaganda targeted the morale of troops and civilian populations in Germany and Japan. These efforts included fake radio broadcasts and newspapers, subversive literature (leaflets and such), and all manner of rumors about the war effort and the enemy leaders.[3]

Because of a personal dislike of Donovan, a predisposition to demobilize at the end of a war, and a distrust of secret institutions, Harry Truman abolished the OSS in October 1945. Its remnants were dispersed elsewhere in the government. Research and Analysis moved into the State Department. Other elements went to the War Department. For almost two years, the administration studied and experimented with how to manage intelligence. The multiple and at times discordant views reaching the President reminded some of the situation that existed prior to Pearl Harbor. In addition, concern was growing about the Soviet Union's intentions in Eastern Europe and increasing communist influence among groups in Western Europe. The need for a centralized effort to counter potential communist takeovers of governments or such groups as trade unions argued for an institutionalized approach. The result was the National Security Act of 1947 and the creation of the Central Intelligence Agency (CIA).

Beginning the Cold War

The National Security Act of 1947

In addition to collection and coordination of information from human sources, analysis and dissemination of national security intelligence, and management of services of "common concern," the National Security Act of 1947 tasked the CIA with performing "such other functions and duties related to intelligence affecting the national security as the President or the National Security Council may direct."[4] With this obscure phrasing, covert action was passed (more or less) to the CIA. In the months that followed the Act's signing on July 26, 1947, the conduct of covert actions could have come to rest in either the State or Defense departments. However, neither the diplomats nor the military wanted anything to do with running peacetime covert operations. They were also not happy about letting the new-kid-on-the-block CIA run them. Nevertheless, the idea of "containment," as first articulated by George F. Kennan, was making its way from concept to becoming the administration's doctrine for confronting the Soviet Union. In this atmosphere, further directives and legislation institutionalized covert action as an instrument of U.S. policy and centralized it in the CIA where it became an integral part (some argue, a defining part) of the organizational structure. (See sidebar, "*Presidents and Covert Action*.")

Presidents and Covert Action

Every President from Truman to the present has used the CIA to intervene covertly in the affairs of other countries, groups, or individuals. Certainly, some Presidents and their staffs have had a greater affinity for the use of covert operations than others (Kennedy and Reagan). Some were less active than others in choosing covert action as a policy option (Clinton). Some in fact came to office with moral objections to the use of such techniques in managing the affairs of state (Carter). But, in the end, they all found reason and need to resort to covert action in fulfilling their oath to defend the U.S. Constitution. From 1947 until 1974 covert action was almost exclusively a matter between Presidents and the CIA. After 1974 and increasingly through the 1990s, congressional oversight of and involvement in intelligence matters in general—and covert action in particular—increased significantly. In the main, however, it is possible to suggest that when a President's policy direction on a given issue has broad support among the public and in Congress, conducting covert action activities (and keeping them covert to some extent) is a great deal easier than on those matters for which a policy consensus is lacking.

Europe

The centerpieces of U.S. national security policy in the immediate post-World War II years were the European Recovery Program (the Marshall Plan) to sustain and rebuild the European economies and the North Atlantic Treaty Organization (NATO) to defend Europe in alliance with the countries of Western Europe. That these two policy initiatives were simultaneously idealistic and pragmatic had much to do with their success. In 1947–1948, the war-devastated countries seemed to be so vulnerable that democratic processes might actually bring antidemocratic communist parties to power. U.S. policymakers were particularly concerned about Italy and France. NSC-4A of December 1947 authorized the CIA to initiate and conduct covert psychological operations. Preventing a Communist Party victory in Italy's national elections in 1948 was the first goal. Much of that effort was quite open. Large quantities of food and other supplies flowed into Italy, Italian-Americans engaged in a letter-writing campaign, and President Truman threatened to withhold aid to any government that included communists. The CIA's covert effort included the use of psychological warfare and propaganda tactics. The fall of Czechoslovakia to communist rule in February 1948 was used to fan the flames of a campaign built around fear of the communists. Millions of dollars were funneled to centrist political parties. When the Christian Democrats obtained a parliamentary majority, the United States had an early victory in the Cold War. (The support of Italy's democratic parties was not a one-shot affair; covert financial assistance continued until 1967.) Similar successes in arming anticommunist forces during the civil war in Greece and supporting moderate labor unions in France helped establish the covert option as a tool for countering communist influence.[5]

In June 1948, NSC-10/2 articulated the concept of plausible denial, gave a sweeping definition to covert operations, and created the Office of Policy Coordination (OPC) to plan and conduct covert operations. OPC was a strange bureaucratic entity. Its head was to be nominated by and accept direction from the Secretary of State, but was to report to the DCI—while operating independently of other CIA components. This lasted until 1952 when OPC was merged with the CIA's intelligence gathering unit, the Office of Special Operations (OSO), to form the Directorate of Plans (later the Directorate of Operations). Frank G. Wisner, an OSS veteran working in the State Department, was named to head OPC. The OPC developed the whole range of covert actions, from propaganda to support for armed resistance groups. Approval for OPC-proposed projects came through a consultation and review process involving a special panel of State and Defense department officials. (Executive Branch panels to review proposed covert actions have continued across administrations, although their names and composition have shifted in keeping with presidential wishes.)

In the early years of the Cold War, there was some hope that the Soviet advances into the East European countries could be reversed. The European war had pushed tens of thousands of people from their lands; they were now parked in "displaced persons" camps. Many were opportunists who had collaborated with the Nazis as they came through, and fled in fear of Soviet retribution. Others were ardent nationalists, who had fought both communists and Nazis and wanted to free their countries and reassert independent nationhood. From these ragtag elements, the covert action activists tried to fashion resistance forces that would operate within the USSR and the occupied countries. Their plans for underground movements, insurrections, and sabotage behind the Iron Curtain failed. Efforts to create, infiltrate, and support anti-Soviet groups in the Eastern Bloc countries all floundered at the cost of expatriate lives. Soviet intelligence had thoroughly infiltrated the émigré groups. The Russians controlled some operations, as in Poland, by using double agents within the country. To make matters worse, the British Secret Intelligence Service (SIS or MI6) liaison officer in Washington, H.A.R. "Kim" Philby, was a Soviet agent. However, failure did not come from lack of trying; and efforts continued into the 1950s.[6] Other aspects of the covert struggle in Europe, which was much broader than paramilitary operations, had a better success rate.

The vehicles for OPC/CIA's efforts to organize for covert activities in Europe were ostensibly private corporations—the National Committee for a Free Europe, the American Committee for the Liberation of the Peoples of the USSR, and national councils for individual countries. These were cover organizations whose funding came from the U.S. government. From these efforts, two symbols of the anticommunist movement emerged—Radio Free Europe (RFE) and Radio Liberty (RL). Their role was to tell the peoples of Eastern Europe and the Soviet Union what was going on in the world beyond the view supplied them by their government-controlled media. Programming included talks by exiles, replies to mail from their audiences, news embarrassing to the communists, and Western music banned in the USSR and its satellites. The low point came when the Soviet Union crushed the 1956 Hungarian revolt and RFE was criticized for holding out false hopes to the Hungarians of U.S. intervention on their behalf. The radios continued to broadcast the news of world events even beyond the end of the Cold War, although they had long passed from CIA tutelage to a congressionally established public board.

While efforts were being made to subvert the Soviet hold on Eastern Europe, a "cultural Cold War" was going on in the West. To counter a Soviet drive to dominate international labor, youth, and other mass opinion organizations, CIA became the conduit for U.S. government funding to noncommunist political parties (moderate conservative and moderate left), newspapers, labor unions, youth groups, and literary endeavors. Leading the anticommunist intellectual offensive was the Congress for Cultural Freedom (CCF). Through its sponsorship of such magazines of political commentary as *Encounter* and *De Monat*, the CCF assisted Europe in reconstituting its intellectual and cultural base, much as the Marshall Plan helped to rebuild the industrial base and other covert actions worked to shore up the political base. When the writings of Russian dissidents (*samizdat*) began to make their way into the West in the 1960s, the CCF's mechanisms for subsidizing their publication were already in place. Similarly, subsidies to the U.S. National Student Association enabled it to sustain the democratically based International Student Conference in its struggle with the communist-controlled International Union of Students.

Exposure in the media in 1967 of the covert funding of voluntary and educational organizations ended these activities. The revelations brought down condemnation on the CIA from all sides of the political spectrum. Most of the commentary ignored the fact that four different presidents had approved the programs. The Soviets denounced the subversion of innocent youth by the capitalist system. The noncommunist left attacked the subversion of the democratic process that government money, especially from the CIA, represented. The right was incredulous that the government was funding an organization like the National Student Association that was so un-American as to be critical of the Vietnam War. And even within the CIA, there were some who groused that the programs had been allowed to go on too long to remain covert. As to charges that the CIA dictated what these organizations did, the head of the CIA's Covert Action Staff, Cord Meyer, has argued vehemently that the leaders of the private organizations, who chose to cooperate with their government, "jealously guarded their independence and organizational integrity. As a result, secret funds did not become a corrupting influence . . . . I cannot remember a single incident in which the Agency was accused of attempting to manipulate or unfairly influence the policies or activities of those with whom we dealt."[7]

Asia

Europe was not the only region where the covert Cold War was waged. Asia also had its share of covert activities designed to limit the influence of communism. After the United States granted the Philippines independence in 1946, the new government faced an armed insurrection from communist guerrillas. By 1950, the Hukbalahap (People's Liberation Army or Huks) were in control of a significant part of the main island of Luzon and represented a threat to Manila, the capital. OPC station chief and OSS veteran Edward G. Lansdale set out to win the support of the rural population for the national government. Working with the country's defense minister, Ramón Magsaysay, Lansdale launched a psychological and political action campaign that included establishing community centers where such things as modern agricultural methods and health care were taught. Combined with Magsaysay's reforms in the Filipino military, these actions gradually reduced the insurgency as a serious threat.

In 1949 the Chinese communists gained control of China, expelling the Nationalist forces to the island of Taiwan. The shock of that communist victory in Asia's most populous country was followed by the North Korean invasion of the South in June 1950. By November, the United States was at war with China, unofficially but real nonetheless, as several hundred thousand Chinese "volunteers" poured into Korea. On the Korean peninsula, the CIA's covert action role was mainly one of establishing escape and evasion routes for U.S. pilots shot down over enemy territory, and equipping and training refugees from the North to conduct guerrilla operations behind the lines. The OPC/CIA also ran several substantial—but largely diversionary—covert operations against the

Chinese communists. The objective was to try to impede the consolidation of their hold on China and thereby draw their attention away from involvement in Korea. These operations included support, such as weapons and communications equipment, to so-called "third force" guerrillas (anticommunist Chinese who were not affiliated with the Nationalists). The ferrying of supplies to these groups (many deep within China) and the insertion and retrieval of clandestine agents was done by CIA-proprietary airlines, such as Civil Air Transport (CAT), in truly hazardous circumstances. Another group receiving U.S. support was the remnants of Nationalist forces left isolated along the border with Burma when the communists took over. As these forces proved better at banditry than in harassing the communists, they eventually had to be evacuated to Taiwan.

Elsewhere, the OPC/CIA ran a proprietary or front organization named Western Enterprises Incorporated (WEI), which trained and equipped paramilitary forces for guerrilla operations into mainland China from the offshore islands that remained under Nationalist control. The operations began with airdrops of individuals and small groups into China, with the hope that they would hook up with anticommunist stay-behind forces in the more remote regions. Much as occurred with airdrops into Albania and Russia (and later in Vietnam), those dispatched in this way disappeared almost as soon as they hit the ground. They were heard from again only if their captors chose to present them to the world media or to have a show trial. WEI quickly adopted hit-and-run attacks on more isolated coastal areas as the preferred mode of operation. Here, there was more success; it appears the Chinese Communists responded by rotating some experienced troops returning from Korea into areas along the coast. Except for intelligence gathering, operations from Quemoy and other islands largely ended after the shooting part of the Korean conflict was over.[8]

From 1953 to 1974

In 1953, Dwight D. Eisenhower succeeded Harry Truman as U.S. President. Over the next twenty years, four different Presidents authorized covert actions that reached beyond the boundaries of the main communist countries. An early political action authorized by Eisenhower was the overthrow in 1953 of the communist-supported regime of Iranian Prime Minister Mohammed Mossadegh. Iran was in a state of near chaos in the wake of the pull out of the British-owned Anglo-Iranian Oil Company, following its nationalization by Mossadegh. Washington feared a communist-dominated government or even direct Soviet intervention. The President approved a joint MI6-CIA plan for returning control to the Shah. A CIA-funded propaganda campaign linking Mossadegh and the Iranian communists to the threat of a Soviet takeover laid the groundwork. In the end, the ouster of Mossadegh and the Shah's return did not take much effort—some money to local leaders capable of getting demonstrators into the streets, some equipment to the Iranian Army to provide backbone at the crucial moment, and convincing the Shah that his people needed him. The ease of it all may have been seductive, because the next year the administration decided to overthrow another national government.

Like Mossadegh, Guatemalan President Jacobo Arbenz Guzmán was more a nationalist than a communist; but, politically, he made common cause with the communists. Arbenz also had nationalized a major foreign-owned company, the United Fruit Company. For years, debate has raged about whether the company influenced the administration in supporting a coup. It is more likely that concern about allowing a communist foothold in the southern hemisphere was what drove the decision. This was as much a propaganda activity as a paramilitary operation. The effort began with clandestine short-wave radios broadcasting from Honduras and Nicaragua, while representing themselves as being in Guatemala. The idea was to intimidate Arbenz's followers and rally support for an insurgent force being armed and trained in Honduras. When a cargo ship with several thousand tons of Czechoslovakian weapons arrived in Guatemala, the paramilitary side of the operation was initiated. In mid-June 1954, Carlos Castillo Armas led a few hundred troops across the border into Guatemala. The "invasion" was a bluff. The clandestine Voice of Liberation announced that Castillo Armas was marching on Guatemala City at the head of several thousand troops and scoring great victories along the way. Planes flown by CIA-contract pilots bombed a fuel depot and other visible points, and dropped propaganda leaflets. Convinced that he faced an overwhelming force and without the support of his army, Arbenz fled, and was replaced by a military junta that accepted Castillo Armas as president.[9]

Other covert operations approved by Eisenhower saw both successes and failures. From the Japanese elections in 1958 until 1964, the Eisenhower, Kennedy, and Johnson administrations sought to reinforce democratic developments in Japan by authorizing covert financial support and advice for a small number of politicians. Also in Japan, a covert program focused on propaganda and social action, designed to counter the influence of the extreme left, continued until 1968. On the other hand, a covert paramilitary effort against Indonesian President Sukarno in 1958 was ended abruptly and without coming close to its goal. The operation was forced into the open—that is, lost its deniability—when a contract pilot flying bombing runs to support rebel Indonesian army officers was shot down, captured, and traced back to the CIA. Another covert action in Asia was meant purely to harass the Chinese communists, with no anticipation of regime change. From 1956 to 1969, that is, in four administrations, the CIA provided weapons, communications equipment, and training to Tibetan guerrillas who had revolted against their Chinese occupiers. The support to the Tibetans was ended as part of the lead up to President Nixon's opening to China.[10] However, the biggest covert action failure was passed in its planning stage from Eisenhower to the new administration.

John F. Kennedy came to office in 1961 supporting the development of unconventional warfare capabilities as an alternative in confronting communist insurgencies. Although he inherited a flawed covert action plan to overthrow Cuban leader Fidel Castro, he introduced additional flaws in the project before it was undertaken. The program approved by Eisenhower in March 1960 envisaged creating a unified opposition among Cuban refugees, a guerrilla organization inside Cuba, and a paramilitary force outside Cuba. However, there was no organized opposition force in Cuba; and efforts to establish one through covert insertions met the same kind of dead end as had occurred earlier in Russia and China (and would occur again in Vietnam). Also, any covertness disappeared with coverage of the guerrilla force by U.S. media. In April 1961, what had begun as a guerrilla-led operation to ignite internal opposition to Castro ended at the Bay of Pigs as an ill-supported amphibious landing of 1,400 anti-Castro Cubans in the wrong place. The Cuban Brigade was crushed at its beachhead. The result was a political disaster for the new President.[11] Nevertheless, both he and, later, Lyndon Johnson continued to turn to covert operations when action other than military engagement seemed in order. Kennedy's desire to get rid of Castro's regime led him to support (some argue, demand) a high level of efforts to try to destabilize Cuba economically and even to assassinate Castro (an action contemplated previously by Eisenhower).

From the mid-1950s, the CIA increasingly became "an all-purpose instrument of action" in Southeast Asia, much like the OSS in World War II.[12] Kennedy charged the CIA with upgrading its operations against North Vietnam. Support from the North was viewed as central to the Viet Cong's efforts to gain control in the South of that divided country. At the time, CIA-trained paramilitary forces drawn from local tribes were engaged in cross-border, hit-and-run sabotage raids. When the CIA failed to generate a guerrilla force in the North, the President in mid-1962 ordered the military to take over and escalate the covert war. The vehicle for doing so was the Military Assistance Command Vietnam's Studies and Observation Group (SOG). Until it was disbanded in 1972, SOG attempted to establish agent networks in the North (unsuccessful, as were similar CIA efforts), created a fictitious resistance movement that formed the basis for a substantial psychological warfare campaign, conducted coastal interdiction and sabotage operations, and eventually carried out cross-border reconnaissance operations in Laos and Cambodia with U.S.-led teams of indigenous troops. Also in 1962, Kennedy launched the CIA into a paramilitary operation in Laos in an effort to inhibit North Vietnam's use of that country as a supply route (the Ho Chi Minh Trail) to the Viet Cong. The initial concept was to recruit, arm, and train Hmong tribesmen for guerrilla warfare and intelligence gathering. By the time the United States withdrew from Southeast Asia in 1975, the guerrillas had grown into an army numbering close to 50,000.[13]

Beginning in the early 1960s, the CIA had undertaken a series of political actions in Chile to support democratic left and moderate right parties against a radical leftist coalition led by Marxist Salvador Allende. In 1964, Christian Democrat Eduardo Frei was elected president, after receiving U.S. funding and benefiting from a large, CIA-run anticommunist propaganda campaign. In 1970, with Frei ineligible to succeed himself, the Nixon administration decided not to support any candidate directly, but mounted a propaganda campaign against Allende.

When no candidate achieved a majority, the choice between the two top vote getters, Allende and a conservative, rested with the Chilean Congress. Economic pressures, propaganda, and arm-twisting of individual congressmen failed to sway the vote against Allende. The United States, then, launched an all-out effort—overt and covert—to undermine the Chilean economy and build up, maintain, and encourage the internal opposition. Although both the CIA and the military had continuing contact with various coup plotters, there is no evidence that any U.S. entity had a direct role in General Pinochet's 1973 coup that resulted in Allende's death. Nevertheless, the concerted efforts to subvert Allende's government, the encouragement that plotters derived from their U.S. contacts (whether intended or not), and the open hostility of the American government to Allende certainly contributed to the environment that produced the 1973 coup and the years of repressive government that followed.[14]

Congress Steps In

The Founders clearly understood the need for secrecy in some government activities and the desirability of the President having some leeway in managing matters regarding national security. This view held sway for 200 years. What challenges there were tended to be short-lived. Broad deference to the President continued even when intelligence and covert action were institutionalized after World War II. Following passage of the National Security Act of 1947, the House and the Senate placed the responsibility for intelligence oversight with special subcommittees of their respective Appropriations and Armed Services committees. The subcommittees worked in what today would be seen as a remarkably nonpartisan manner, and their relationship with intelligence officials was largely collegial and supportive in nature. A high level of trust generally dominated interactions, even in the critical appropriations arena. That began to change in the 1970s as dissension over the Vietnam War eroded the American consensus on national security policy. The loss of that consensus, coupled with the disillusionment generated by the Watergate affair, media revelations about domestic spying, and disagreements over the covert actions in Chile, created an atmosphere in which many aspects of the U.S. governance process were subjected to review and criticism. Intelligence in general and covert action in particular ended up as the centerpiece of a tug of war between the President and Congress.

The initial move to restrict a President's freedom to undertake covert actions without the knowledge of Congress came in 1974 with passage of the Hughes-Ryan Amendment (Section 622 of the Foreign Assistance Act). Individual parts of Hughes-Ryan have been modified over the ensuing years, but its core concepts of presidential accountability and notification of Congress remain in effect. Using Congress's "power of the purse," Hughes-Ryan mandated that, except for intelligence-gathering activities, the CIA could not spend appropriated funds for covert operations until the President found that each such operation was important to U.S. national security. In addition, the President was to provide the appropriate committees of Congress with a description of the operation in advance of undertaking a covert action. The required presidential decision quickly came to be called a "finding."

The Intelligence Authorization Act of 1991 established the current statutory framework that surrounds legislative oversight of covert action. The legislation requires that:

- The President must determine that the conduct of a covert action by any entity of the U.S. Government (originally just the CIA) supports "identifiable foreign policy objectives" and is important to U.S. national security.
- A finding must be in writing. In an emergency situation, a written finding must be produced within forty-eight hours of the decision. With that exception, no finding may be retroactive.
- Any U.S. Government entity or "third party" (such as, a foreign government) that may be involved in funding or otherwise participating in the covert action must be identified in the finding.
- No action that would violate U.S. laws or the Constitution may be authorized.
- The Director of National Intelligence (changed from the DCI by the Intelligence Reform and Terrorism Prevention Act of 2004) and the head of any U.S. Government entity involved in a covert action must keep the intelligence committees "fully and currently" informed and provide the committees with any information that they might request.
- Findings must be reported to the intelligence committees prior to initiating a covert action. In extraordinary circumstances, the report of the finding may be limited to the House Speaker and minority leader, the Senate majority and minority leaders, and the chairs and ranking minority members of the intelligence committees (the so-called Gang of Eight). When access is limited in this manner, the President must provide a statement as to the reasons for do so.
- When a finding is not reported prior to initiation of a covert action, the President must still inform the committees in a "timely fashion" of the finding and provide a statement as to why prior notice was not given.
- The President must ensure that any significant change to a previously approved covert action is reported to the committees or, if necessary, the specified members of Congress.
- Covert actions may not be used to influence U.S. political processes, public opinion, policies, or media.[15]

The changes in the law governing approval of covert actions make clear that such acts belong to the President who approves them. Thus, plausible deniability no longer exists—Presidents may no longer disclaim any knowledge of covert actions. If they have no knowledge of an operation, that means it was not approved, that no appropriated funds can be spent on that operation, and that any funds spent on an unapproved covert action would represent the misappropriation of government funds. This is a powerful disincentive against "rogue" operations. In addition, while presidential findings technically only provide notice of a covert action and are not a request for approval, Congress's authority to authorize and appropriate public funds provides a ready tool to close down an unpopular operation. The Boland amendments of 1982 and 1984, which prohibited the expenditure of U.S. funds for the overthrow of the Nicaraguan Sandinista government, are a prime example of Congress flexing its budgetary authority as a tool for influencing policy. The committees and their members have other options for expressing objections to or even derailing covert actions. These include trying to talk the President out of a particular action, taking a dispute to the floor of the relevant chamber in secret session (whether anything could remain covert in such circumstances is doubtful), or in extreme cases leaking information about a covert action to the media. However, inclusion of the intelligence committees in the covert action process, if only in the sense that notification is made, also raises possibilities for obtaining additional support for the proposed activity. The covert support to the Mujahideen in Afghanistan, for example, had the enthusiastic support of Congress (some suggest an overenthusiastic support from certain members).

Business Continues

At the same time that the debate was going on over approvals for covert actions and while congressional committees were exploring a range of questionable activities by intelligence agencies, the Ford administration launched a new covert action. Controversial from its beginning (Assistant Secretary of State for African Affairs Nathaniel Davis resigned in protest), the program provided funding and arms to two factions in the Angolan civil war. A third group was supported by the Soviet Union and Cuba, with the latter supplying tens of thousands of troops to the power struggle. This is a clear case where policymakers (primarily Secretary of State Henry Kissinger) chose covert action in the absence of a willingness to take more direct action to confront the Soviet proxies. Nevertheless, the program was too small to be effective and too large to remain covert. That South Africa was supporting the same factions was a burden on the credibility of the U.S. involvement. Exposure in the news media came in mid-December 1975; and within a month, Congress terminated funding for the operation (the Clark-Tunney Amendment).[16]

Despite his view that such operations were inherently undemocratic, Jimmy Carter found that acting covertly was at times the best (perhaps, the only) way to advance his international agenda. Early in his administration, Carter approved a covert action for smuggling books and other written material into the USSR. There was also an effort focused on supporting publication and dissemination of the underground writings (*samizdat*) of dissidents inside the Soviet Union and in exile in Western Europe. In addition, assistance was approved for some Western groups to counter Soviet propaganda against the planned deployment of the neutron bomb and to press the USSR on human rights issues. A July 1979 finding provided for paramilitary assistance to the Yemen Arab Republic in its ongoing border dispute with its Marxist neighbor, the People's Democratic Republic of Yemen. Another finding in July 1979 authorized covert support to the opposition in Grenada following the seizure of power there by a pro-Cuban Marxist. This covert action was shot down when the Senate Select Committee on Intelligence (SSCI) refused to support the proposal. Also, in mid-1979, soon after the Sandinistas gained control in Nicaragua, the flow of arms and other material from Cuba led Carter to approve funding and political assistance to the regime's opponents. Similarly, a finding authorized covert support to El Salvador in dealing with an insurgency that was originating in Nicaragua and had Cuban involvement.

Two issues that began barely a month apart—both of which brought on covert actions—colored much of the last year of Carter's presidency. These were Iran and Afghanistan. When radical Iranian "students" seized the U.S. Embassy in Tehran in November 1979, the sixty-six Americans taken hostage became a problem that bedeviled the President until his last day in office (and, perhaps, cost him reelection). A secret military effort in April 1980 to rescue the hostages failed, with a loss of American lives, when two aircraft collided after the mission was aborted short of its target. A happier result had been obtained in January 1980, when a CIA covert operation extracted six Americans from Tehran. The six had escaped notice by the Iranians and found refuge in the Canadian Embassy. Even before the Soviet Union invaded Afghanistan at Christmas 1979, the administration was funneling covert aid, primarily money and nonmilitary supplies, from the CIA through Pakistan to the Mujahideen fighting Afghanistan's pro-Soviet, Marxist government. With the invasion, the flow of covert aid increased dramatically and included the provision of weapons.[17]

Ronald Reagan brought to the presidency strong anticommunist beliefs. His DCI, William Casey, shared those beliefs and was an activist by nature. Covert action became a tool for countering both the Soviet Union on its own turf and Marxist regimes beyond the Warsaw Pact. Poland was a crisis in the making during the transition from Carter to Reagan. After over a year of back-and-forth near-crises between the communist government and the Solidarity reform movement, martial law was declared in mid-December 1981. It is exciting to speculate that Pope John Paul II and the CIA worked together to keep Solidarity functioning following the communist crackdown. It is much more likely, however, that while both worked toward the same goal—Polish freedom—they did so on their own and with a minimum of keeping the other informed. In any event, the CIA launched a covert operation to provide Solidarity with the tools needed to wage an underground political campaign. This included enhancing Solidarity's ability to communicate with the Polish people—printing presses, copiers, the materials to produce clandestine newspapers, and a radio transmitter. Propaganda materials produced in the West were smuggled into Poland. Speeches by underground leaders were reprinted in Europe and sent back into the country, where they were given wide, if underground, distribution. The battle for Poland's soul ended in late summer 1989, when a noncommunist government took power in Warsaw.

In Afghanistan, covert assistance to the Mujahideen continued throughout the 1980s, until the Russians completely withdrew in early 1989. For many people, the turning point in the war (and in U.S. assistance that in the end totaled billions of dollars) came with the decision in 1986 to provide the Mujahideen with the

Stinger antiaircraft missile. In the same timeframe, Congress revoked its ten-year-old prohibition on support to Jonas Savimbi's UNITA insurgents in Angola; and they were also given Stinger missiles, as well as other weapons and supplies, in their ongoing struggle with the Soviet and Cuban-supported government. Similarly, with regard to Nicaragua, the Reagan administration initially continued and then began to increase both the amount and the lethality of support to the anti-Sandinista forces. By late 1981, training of Contra guerrilla forces was underway in Honduras and Argentina. Cross-border and sabotage attacks into northern Nicaragua from Honduras began in early 1982. Later that year, trust between the administration and the Congress had eroded to such an extent that the House enacted the Boland amendment (named for HPSCI chairman Edward Boland), prohibiting the use of appropriated funds to overthrow the Nicaraguan government. In October 1984, Congress cut off all aid to the Contras. Funding for paramilitary assistance resumed in 1986, and 1987 saw the Contras resume sabotage operations. Covert aid ended after the 1987 ceasefire between the Contras and the Sandinistas.

When Congress cut off funding for the Contras, the administration attempted to fill the gap through nontraditional covert activities managed by National Security Council (NSC) staff members. This was essentially an "off-the-books" operation that began with an effort to identify funding from private donors and third countries and included a "private" pipeline for supplying arms to the Contras. At the same time, the NSC staff became involved in a plan whereby the United States would sell weapons (using Israel as an intermediary) to Iran in return for that country's assistance in freeing American hostages being held in Lebanon. (Congress had earlier embargoed arms sales to Iran.) The NSC staff managed the undertaking, because use of the CIA would have required a finding and notification of Congress. Later, the CIA was brought in to handle the logistics of moving the weapons. A retroactive finding authorized the CIA involvement, but ordered that Congress not be informed. Congress did not receive the finding until ten months after Reagan had signed it. In other words, both of the pieces of the scandal that became known as Iran-Contra began as efforts to get around Congress's restrictions on the President's freedom to initiate covert actions. The intertwining of the two by the decision to divert some of money derived from overcharging the Iranians to support the Contras bears the taint of impropriety and even illegality. Multiple investigations aired most of the facts of the affair, with the result that the accomplishments of Reagan's administration may be overshadowed by Iran-Contra. Congress reacted to the efforts to short-circuit the finding process by passing the Intelligence Authorization Act of 1991 (see above).[18]

Old and New Enemies

The Cold War was winding down as George H.W. Bush assumed the presidency in January 1989. As one-by-one the Bloc countries replaced their communist regimes, aid to the new governments could be handled in the open. Thus, when the curtain was rung down on the Soviet Union on December 26, 1991, many of the older covert action findings were ended. In addition, the number of new findings dropped; and their thrust changed. Findings began to focus more on multinational issues, such as nuclear proliferation, weapons of mass destruction, terrorism, narcotics, international criminal enterprise, and technology transfer. One of the problems left over not just from the previous administration, but also from Bush's time as DCI (1976–1977), was Panamanian strongman Manuel Noriega. Noriega may have been a paid CIA source from as early as the late 1950s, with a break during Adm. Stansfield Turner's tenure as DCI (1977–1981). After Noriega was indicted in February 1988 for drug dealing, there were at least four separate findings dealing with Panama, the exact contents of which remain classified. Nevertheless, covert efforts to build an opposition in Panama went nowhere. The impediments to action included U.S. military concern about putting Americans in the Canal Zone at risk, the CIA's reluctance to support a coup that might lead to Noriega's assassination, and leaks to the media about proposed activities. Eventually, the administration chose to forego covert action against Noriega and opted for the most overt of actions—a military invasion of Panama in December 1989.[19]

Investigative journalist Mark Perry describes a covert action running from the late 1980s to 1990, which was successful in disrupting the organization and activities of the Abu Nidal terrorist group. That operation included close cooperation with the Palestinian Liberation Organization (PLO). Perry also details a covert effort to rescue pro-democracy leaders from China after the crackdown that followed the Tiananmen Square massacre in June 1989. The British and French intelligence services were involved in this effort. Immediately after Iraq invaded Kuwait in August 1990, President Bush ordered the CIA to prepare a plan to destabilize Saddam Hussein's government. In response to this finding, the CIA opened up contacts with Iraqi exile groups, and began to develop relationships with other dissidents, especially the Kurdish minority in northern Iraq. Media reporting over the next twelve years indicates that efforts to oust Saddam Hussein from power continued into and through Bill Clinton's presidency, often at the urging of Congress. However, the existence of such reporting suggests that the concept of "covert action" has been drained of much of its previous meaning. At most, the details of what was being done were hidden, but not the fact of the target and certainly not the activity's sponsor. In a severe setback, Saddam Hussein's army crushed the CIA-funded opposition forces in northern Iraq in 1996. At that time, the decision was made by the White House not to use U.S. airpower to interdict the movement of Iraqi forces into that region. Follow-on activities were undertaken, nevertheless, to rebuild the Iraqi opposition. These efforts were highlighted by the passage of the 1998 Iraq Liberation Act, setting aside $97 million for the overthrow of Saddam Hussein's regime. This was a clear example of an overt commitment to wage covert war against the leadership of another country. President George W. Bush directed the strengthening of those activities in 2002, prior to the decision to invade Iraq.[20]

Much of the 1990s was spent with Washington policymakers trying to capture the "peace dividend" that was expected to come with the end of the Cold War. The national defense and intelligence budgets generally and dollars and personnel devoted to covert capabilities specifically took deep cuts over the next several years. In fact, a shift away from large-scale, CIA-sponsored paramilitary actions had already begun following the end of the Vietnam War. In the 1980s (despite the commitment in Afghanistan) that shift was reinforced by a move toward a greater dependence on direct military action, exemplified by the raid on Libya in 1986 and the invasion of Panama in 1989. Instead, covert actions more frequently involved such techniques as identifying and cutting off the flow of money to—and in other ways disrupting the activities of—terrorists, arms traffickers, international criminal enterprises, drug smugglers, and rogue governments. In 1998, the downsizing trend began to be reversed. However, many experienced covert operators had retired or left the CIA in disenchantment during the intervening years. Nevertheless, when the decision was made after the 9/11 attacks to go after Osama bin Laden and al Qaeda and their Taliban protectors in Afghanistan, the CIA retained sufficient paramilitary expertise to be the lead element in planning and executing the first steps in the war on terrorism.

On September 19, 2001, eight days after the 9/11 attacks, the CIA's Northern Afghanistan Liaison Team (NALT) departed the United States. The work of the Counterterrorism Center (CTC) in putting Operation JAWBREAKER together showed flexibility at a critical moment. It took the team a week to make its way to Afghanistan's rugged northeast. There, it joined up with the forces of the Northern Alliance, a loose collection of tribal warlords, which represented the only serious opposition to the Taliban regime. The team's role was to enlist the Alliance's cooperation with the CIA and follow-on U.S. military forces that would assist the Alliance in taking on the Taliban preparatory to going after bin Laden and al Qaeda. Although its presence and the contacts that the CIA had maintained over the years with the Northern Alliance leaders were the team's most important weapons, the $3 million in cash that it carried was not far behind. By the time the first Special Forces' A-team arrived on October 19, 2001, the way had been paved for the cooperative effort, despite such issues as the Afghanis not getting their wishes that the U.S. troops not be in uniform. Backed by U.S. airpower, Northern Alliance forces captured Kabul on November 14, 2001. The Taliban regime was ousted and al Qaeda's safe haven eliminated. However, the effort failed to capture bin Laden, who remained at large as a terrorist rallying point.[21]

Almost an afterthought in military planning for decades, Special Operations Forces (SOF) have a central role in both the overt and covert war on terrorism. In 1987, Congress legislated the creation of a joint command structure for special operations—the U.S. Special Operations Command (SOCOM)—and gave it the primary role of supporting combatant commands. SOCOM reports to the Defense Secretary, and is not part of the Intelligence Community structure overseen by the DNI. The Defense Secretary's designation of SOCOM as the lead element in planning the war on terror has led to some friction within the national security apparatus. As military special operators increasingly engage in the type of covert activities that for the CIA require a Presidential finding and notification of Congress, the absence of a similar requirement for military-initiated activities remains a cause of concern. Also, there have reportedly been some hard feelings among officers in the military's regional war-fighting commands that previously had responsibility for the counterterrorism mission. In addition, SOCOM has been sending teams of disguised SOF troops into certain countries, as well as placing small teams in U.S. embassies, to gather intelligence on terrorists and prepare for potential missions against them. That these actions initially occurred without the concurrence of U.S. ambassadors or coordination with the CIA is worrisome to some members of Congress, as well as Foreign Service and intelligence officers.

Much of the war on terror is waged sufficiently outside normal view that we get only occasional glimpses of the kinds of covert operations that are being carried out. It has been acknowledged that CIA-controlled Predator unmanned aerial vehicles armed with Hellfire missiles were used against al Qaeda forces in Afghanistan, and in November 2002 a Predator-fired missile was used to kill a senior al Qaeda leader in Yemen. Media reports suggest that Predators have also been used for lethal strikes against al Qaeda personnel in Pakistan. In addition, there are reports of combined CIA and SOF teams working with Pakistani forces in the hunt for bin Laden and al Qaeda leaders in the Afghanistan-Pakistan border region. The military and CIA are also reportedly supporting local forces battling Islamist militia in Somalia, and providing counterterrorism training and equipment to troops from African countries from a base in Djibouti.

Do We Still Need It?

The covert operations that changed the governments in Iran and Guatemala are linked together not just in time but also by a phenomenon whereby actions regarded as successful in their day are retrospectively treated by some as failures. The same holds true for the supply of arms, especially Stinger missiles, provided to the Mujahideen in the war against the Soviet Union. In the case of Iran, much of the anger directed against the United States since the fall of the Shah (including the storming of the U.S. Embassy and the taking of its occupants as hostages) is attributed to resentment associated with U.S. actions in 1953 and support over time of the Shah's regime. For Guatemala, the argument is that forty years of internal warfare and oppressive rule followed the removal of Arbenz. And in Afghanistan, the concern is that the weapons provided to fight the Russians have now found their way into the hands of terrorists. All of these criticisms contain elements of truth, but the critics miss a number of points. In the first place, they are not taking into account either the tenor of the times in which the actions took place or judging the action on the basis of what was known at the time. Also, covert action is a tool of the moment, resorted to when talking is not achieving the desired effect and overt warfare does not seem like a good idea. It is meant to deal with the now, not necessarily to produce an outcome that will fix everything for all time.

In the cases of Iran, Guatemala, and Afghanistan, it did just what it was meant to do. However, covert action cannot replace policy, although it has certainly been used as a substitute when a well-articulated policy was lacking.

Given that there really is no way to determine what might have transpired in the long-term without the American intervention, the proper targets for debate are the policies in the furtherance of which U.S. presidents resorted to covert action. When that debate takes place between open-minded and well-informed individuals, they often can agree with the conclusions of the Twentieth Century Fund Task Force on Covert Action and American Democracy. The Task Force, with its panel of distinguished individuals from both the public and private sectors, mirrored the same tensions that mark American attitudes toward covert action in general. The Task Force concluded that:

> covert action inherently conflicts with—is in constant tension with—our democratic aspirations, not merely because it is secret and deceptive but because it is intended to avoid public accountability, a fundamental principle of constitutional democracy. At the same time, the world remains a dangerous place in which threats to the United States, its interests, and it citizens continue to exist . . . . Therefore we also conclude that covert action may be justified when a prospective threat creates a compelling national interest that cannot be met prudently by overt means alone.[22]

Notes

1. "Intelligence Operations," in *Intelligence in the War of Independence* (Washington, DC: Central Intelligence Agency, 1976), https://www.cia.gov/cia/publications/warindep/main.html.

2. See Stephen F. Knott, *Secret and Sanctioned: Covert Operations and the American Presidency* (New York: Oxford University Press, 1996), 61–136; and Charles D. Ameringer, *U.S. Foreign Intelligence: The Secret Side of American History* (Lexington, MA: Lexington Books, 1990), 73–87.

3. See Michael Warner, *The Office of Strategic Services: America's First Intelligence Agency* (Washington, DC: Central Intelligence Agency, n.d]), https://www.cia.gov/cia/publications/oss/.

4. *National Security Act of 1947*, July 26, 1947, Sec. 103(d) (1)–(5), http://www.intelligence.gov/0-natsecact_1947.shtml.

5. See Thomas Powers, *The Man Who Kept the Secrets: Richard Helms and the CIA* (New York: Knopf, 1979), 29–31; and Sallie Pisani, *The CIA and the Marshall Plan* (Lawrence, KS: University Press of Kansas, 1991), 81–105.

6. See Peter Grose, *Operation Rollback: America's Secret War behind the Iron Curtain* (Boston, MA: Houghton Mifflin, 2000), 121–189.

7. Cord Meyer, *Facing Reality: From World Federalism to the CIA*, 2nd ed. (Washington, DC: University Press of America, 1982), 109.

8. On Korea, see Michael E. Haas, *In the Devil's Shadow: U.N. Special Operations during the Korean War* (Annapolis, MD: Naval Institute Press, 2000). On WEI, see Frank Holober,

Raiders of the China Coast: CIA Covert Operations during the Korean War (Annapolis, MD: Naval Institute Press, 1999).

9. On Iran, see Kermit Roosevelt, *Countercoup: The Struggle for the Control of Iran* (New York: McGraw-Hill, 1979). On Guatemala, see Nick Cullather, *Secret History: The CIA's Classified Account of Its Operations in Guatemala, 1952–1954* (Stanford, CA: Stanford University Press, 2000).

10. On Japan, see U.S. Department of State, Office of the Historian, ed., Karen L. Gatz, *Foreign Relations of the United States, 1964–1968, Japan*, Vol. XXIX, Part 2 (Washington, DC: GPO, 2006), http://www.state.gov/r/pa/ho/frus/johnsonlb/xxix2/index.htm. On Indonesia, see Kenneth Conboy and James Morrison, *Feet to the Fire: Covert Operations in Indonesia, 1957–1958* (Annapolis, MD: Naval Institute Press, 1999). On Tibet, see John Kenneth Knaus, *Orphans of the Cold War: America and the Tibetan Struggle for Survival* (New York: Public Affairs, 1999).

11. See Peter Kornbluh, ed., *Bay of Pigs Declassified: The Secret CIA Report on the Invasion of Cuba* (New York: New Press, 1998).

12. Harry Rositzke, *The CIA's Secret Operations: Espionage, Counterespionage, and Covert Action* (New York: Reader's Digest Press, 1977), 180.

13. On SOG, see Richard H. Shultz, Jr., *The Secret War against Hanoi: Kennedy and Johnson's Use of Spies, Saboteurs, and Covert Warriors in North Vietnam* (New York: HarperCollins, 1999). On Laos, see Kenneth Conboy and James Morrison, *Shadow War: The CIA's Secret War in Laos* (Boulder, CO: Paladin Press, 1995).

14. See Nathaniel Davis, *The Last Two Years of Salvador Allende* (Ithaca, NY: Cornell University Press, 1985); and U.S. Congress, Select Committee to Study Governmental Operations with Respect to Intelligence Activities [Church Committee], "Covert Action in Chile: 1963–1973," *Staff Report* (Washington, DC: GPO, 1975), http://www.fas.org/irp/ops/policy/church-chile.htm.

15. 50 U.S.C. 413b(b), http://www.law.cornell.edu/uscode/html/uscode50/usc_sec_50_00000413-b000-.html. See Frank J. Smist, Jr., *Congress Oversees the United States Intelligence Community, 1947–1989* (Knoxville: University of Tennessee Press, 1991).

16. See Gregory F. Treverton, *Covert Action: The Limits of Intervention in the Postwar World* (New York: Basic Books, 1987), 148–160.

17. For the Carter administration, see William J. Daugherty, *Executive Secrets: Covert Action and the Presidency* (Lexington, KY: University Press of Kentucky, 2004), 183–192; Robert M. Gates, *From the Shadows: The Ultimate Insider's Story of Five Presidents and How They Won the Cold War* (New York: Simon & Schuster, 1996), 135–169 (hereinafter Gates, *From the Shadows*); and Stanfield Turner, *Burn Before Reading: Presidents, CIA Directors, and Secret Intelligence* (New York: Hyperion Books, 2005), 157–188 (hereinafter Turner, *Burn Before Reading*).

18. For Iran-Contra, see Gates, *From the Shadows*, 390–403; and Bob Woodward, *Veil: The Secret Wars of the CIA, 1981–1987* (New York: Simon & Schuster, 1987). On Poland, see Gates, *From the Shadows*, 162–168, 226–239, 358, 450–451, 464–467. On Afghanistan, see Milt Bearden and James Risen, *The Main Enemy: The Inside Story of the CIA's Final Showdown with the KGB* (New York: Random House, 2003), 207–367; Steve Coll, *Ghost Wars: The Secret History of the CIA, Afghanistan, and Bin Laden, from the Soviet Invasion to September 10, 2001* (New York: Penguin, 2004); and Gates, *From the Shadows*, 319–321, 348–350, 428–433. On Angola, see Gates, *From the Shadows*, 346–348, 433–434. On Nicaragua, see Gates, *From the Shadows*, 293–316, 434–436; and Jeffrey T. Richelson, *The U.S. Intelligence Community*, 2nd ed. (New York: HarperCollins, 1989), 346–350.

19. Turner, *Burn Before Reading*, 211–213. Mark Perry, *Eclipse: The Last Days of the CIA* (New York: Morrow, 1992), 104–135, 251–295 (hereinafter Perry, *Eclipse*).

20. Perry, *Eclipse*, 191–193 (Abu Nidal); 246–250 (China); 361–362 and 370–371 (Iraq). See also, Don Oberdorfer, "A Carefully Covert Plan to Oust Hussein," *Washington Post National Weekly Edition* (January 25–31, 1993): 19; Tim Weiner, "Iraqi Offensive into Kurdish Zone Disrupts U.S. Plot to Oust Hussein," *New York Times* (September 7, 1996): A1, A4; R. Jeffrey Smith and David B. Ottaway, "Anti-Saddam Operation Cost CIA $100 Million," *Washington Post* (September 15, 1996): A1, A29–A30; and Thomas W. Lippman, "A Blueprint to Overturn Iraq," *Washington Post National Weekly Edition* (August 10, 1998): 14; Bob Woodward, "President Broadens Anti-Hussein Order: CIA Gets More Tools to Oust Iraqi Leader," *Washington Post* (June 16, 2002): A1.

21. See Gary Berntsen, and Ralph Pezzullo, *Jawbreaker: The Attack on Bin Laden and Al Qaeda: A Personal Account by the CIA's Key Field Commander* (New York: Crown, 2005); and Gary C. Schroen, *First In: An Insider's Account of How the CIA Spearheaded the War on Terror in Afghanistan* (Novato, CA: Presidio, 2005).

22. Twentieth Century Fund, *The Need to Know: The Report of the Twentieth Century Fund Task Force on Covert Action and American Democracy* (New York: Twentieth Century Fund, 1992), 5.

CHAPTER 6

Where Do We Go from Here?

A Continuing Need

The end of the Cold War opened the door to a certain amount of wishful thinking that perhaps the "dirty business" of intelligence was no longer necessary. A U.S. Senator could even argue for abolishing the Central Intelligence Agency (CIA). The belief that there was a "peace dividend" to be gained led to continuing reductions in intelligence budgets and personnel throughout most of the 1990s. However, life and events have shown that those who speculated on a less dangerous world were wrong. The disappearance of the Soviet Union did not remove all threats to U.S. national security or to American lives and peace of mind. In many ways, the current world scene is more complex and difficult to understand and deal with than was the seemingly stable bi-polar Cold War. New threats have arisen, while old threats have mutated in ways that seem new and even more dangerous. Terrorism was a serious matter long before September 11, 2001 (the CIA's Counterterrorism Center was formed in 1986 and its Osama bin Laden unit was created in 1996), but the 9/11 events have changed how we view and react to terrorism. Regional conflicts (whether in the Middle East, between India and Pakistan, or elsewhere) are certainly nothing new, but we have seen new regions (including the Balkans and Africa) burst into extreme violence. Concerns about the spread of nuclear weapons have existed through multiple administrations, but we have now seen India and Pakistan add the weapons to their arsenals and other nations (North Korea and Iran) prepare to do so.

It seems obvious that in the face of continuing, new, and yet-to-be threats, U.S Presidents and the civilian and military decision makers who support that office need to be kept as well informed as humanly possible. That is the job of the organizations that comprise the loosely organized entity we call the U.S. Intelligence Community. No matter how ubiquitous they become, the Internet, cable news, privately owned imaging satellites, and open-source data mining will not suffice either for national-level decision-making or in-the-field support to deployed military forces. Informed decision-making seems preferable to the uninformed version and can be regarded as a necessity in seeking to maintain and enhance U.S. national security in the twenty-first century. As stated by the National Commission on Terrorist Attacks Upon the United States (the 9/11 Commission): "Not only does good intelligence win wars, but the best intelligence enables us to prevent them from happening altogether."[1] We can conclude, therefore, that accurate intelligence is needed as a foundation for the complex political, economic, and military decisions that will confront American leaders in the future. In addition, the military's increasing reliance on the use of "smart" weapons creates very real issues of immediacy of information delivery and direct battlefield access. These issues will continue to put stress on intelligence-collection systems that must meet the sometimes-conflicting needs for long-term national-level strategic planning and for shooting at a target of opportunity when it is available. Choices and tradeoffs on what is to be done and by whom will remain a significant feature of American intelligence.

Centralized Management?

It is ironic that intelligence, so strongly rooted in secrecy, has since World War II been one of the government's most frequent targets of official and nonofficial inquiries. Issues concerning how to manage the government's diverse (and, over time, growing) collection of civilian and military intelligence agencies have been reviewed and debated literally dozens of times by serious-minded and well-intentioned task forces, commissions, and committees.[2] The question of how much centralization or, conversely, decentralization should be applied to the intelligence agencies has pervaded such discussions from the earliest studies to the present. The three central questions within that debate have been (1) whether there needs to be a single head of the Intelligence Community; (2) if a single head is warranted, how much authority should the position have ("czar" or moderator); and (3) where should such a head be located in the government structure. In creating a Director of Central Intelligence (DCI), the National Security Act of 1947 had the position reporting to the President through the National Security Council (NSC) and gave it three broad responsibilities: coordinator of U.S. intelligence activities, chief intelligence adviser to the President, and head of the CIA. Former DCI Adm. Stansfield Turner describes succinctly and candidly the situation that existed for the fifty-seven years after 1947 with regard to efforts to coordinate and guide America's diverse intelligence agencies: "Despite the best efforts of a number of DCIs and presidents, no DCI has ever had sufficient authority to manage the Intelligence Community effectively."[3]

Among the numerous groups that have undertaken reviews of the organization and leadership of U.S. intelligence, it has been a rare event when the final product of their work did not include recommendations for change. Such groups find it very difficult to suggest that a great deal of effort and thought have been expended only to find that everything is fine and no change is necessary. Most of the studies of U.S. intelligence (often launched after some event has cast the system in a bad light) have in some way addressed the DCI's role. Not one of the studies has argued that the DCI's authority was too great and should be diminished. Beyond that, however, there has been little agreement. Some studies have come down on the side of broadened and strengthened authorities, while others have favored splitting the position into two jobs—one position serving as the head of the Intelligence Community and the other as head of the CIA. Two examples from the 1990s (although there are plenty of others) illustrate the point. Both cases focus on issues of control of the intelligence budget as a critical element in establishing a more centralized environment in the Intelligence Community.

With small exceptions, the allocations that account for the dollars spent by American intelligence agencies constitute a secret budget, hidden from public view within the defense budget. (The exception is the release of the overall figures for fiscal years 1997 and 1998—$26.6 billion and $26.7 billion, respectively.) That does not mean, however, that the intelligence budget is hidden from the government's multilayered budgeting process. The budget that contains the funds for U.S. intelligence activities goes through basically the same review process, involving the Office of Management and Budget (OMB) and the congressional authorization and appropriations committees, as the budgets of all other federal agencies. The intelligence budget is actually three separate budgets, with some 80 percent of the dollars controlled by the Defense Secretary and only 20 percent by the (until 2004) DCI:

- The National Foreign Intelligence Program (NFIP; renamed the National Intelligence Program or NIP in 2004) consists of the budgets of activities that involve more than one agency or are not in the defense budget. The NFIP/NIP budgets include the CIA, specific Defense Department agencies (the National Security Agency [NSA], the National Reconnaissance Office [NRO], the National Geospatial Agency [NGA], and part of the Defense Intelligence Agency [DIA]), and the intelligence units of other, non-intelligence agencies and departments (such as, the Federal Bureau of Investigation [FBI], State Department, and Treasury Department). Depending on the national priorities of the moment, the NFIP absorbs 45–55 percent of the intelligence dollars.
- The Joint Military Intelligence Program (JMIP) encompasses Defense Department programs that reach beyond the individual military services. Activities within the JMIP include the Defense Airborne Reconnaissance Program (DARP) and the Defense Space Reconnaissance Program (DSRP). The JMIP will normally be allocated between 10 and 15 percent of the intelligence budget.
- The Tactical Intelligence and Related Activities (TIARA) Program includes the individual intelligence programs of the Air Force, Army, Marine Corps, Navy, and Special Operations Command (SOCOM). The funds expended on TIARA usually run between 33 and 40 percent of the overall intelligence budget.

In 1992, the chairmen of the House and Senate intelligence committees introduced separate-but-companion legislative proposals for reorganizing U.S.

intelligence. Both bills envisaged the creation of an "intelligence czar," separate from the CIA and with enhanced authorities, particularly with regard to budgetary matters. In this scenario, a "director of national intelligence" would serve as the President's principal intelligence adviser and coordinator of the Intelligence Community. While individual agencies would retain control of their existing "assets," their budgets would be subject to the director's authority. The director would develop the NFIP budget, and allocate, obligate, expend, and reprogram all NFIP funds.[4] Although these proposals were not enacted at the time, portions of them found their way into various pieces of legislation; and they were widely discussed and dissected. Their main thrust—separating the Community function (whether coordination or control) away from the role of CIA Director—would find new resonance in 2004's reorganization legislation.

A wide-ranging study of the role, functions, and structure of the Intelligence Community by the staff of the House Permanent Select Committee on Intelligence (HPSCI) was released in April 1996. The study proposed that the DCI be given a stronger Community-management role. The position would have "the authority to transfer limited amounts of money within the NFIP without program managers' approval"; the DCI's "advice and concurrence" would be required for the appointment of the heads of Defense Department agencies funded within the NFIP; and the DCI's authority over NFIP agencies' personnel would be expanded to include the right to move personnel across agencies as needed. The study also suggested linking the DCI closer to the DIA. The study envisaged that the DIA Director would become the Director of Military Intelligence (DMI). The position would simultaneously be the Defense Secretary's senior military intelligence officer and "be accountable to the DCI" for Intelligence Community matters.[5] As with most such recommendations, these ideas were not converted directly into legislation; but the House study, like others, helped frame the debate about intelligence structure in the aftermath of 9/11.

The 9/11 Commission

The bipartisan 9/11 Commission issued its public *Final Report* on July 22, 2004. The blue-ribbon panel (see sidebar, "*9/11 Commission Members*") had spent a year and a half in hearings and interviews. The Commission was fulfilling a congressional and presidential mandate "to prepare a full and complete account of the circumstances surrounding the September 11, 2001 terrorist attacks, including preparedness for and the immediate response to the attacks." It was also charged with providing "recommendations designed to guard against future attacks." The Commission's Report is in many ways an extraordinary document. It has sustained narrative power (commentators have used such terms as riveting and enthralling); its language is clear and, for such a lengthy document, readable; and its tone is straightforward and evenhanded (some suggest, too much so). The Commission recommended a reorganization of U.S. national security institutions, and its guiding concept was centralization or "jointness" in the terminology it borrowed from the military. Its recommendations drove the debates that followed in and among the White House, Congress, the media, and the public in the months after release of the report.

9/11 Commission Members

Chair, Thomas H. Kean, president of Drew University and former governor of New Jersey; Vice Chair, Lee H. Hamilton, president and director of the Woodrow Wilson International Center for Scholars and former congressman from Indiana; Richard Ben-Veniste, attorney, former assistant U.S. attorney, and chief of the Watergate Task Force; Fred F. Fielding, attorney and former White House counsel; Jamie S. Gorelick, attorney and former U.S. deputy attorney general; Slade Gorton, attorney and former Senator from Washington state; Bob Kerrey, president of New School University and former Senator from Nebraska; John F. Lehman, chairman of a private equity fund and former Secretary of the Navy; Timothy J. Roemer, president of the Center for National Policy and former congressman from Indiana; James R. Thompson, attorney and former governor of Illinois.

In its lead structural recommendation, the 9/11 Commission put forward the concept of combining all-source, strategic intelligence analysis with joint operational planning in a National Counterterrorism Center (NCTC). The Commission saw this organization as the civilian equivalent of a unified joint command for counterterrorism. The NCTC would take over many of the analytical personnel in the CIA's Counterterrorist Center and the DIA's Joint Intelligence Task Force-Combating Terrorism (JITF-CT). The Center would also develop joint operational plans and assign responsibilities for execution of those plans to lead agencies, such as the CIA, the Defense Department and its combatant commands, the FBI, the Homeland Security Department, the State Department, or other departments or agencies. The NCTC would track the implementation of operations; but it would not run or direct them, leaving that to the agencies. Nor would it be a policymaking body, instead taking its policy direction from the president and the NSC. The Commission wanted the NCTC head to have the right to concur in the choices of the heads of the counterterrorism entities of the departments and agencies, specifically the heads of the CIA, FBI, and State Department counterterrorism units and the commanders of SOCOM and Northern Command (see sidebar, "*U.S. Northern Command*"). It also anticipated that the NCTC head would develop the president's counterterrorism budget.

The 9/11 Commission also pointed toward greater centralization in its recommendation that the DCI be replaced with a national intelligence director. (This title would be changed to Director of National Intelligence or DNI in the follow-on legislation, and DNI is used throughout this discussion.) The new position would have three main responsibilities. One would be overseeing national intelligence

U.S. Northern Command

NORTHCOM's formation in October 2002 was a direct reaction to the 9/11 attacks. It provides command and control of the Defense Department's homeland security activities and, as directed by the President or Defense Secretary, coordinates military support of civil authorities. It is responsible for the air, land, and sea approaches to the continental United States, Alaska, Canada, Mexico, and the surrounding water out to approximately 500 nautical miles, including the Gulf of Mexico and the Straits of Florida. Although NORTHCOM "plans, organizes and executes homeland defense and civil support missions," it has few permanently assigned forces, relying on "assigned forces" as needed. It is when a domestic disaster relief emergency exceeds the capabilities of local, state, and other federal agencies that NORTHCOM becomes involved. Its headquarters are located at Peterson Air Force Base in Colorado Springs, Colorado. NORTHCOM has a Web site at: http://www.northcom.mil/.

centers (such as the NCTC), which would be organized to provide all-source analysis and to plan intelligence operations on major problems for the whole U.S. government. The second would be to serve as the President's principal intelligence adviser. And third, the DNI would "manage" the national intelligence program and "oversee" the agencies that comprise the Intelligence Community. The DNI would be responsible for submitting a "unified budget for national intelligence" and for apportioning the funds appropriated to the agencies. The budgetary authority of the DNI would include the authority to reprogram funds among the national intelligence agencies "to meet any new priority." Under this proposal, the CIA Director would become one of three of the DNI's deputy directors. Nominations of individuals to head the CIA, DIA, NSA, NRO, and NGA, as well as the intelligence offices of the FBI, Homeland Security, and other offices engaged in national intelligence activities, would require the approval of the DNI prior to their presentation to the President. Responsibility for the military intelligence programs—JMIP and TIARA—would remain with the Defense Secretary.

One of the salient features of the Commission's Report was something it did not do. The Commission expressed concern that the FBI's fifty-six field offices are not completely onboard with shifting the Bureau to a more "preventive counterterrorist posture." The goal here would be to move the FBI's priorities away from lower-priority criminal justice cases to a focus on national security requirements. Nonetheless, the Commission chose not to recommend creation of a new agency dedicated to domestic intelligence collection and analysis. It did stress that to do the job the Bureau would need to make an all-out effort to institutionalize the change in priorities. It recommended creation of a trained and appropriately rewarded domestic intelligence workforce within the FBI to ensure the development of an institutional culture compatible with intelligence and national security work. The Commission believed that it would be especially important for each FBI field office to have an official at the deputy level to focus on national security matters.

Other recommendations from the 9/11 Commission included moving responsibility for covert paramilitary operations from the CIA to SOCOM; making public the aggregate national intelligence budget and the overall budgets of the intelligence agencies; and promoting greater information sharing horizontally, with databases searchable across agencies. In addition, the Commission found that the Department of Homeland Security, established by the Homeland Security Act of 2002, lacked the capacity "to assimilate and analyze information" from its own component agencies, such as the Coast Guard, Secret Service, Transportation Security Administration, Immigration and Customs Enforcement, and Customs and Border Protection. However, it made no substantive recommendations regarding that area of the counterterrorism problem. Whether the Commission found the continuing disarray in the Department of Homeland Security too difficult a problem to tackle or simply one that extended beyond the outlines of its charter is not clear.

In what may become its most ignored statement, the Commission declared (in the clearest possible terms) that congressional oversight of intelligence—and, by extension, of counterterrorism—was dysfunctional. It stated unambiguously that creating a DNI and a national-level counterterrorism center would not work without a change in the oversight regime. The Commission suggested either a joint House-Senate committee or single committees in each chamber with combined authorizing and appropriating authorities. It is interesting that Congress felt collectively comfortable with orally endorsing the 9/11 Commission's analysis and recommendations—and adopting many of them, with some modification—but showed almost no interest in addressing the aspect that the Commission declared to be most significant. Similarly, the Commission argued for consolidating congressional oversight of the Department of Homeland Security, finding that department officials at present must deal with eighty-eight committees and subcommittees.

Initial Reactions

Early reactions to the 9/11 Commission's report illustrate the dangers of proposing sweeping changes to bureaucracies in the closing phase of a presidential electoral campaign. The public pressure to accept and endorse the Commission's findings was such that the major parties' candidates, the Democrat John Kerrey and the incumbent Republican George W. Bush, felt compelled to do so quickly and uncritically. Similarly, Senators John McCain (Republican from Arizona) and Joseph I. Lieberman (Democrat from Connecticut) put forward a legislative package that would have enacted almost all of the Commission's recommendations. Their proposal received the immediate endorsement of Commission Chairman Thomas H. Kean. On the other hand, the chairman of the Senate Select Committee on Intelligence, Sen. Pat Roberts (Republican from Kansas), sought to move even closer to true centralization of the management of U.S. intelligence. He proposed the creation of a national intelligence director with direct control over most of the country's major intelligence-gathering operations and their budgets. NSA, NRO, and NGA would be taken from the Pentagon; the CIA's analytic, human intelligence, and scientific components would each become separate agencies; and all would answer to the national intelligence director. Other senators and representatives, as well as former DCIs, former heads of other intelligence and defense agencies, and major media outlets, weighed in with pros and cons about reorganizing intelligence generally and creating an "intelligence czar" specifically.

Although he later signed the Intelligence Reform and Terrorism Prevention Act, there is little doubt that President Bush would have preferred to keep the recalibrating of intelligence in his own hands. In a move intended to show the administration's responsiveness to the 9/11 Commission's recommendations and perhaps to short-circuit the momentum for new legislation, the President initiated his own reform measures in August 2004 by issuing a series of Executive Orders. Congress virtually ignored the President's effort, but his actions further illustrate the divergences in thinking about the future of U.S. intelligence.

Executive Order 13355, "Strengthened Management of the Intelligence Community," sought to shore up the DCI's position and role. It reaffirmed the DCI's responsibility as the "principal adviser" to the President and the NSC "for intelligence matters related to the national security," and added the same role for the Homeland Security Council. Among other responsibilities, it tasked the DCI with:

- developing "objectives and guidance for the Intelligence Community necessary . . . to ensure timely and effective collection, processing, analysis, and dissemination of intelligence";
- establishing, operating, and directing "national centers" of intelligence concerning "matters determined by the President . . . to be of the highest national security priority";
- developing, determining, and presenting, "with the advice of the heads of departments or agencies that have an organization within the Intelligence Community," the annual consolidated NFIP budget; and
- participating in the development by the Defense Secretary of the JMIP and TIARA budgets.

Executive Order 13355 also gave the DCI the authority to transfer funds from one NFIP appropriation to another or to another NFIP component, and to monitor and consult with the Defense Secretary on reprogramming or transferring funds "within, into, or out of" appropriations for the JMIP and TIARA. In addition, the DCI was given veto power over appointments to head organizations within the Intelligence Community, and required to make a separate recommendation for presidential appointments to such positions.

Issued at the same time, E.O. 13354 established the National Counterterrorism Center (NCTC), with a director appointed by the DCI with the approval of the President. The NCTC would be the government's primary organization "for analyzing and integrating" intelligence pertaining to terrorism and counterterrorism, except for "purely domestic counterterrorism information." It would conduct "strategic operational planning" and assign "operational responsibilities to lead agencies for counterterrorism activities," but not direct "the execution of operations." The NCTC would also serve as "the central and shared knowledge bank on known and suspected terrorists and international terror groups."

The third Executive Order, E.O. 13356, focused on one of the 9/11 Commission's major concerns—the sharing of information about the terrorist threat among and across governmental units and levels. The order directed the DCI to "set forth . . . common standards for the sharing of terrorism information" among federal agencies and, "through or in coordination with the Department of Homeland Security, appropriate authorities of State and local governments." The common standards were to include preparing reports for distribution at lower classification levels, including in unclassified form; sharing of terrorism information without the originating agency retaining control over its further dissemination; and minimizing the use of compartmentalization in dealing with terrorism information. E.O. 13356 also established the Information Systems Council "to plan for and oversee the establishment of an interoperable terrorism information sharing environment to facilitate automated sharing of terrorism information among appropriate agencies."[6] If his goal was to preclude legislative action, the President's effort proved futile.

Congress Takes Over

Between its founding in 1947 and the changes of 2004, the CIA's organization, its role in the U.S. intelligence community, and the performance of American intelligence agencies in general were, as noted previously, examined dozens of times by both governmental and private investigative bodies. Nevertheless, except for relatively modest changes at the margin (usually coming in the budgetary process), Congress had left the structure laid out by the National Security Act of 1947 relatively intact. That does not mean there had not been changes, but those that had occurred had come primarily through actions by and within the executive branch. Not this time, however. On December 17, 2004, President Bush signed into law the Intelligence Reform and Terrorism Prevention Act of 2004.[7] (Excerpts in "*Key Documents*.") This was less than five months after the 9/11 Commission released its report. The legislation approved by Congress and accepted by the President was driven by the political dynamic arising from the perceived need to "do something" given the shock of the 9/11 attacks, pressure from victims' families, and the wide and aggressive publicity given the Commission's recommendations. As enacted, this legislation represents another compromise in a long history of compromises surrounding the organization of American intelligence. The speed with which Congress acted, coupled with the relative absence of floor debate and dissent, is not only amazing in a deliberative body not known for its capacity for moving legislation rapidly, but also troubling—perhaps portending the creation of as many or more problems than it solved.

The title and substance of the Intelligence Reform and Terrorism Prevention Act links two subjects—intelligence reform and terrorism prevention—in such a way as to leave the impression that intelligence was being "reformed" primarily (perhaps, solely) for the purpose of preventing terrorism. In pursuit of prevention (a probably unattainable goal), the law addresses a wide range of terrorism and domestic security matters. These include transportation security (aviation, air cargo, and maritime); border protection, immigration, and visa matters; money laundering; criminal background checks; grand jury information sharing; pretrial detention of terrorists; and national preparedness. If the reform-terrorism linkage is truly the intent of the legislation (as opposed to merely the result of a rush job to legislate on the various topics), there are multiple implications for the future of U.S. national security. One such is that intelligence resources are expected to be directed at a single, overriding target—terrorism. Such a laser-like focus increases the possibility that the next crisis—that is, the next beyond terrorism—will be missed. It also may run counter to the military's increasing insistence on a high degree of commitment to intelligence in support to military operations. In addition, it implies that it will be necessary for Congress to "reform" the intelligence structure every time there is a change in what is believed to be the central threat. Another implication is that it is now Congress, not the President, which will decide how U.S. intelligence is going to be organized. In other words, Congress has asserted that it is at least an equal partner in organizing the Intelligence Community, despite the long-time acceptance of the view that intelligence is predominantly the business of the executive branch.

New Boxes, Old Solutions?

In configuring the Intelligence Reform and Terrorism Prevention Act, Congress accepted the much-discussed concept of splitting the jobs of coordinating the Intelligence Community and directing the CIA. The legislation replaces the DCI with two positions—the Director of National Intelligence (DNI) and the Director of the CIA (DCIA). The DNI's first two principal duties were transferred directly from the former DCI position as defined by the National Security Act of 1947. The DNI is now charged with heading the intelligence community and acting as the President's principal intelligence adviser. The law also tasks the DNI with:

- overseeing and implementing the National Intelligence Program (NIP, formerly the NFIP);
- providing guidance to department and agency heads for developing their portions of the NIP budget and, on the basis of their proposals, developing and determining the annual consolidated NIP budget;
- participating in the development by the Defense Secretary of the annual JMIP and TIARA budgets; and
- establishing objectives and priorities and managing and directing tasking for the collection, analysis, production, and dissemination of national intelligence.

The DNI's authorities include the power to transfer or reprogram funds (with limitations) from one NIP program to another. The Defense Secretary is required to "consult" with the DNI prior to transferring or reprogramming funds within the JMIP. The TIARA program remains solely under the purview of the Defense Secretary. The DNI is given the authority to create national intelligence centers "to address intelligence priorities," and to transfer personnel (not more than a hundred) from community elements to any newly established national intelligence center. The DNI may also transfer personnel (again, with limitations) from one element to another for two years or less. In the interest of greater information sharing, the DNI has "principal authority" to ensure maximum availability of information within the Intelligence Community. In another duty transferred from the former DCI, the DNI is given the responsibility for coordinating the relationships between U.S. intelligence agencies and the intelligence or security services of foreign governments or international organizations.

The legislation gives the DNI a Principal Deputy Director (a presidential appointment) and up to four Deputy Directors to be appointed by the DNI. The National Intelligence Council (NIC), which produces the national intelligence estimates, is placed under the DNI's authority, as is the existing National Counterintelligence Executive (NCIX). Other legislatively created components of the DNI's office include a Civil Liberties Protection Officer, a Director of Science and Technology, a Director of the National Intelligence Science and Technology Committee, and a presidentially appointed General Counsel. The staff of the Office of the Deputy Director of Central Intelligence for Community Management is transferred wholesale to the DNI, to support that office's community-management role.

After converting the DCI position into a DNI with two of the DCI's three primary responsibilities, the Intelligence Reform and Terrorism Prevention Act created the position of DCIA, who reports to the DNI. In reality, the CIA is the only line intelligence agency that reports directly to the DNI. The DCIA is charged with collecting "intelligence through human sources and by other appropriate means"; correlating, evaluating, and disseminating (the legislation does not use the term analysis in this context) intelligence related to the national security; and providing "overall direction for and coordination of the collection of national intelligence outside the United States through human sources by elements of the intelligence community."

The Act created a National Counterterrorism Center (NCTC), which had already come into existence under Executive Order 13354. The NCTC director reports to the DNI with regard to the Center's budgets, programs, and analysis activities. However, the director is also supposed to report directly to the President on the "planning and progress" of joint counterterrorism operations other than intelligence-collection operations. The legislation goes so deeply into detail as to define the NCTC's two-pronged organizational structure, perhaps to legislatively recognize the arrangements already in place. A Directorate of Intelligence has "primary responsibility" within the U.S. Government for "analysis of terrorism and terrorist organizations," with the exception of "purely domestic" terrorism and organizations. A Directorate of Strategic Operational Planning provides "strategic operational plans" for counterterrorism operations. However, this is purely a planning activity, as the NCTC director "may not direct the execution of counterterrorism operations." The DNI was also mandated to establish within eighteen months a National Counterproliferation Center (NCPC). In addition, Congress expressed its belief ("It is the sense of Congress . . . ") that the DNI "should" set up an intelligence center to coordinate the "collection, analysis, production, and dissemination of open-source intelligence."

Recognizing that additional powers at the Federal level might be needed to conduct the war on terrorism and that such a "shift of power and authority" could place strains on American liberties, Congress also created a Privacy and Civil Liberties Oversight Board. A part of the Executive Office of the President, the Board's role is to serve as "an enhanced system of checks and balances" to protect those liberties. It is charged with reviewing laws, regulations, and executive branch policies relevant to the effort to protect the United States from terrorism. It is also supposed to review government information-sharing practices to determine whether privacy and civil liberties are being protected. The President appoints all five members of the Privacy and Civil Liberties Oversight Board, but the chairman and vice chairman require the advice and consent of the Senate. After some concern was heard about slowness in getting the Board up and running, the full membership was sworn in and held its first meeting in March 2006.[8]

Echoing the *Final Report* of the 9/11 Commission, which called for the FBI to "fully institutionalize the shift of the Bureau to a preventive counterterrorism posture," the Intelligence Reform and Terrorism Prevention Act urges the FBI to improve its intelligence capabilities and "to develop and maintain" its own "national intelligence workforce." Not stated in clear terms but nonetheless the intention is an admonition for the FBI to create and nurture a *domestic* intelligence capability beyond anything that has previously existed in the United States. In a clear effort to move the FBI away from the dominance of its engrained law enforcement culture, Congress charged the FBI Director with creating a multifaceted intelligence workforce "consisting of agents, analysts, linguists, and surveillance specialists who are recruited, trained, and rewarded in a manner" that ensures the existence within the FBI of "an institutional culture with substantial expertise in, and commitment to," the Bureau's intelligence mission. In addition, the FBI Director is told to establish a budget structure that reflects the Bureau's reordered principal missions: (1) intelligence; (2) counterterrorism and counterintelligence; (3) criminal enterprises/federal crimes; and (4) criminal justice services. The legislation also raises the status of the FBI's Office of Intelligence to the level of a Directorate of Intelligence. It is charged with supervising the Bureau's "national intelligence programs, projects, and activities"; overseeing "field intelligence operations"; coordinating collection against national intelligence requirements; performing strategic analysis; and developing and maintaining the intelligence workforce.

Change in Perspective

As has been noted, the organizational structure of U.S. intelligence has undergone multiple incremental changes since 1947. The National Security Agency (NSA) was created in 1952, followed by the Defense Intelligence Agency (DIA) and the National Reconnaissance Office (NRO) in 1961. All three of these creations were the result of executive branch action, and did not have a legislative base. Congress asserted a more active role in determining the organization of the components of national security with passage of the Goldwater-Nichols Department of Defense Reorganization Act of 1986.[9] Goldwater-Nichols centralized military advice to the President in the Chairman of the Joint Chiefs of Staff ("principal military adviser to the President, the National Security Council, and the Secretary of Defense"), rather than resting with each of the individual service chiefs. The legislation sought to reduce what was seen as counterproductive interservice rivalries by decreeing that the services would practice "jointness." The emphasis here is the need for the services to coordinate with each other on everything from war-fighting doctrine to procurement of mutually compatible equipment. The mid-1990s also saw some wide-reaching rearrangements of responsibilities and authorities within the intelligence community. The NRO was reorganized to give primacy to the Defense Department and the organization's military-support role; the Defense HUMINT Service was established in the DIA; and the National Imagery and Mapping Agency (NIMA) was created out of existing intelligence and nonintelligence units and placed under the Defense Secretary. However, the rapidity and magnitude of change—both in theory and in practice—was accelerated at an unprecedented pace in the aftermath of the 9/11 attacks. Between October 2001 and December 2004, three sweeping pieces of legislation impacted how the U.S. government is going to defend America against terrorist attacks and how it will organize to wage the war on terrorism.

On October 26, 2001, less than fifty days after the 9/11 attacks, President Bush signed into law the Uniting and Strengthening America by Providing Appropriate Tools Required to Intercept and Obstruct Terrorism Act of 2001, officially the USA PATRIOT Act but most often referred to as the Patriot Act.[10] Passed in Congress with minimal opposition (a single dissenting vote in the Senate), the Patriot Act expanded the authority of U.S. law enforcement in the fight against terrorists in the United States and abroad. It also focused on eliminating the wall between law enforcement and intelligence in the sharing of information, a theme that reappeared in the 9/11 Commission's report, the Intelligence Reform and Terrorism Prevention Act, and the report of the Commission on the Intelligence Capabilities of the United States Regarding Weapons of Mass Destruction (the WMD Commission).

Then, a year later, in November 2002, President Bush signed the Homeland Security Act of 2002, creating the Department of Homeland Security (DHS).[11] In what was the largest government reorganization since the Defense Department was formed more than fifty years before, over 170,000 employees from twenty-two agencies were folded into the new department. The goal was to consolidate executive branch organizations with "homeland security" responsibilities into a single, cabinet-level department in order to strengthen the nation's defenses against terrorism. It is noteworthy that in defining the department's "primary mission," the legislation lists three activities—preventing terrorist attacks within the United States, reducing U.S. vulnerability to terrorism, and minimizing the damage and assisting in the recovery from any terrorist attacks that do occur—before it takes note that the entities being amalgamated in DHS have significant responsibilities other than dealing with the threat of terrorist attacks. Here, we see a huge and potentially disruptive governmental reorganization taking place with a singular focus, while the disparate pieces being shuffled around remain responsible for other and often unrelated activities. (See sidebar, "*Transfers to DHS*.") Essentially, the creation of DHS was an enormous act of centralization of authority (whether centralized control has been achieved in fact is a separate matter). The result of adding an extra layer of bureaucracy was to demote certain functions—those of the Federal Emergency Management Agency (FEMA), for example—further down the bureaucratic hierarchy and, thereby, impede or even interrupt the flow of critical information. This is at least a partial explanation of FEMA's failures in the wake of Hurricane Katrina.

Transfers to DHS

(Units in parentheses are representational only; some departments lost multiple activities.) The activities folded into DHS came from the departments of Justice (Immigration and Naturalization Service), Energy (advanced scientific computing research program at Lawrence Livermore National Laboratory), Defense (National Bio-Weapons Defense Analysis Center), Agriculture (agricultural import and entry inspection), Treasury (Customs Service and U.S. Secret Service), Transportation (Transportation Security Administration), and Health and Human Services (National Disaster Medical System). Also, giving up functions were the General Services Administration (Federal Protective Service), the National Oceanic and Atmospheric Administration (Integrated Hazard Information System), and the FBI (National Domestic Preparedness Office). In addition, all of the Federal Emergency Management Agency (FEMA) was moved into DHS.

Even passage of the Intelligence Reform and Terrorism Prevention Act did not constitute the last word on relationships and structures within and among the national security agencies. At a minimum, a process of filling in the blank spaces left by the legislation was (and remains) ongoing; but, beyond that, other voices were yet to be heard on how to reorganize U.S. intelligence. Less than six months after the Act was signed into law, the bipartisan Presidential Commission on the Intelligence Capabilities of the United States Regarding Weapons of Mass Destruction (the Silberman-Robb Commission or WMD Commission) issued its final report in both classified and unclassified versions.

The WMD Commission's wide-ranging recommendations covered such matters as creating "Mission Managers" on the DNI's staff, to be responsible for all aspects of the intelligence process with regard to high-priority intelligence issues; establishing a central human resources authority for the Intelligence Community; creating a National Counterproliferation Center (NCPC); creating a Human Intelligence Directorate in the CIA in order to strengthen the Agency's authority to manage and coordinate overseas human intelligence operations across the Community; creating an Open Source Directorate in the CIA; establishing a long-term research and analysis unit under the National Intelligence Council; developing a Community program for training analysts; restructuring the *President's Daily Brief* (PDB), with responsibility for its production resting with the DNI; expanding the Information Sharing Environment (ISE) to include all intelligence information, not just that related to terrorism; and creating a National Security Service within the FBI, encompassing its intelligence, counterintelligence, and counterterrorism units, which would be subject to the DNI's coordination and budget authorities. President Bush used the Commission's recommendations to begin clarifying some aspects that the earlier legislation left ambiguous, specifically the DNI's powers and authorities. In June 2005, the President endorsed seventy of the WMD Commission's seventy-four recommendations, while noting that congressional action may be necessary to implement some of the Commission's classified recommendations. However, many of the endorsements were the political equivalent of, "We are working on it." The President also embraced the recommendations of both the WMD Commission and the 9/11 Commission that Congress should reform its intelligence oversight structures.[12]

Where We Are

A detailed and balanced assessment of the impact of the most recent changes in U.S. security structures—and especially the intelligence component—is probably several years away. Even if the changes turn out over time to have had a salutary effect on protecting U.S. national security, we should not expect to see a clearly positive outcome for some time. Bureaucratic systems and cultures do not change overnight and sometimes not even over years. Indeed, major reorganizations rarely seem to provide immediately constructive results, and, in fact, tend to be disruptive in the short-term and sometimes longer. Whether there is a direct correlation between the 9/11 Commission's narrative and analysis of the fault lines in U.S. intelligence and its recommendations for structural changes is arguable, but it is also a moot point. Congress accepted (superficially, at least) those recommendations as the basis for the Intelligence Reform and Terrorism Prevention Act. Nevertheless, a review of the state of play in the still-changing reorganization shows that the legislation's DNI is not as potentially powerful as the national intelligence director envisaged by the Commission and certainly not as strong as the "intelligence czar" proposed by Senator Roberts. To state it another way, the Intelligence Community has not become as centralized as the Commission seemed to want it to be. Whether this is a good or bad thing is a separate matter.

Former DCI Adm. Stansfield Turner argues that the DNI's authorities under the Intelligence Reform and Terrorism Prevention Act are less than those afforded him by President Jimmy Carter. Executive Order 12036, dated January 24, 1978, gave the DCI "full and exclusive authority for approval" of the NFIP budget to be submitted to the President, as well as "full and exclusive authority for reprogramming" NFIP funds after consultation with the head of the affected department and, as appropriate, with Congress. The DCI's decisions on NFIP budgets and reprogramming matters could be (and, according to Turner, sometimes were) appealed to the President and, thereby, overturned. But that is how things should be, with the President exercising final authority on such matters.[13] Nevertheless, even this level of authority ended with the Carter administration. The point remains, however, that throughout its existence (and increasingly so as the size and complexity of the intelligence establishment grew), the DCI position had more responsibilities than it had power to carry them out. Similarly, the DNI has been handed a full plate of responsibilities. There is some question as to whether the legislation provides sufficient authority for the DNI to accomplish the Community-management tasks the 9/11 and WMD commissions identified as needed.

In a critical analysis of the effects of reorganizing U.S. intelligence, Judge Richard A. Posner presents a worst-case scenario for the DNI position:

> [The DNI] is designated the head of the intelligence community, and the President's principal intelligence advisor. He is to prepare a consolidated budget, overhaul personnel, security, and technology policies, coordinate the different agencies that comprise the intelligence community, ensure that information is fully shared among them, monitor their performance, eliminate waste and duplication [footnote omitted]. So broad is his mandate that should intelligence failures open the way to a new attack on the United States, he'll be blamed. Yet he has not been given the wherewithal to prevent such failures. His budgetary authority excludes major Department of Defense programs.... The DNI can shuffle some money among agencies..., and he can shuffle employees... [with several limitations] among the agencies and veto the appointment of some second-tier intelligence officials. But he cannot hire or fire the agency heads or other agency personnel.... He can issue policies and guidelines to his heart's content, but if the agencies ignore (subvert, "interpret") them he may be helpless. All the agencies except the CIA and the National Intelligence Council report to heads of Cabinet-level departments, who are the DNI's peers and will, if history is a guide, try to protect "their" agencies from him.[14]

Of course, the authorities granted by laws or regulations may not express the full measure of an official's power. If we define it as being able to get things done, power in Washington often has as much to do with relationships as it does with job descriptions. This is especially true the closer a position is to the top of the governmental pyramid. The DNI works for the President and, given the dearth of real authorities in the law creating the position, will be highly dependent on support from the occupant of that office to have any real expectation of coordinating (much less controlling) U.S. intelligence activities. Yet, the most prominent among the other participants in the competition to influence national security policy also work for the President; and some of them bring more to the table than the DNI. The Defense Secretary controls the majority of the agencies, programs, personnel, and funding for intelligence activities and, at one step below the President, is the civilian guardian of the nation's security. Even in the best of circumstances, the holder of that position is a formidable obstacle to any change that is perceived by the military establishment (including members of Congress who sit on the relevant committees) as impinging on the services' ability to do their job. This was the situation that the old DCI position faced throughout its existence; and, in many ways, the DNI is little more than the former without a bureaucratic base from which to work. That latter circumstance, however, may be subject to change as current and future DNIs work to solidify, enhance, and enlarge their role in the broader national security system.

Moving Forward

The first DNI, John D. Negroponte, and his Principal Deputy, Gen. Michael V. Hayden, were sworn in on April 21, 2005; and Congress's reorganization of U.S. intelligence was ready to be tested. When they were nominated for their positions, Negroponte was U.S. Ambassador to Iraq and Hayden was NSA Director (barely a year later Hayden left the deputy job to become CIA Director). During the confirmation process, the White House already had indicated that the DNI would be responsible for producing the intelligence material that the President receives at his morning national security briefing (the *President's Daily Brief* or PDB). Less than a week after taking office, Negroponte began presenting the briefing. The WMD Commission had argued against the DNI's involvement in either the production or delivery of the briefings. Commission members believed that too close an association with the current intelligence process would detract from the DNI's focus on matters of concern to the Intelligence Community as a whole. As noted in Chapter 3, the President's intent may well have been to send a signal that the DNI would have continuing access to the President, an important component of perceived influence in Washington. Nevertheless, there may be legitimate cause for concern in this regard as former DCI Porter J. Goss has publicly stated that he found the time necessary to prepare for the briefings (an estimated five hours a day) overwhelming.[15]

DNI Negroponte moved quickly to begin building his office into a tool for carrying out the duties assigned to him. He immediately ordered CIA chiefs of station to report to him when their activities involve matters relevant to the overall U.S. intelligence community. In early May 2005, he named deputy directors for analysis, collection, and management, and proceeded with setting up his own twenty-four-hour watch office (every office that pretends to importance in the national security arena has its own watch office/operations center—see Chapter 3). In June, the DNI scored a political victory when the House Republican leadership withdrew an amendment to the Intelligence Reform and Terrorism Prevention Act, which would have limited his authority to transfer employees from one intelligence agency to another. Also in June, the DNI's role in domestic security matters was expanded when a presidential order created the National Security Branch (NSB) in the FBI. The move unified the Bureau's domestic intelligence, counterterrorism, and counterintelligence activities in a single unit. Although organizationally a part of the FBI, the branch is theoretically under the DNI's overall direction; therefore, it reports to both the DNI and the FBI Director. Giving the DNI a role in overseeing a portion of a law enforcement organization is a new direction in defining the reach of the heads of intelligence in this country. As noted in Chapter 4, this linking of law enforcement and intelligence activities remains the cause of concern for civil libertarians.[16]

In July 2005, it was reported that DNI Negroponte was expanding the PDB to include more contributions from agencies other than the CIA. In addition, the PDB was combined with what had previously been a separate daily terrorist threat assessment. The DNI published *The National Intelligence Strategy* in October 2005, coinciding with his first six months in office. The document's stated goal is to establish strategic objectives for the Intelligence Community. It projects a more unified and coordinated Community that will seek to capitalize on the comparative advantages of each member organization. The top two objectives focus on defeating terrorists at home and abroad and on preventing and countering the spread of weapons of mass destruction. In response to a "sense of Congress" statement in the Intelligence Reform and Terrorism Prevention Act, the DNI established an Open Source Center (OSC) in early November. This center, while part of the DNI's office, is based at the CIA and administered by the DCIA. And, as directed by the Act, the National Counterproliferation Center (NCPC) was formally inaugurated on December 21, 2005.[17]

Even while the DNI was moving to establish a working organization, criticism of the decisions made in creating the legislation—and of decisions not made—began to mount. This was soon followed by statements of concern about the manner in which the DNI was implementing the legislation. The criticisms came from all directions. Some critics believed that the Act had failed to alter significantly the Defense Department's primacy in terms of number of personnel, size of budget, and level of influence among the departments and agencies with national security and intelligence responsibilities. Of course, some members of Congress had worked hard to produce just that result. A different set of critics were of the opinion that a law put forward as consolidating and streamlining the various agencies had done nothing more than add another layer to the bureaucracy. By early 2006, concern was surfacing in Congress that Negroponte had failed to take charge in the relationship with the Pentagon. Others argued, however, that the DNI had not been given the authority necessary to undertake and enforce such a dominant role.

Turnover at the top of the office charged with creating the so-called Information Sharing Environment (ISE) served to focus attention on the lack of progress in that area. This concern was reinforced in April 2006 by a stinging report from Government Accountability Office (GAO) investigators. Also, in the spring, the rapid growth in the size of the DNI's office (originally envisaged as perhaps 500 officials but already over 1,500) and budget (reaching close to $1 billion) began to draw attention and negative comment from members of Congress. Then, in July 2006, the House Permanent Select Committee on Intelligence published a staff report asserting that there needed to be "a greater sense of urgency in correcting the deficiencies identified by study after study." The report criticized the DNI for "trying to a little bit of everything which slows down improvements in key areas," and urged him to "prioritize activities and have his staff focus on those that are most important. Information sharing and other activities necessary to help in preventing future terrorist attack require more attention."[18]

Beyond issues surrounding the closer linkage of law enforcement and intelligence, the recasting of the FBI's mission and the role of its new National Security Branch (NSB) remain subjects for debate. The NSB concept is one of the ongoing changes that will require substantial time to play out before its efficacy (or lack thereof) can be proved. This is especially the case, because it is clearly an effort to effect cultural change through structural or organizational modification—an approach that is at a minimum arguable. Yet, patience with the FBI's efforts to remake itself is beginning to run short. Judge Posner, in a growing body of analysis and argumentation, has articulately delineated the main concerns with and alternatives to leaving domestic intelligence in the FBI.[19] In September 2006, 9/11 Commission member and former Secretary of the Navy John Lehman declared that "[o]ur attempt to reform the FBI has failed. What is needed now is a separate domestic intelligence service without police powers such as the British MI-5."[20] Although the question of who would staff such a new organization remains germane, the FBI's continuing failure (Is this the old bureaucratic ploy of waiting "them" out?) to adjust away from its culture dominated by law enforcement habits and mores is likely to bring more criticism for both the FBI Director and eventually the DNI.

It seems clear in retrospect that what many members of Congress believed was being accomplished by the Intelligence Reform and Terrorism Prevention Act was not justified by the actual authorities extended to the DNI. The idea that the reconfiguration of the old DCI job with marginally stronger powers would somehow produce a "jointness" comparable to the concept that has been dominant in the military since the Goldwater-Nichols Act in 1986 seems unrealistic at best. In effect, unrealistic expectations are being pushed to the front in a timeframe that borders on the unreasonable. Except for the CIA and those elements directly part of his office, the DNI does not have a command relationship with a major portion of the Intelligence Community. The DNI is not the overall manager of a unitary community, but instead must be prepared to consult, negotiate, and compromise in order to perform even a coordination role. This is a situation that former DCIs must find familiar. In addition, it is not surprising that the DNI's early focus has been on staffing and organizing his office. Taking over as DNI was not like being named to head an already functioning department or agency. He had no organization to begin with and, in addition, was an outsider to both the people and the central functions of the Intelligence Community. To even begin to attack the full plate of responsibilities passed to the DNI required that an office infrastructure be built from scratch. And that does not even take into consideration the absence of established relationships among the people being brought in from other agencies and shoehorned into previously nonexistent but critical positions. Whether Negroponte should also have taken on the creation of a separate analytic capability in his office—thereby duplicating analytic functions already being handled elsewhere—is a separate issue.

In early January 2007, Negroponte announced his decision, after only twenty months as DNI, to leave his cabinet-level position for the subcabinet number two job at the State Department. His departure, coupled with a situation where no one had been nominated to be deputy director of national intelligence in the interval since General Michael V. Hayden's move to the CIA, as well as turnover in other senior positions in the DNI's office, is sufficient to raise serious concerns about the President's commitment to uncompleted arrangements for managing U.S. intelligence. On February 20, 2007, retired Vice Admiral John M. McConnell was sworn in as the second DNI. He assumes the formidable task of trying to make the still-unproven rearrangement of U.S. intelligence work.

The American intelligence system clearly is passing through a period of upheaval. Roles and missions have been cast into doubt. Structural adjustments to the system have been mandated and implemented. Substantive changes are expected to flow from the new structures. Yet, structural and substantive changes are two different matters. New boxes on organizational charts do not generate new intelligence or change mindsets in evaluating data. New layers of bureaucracy do not speed up the flow of information. A high degree of uncertainty is being created at the very time that focus and cohesion within the U.S. national security apparatus would seem to be needed in order to respond effectively to the amorphous and ill-understood threat of terrorism. In addition, there are other concerns on the horizon, with nuclear proliferation by such countries as North Korea and Iran being only the most salient. In this time of uncertainty and even fear, the DNI is going to find it difficult to fully meet the expectations of important constituencies—notably, the President, Congress, and the public. The next "intelligence failure" (that there will be another is a certainty) will come to rest on the shoulders of the occupant of that office. Debate will continue over whether the 2004–2005 reorganization addressed the main problems in U.S. intelligence, as well as over what those problems really are. In fact, it is safe to predict that additional changes will be forthcoming. Yet, the challenge of ensuring that the foreign, domestic, and military intelligence components play their vital role in addressing the potential threats to American national security remains. The bright spot is that a successful response to the challenges facing American intelligence actually rests with the dedicated men and women who carry out the daily and often mundane tasks inside the agencies that make up the Intelligence Community, rather than in organizational charts carefully crafted for purposes other than getting the basic job done.

Intelligence and American Democracy

George Washington clearly understood the value of intelligence and of the secrecy that inevitably surrounds it. (See sidebar "*Advice from Gen. George Washington.*") At the same time, there is little question that the activities of intelligence collection (spying), the internal vigilance associated with counterintelligence and domestic intelligence (snooping), and, especially in the post-World War II years, the use of covert action (dirty tricks) as a policy tool often strain—and sometimes overstep—the bounds of the uneasy and shifting balance between openness and secrecy that we have accepted as necessary to maintain American national security. In essence, as a society, Americans have proved willing to compromise democratic freedoms in order to feel secure against threats to their persons and to the very concept of liberty—but only up to a point. How deeply into freedom that compromise cuts is directly associated with the level of threat perceived at any moment by the U.S. leaders and by the citizenry. When the threat is seen as significant and imminent, the U.S. political process can move quickly, decisively, and with substantial cohesion. As the threat recedes from the collective consciousness, however, that cohesion begins to erode. Doubts as to the wisdom of acting in haste, rather than after due deliberation, begin to surface. Concerns pushed aside in the face of shared danger start to take on greater significance. Most recently, the government's reaction to the horrors of 9/11, clearly illustrates the difficulties inherent in taking dramatic actions that have the potential to push the liberty-security dichotomy out of balance.

> ***Advice from Gen. George Washington, July 26, 1777***
>
> "The necessity of procuring good Intelligence is apparent & need not be further urged—All that remains for me to add is, that you keep the whole matter as secret as possible. For upon Secrecy, Success depends in Most Enterprizes of the kind, and for want of it, they are generally defeated, however well planned & promising a favourable issue."[21]

President George W. Bush signed the Patriot Act (see above) into law on October 26, 2001, less than fifty days after the 9/11 attacks. Passed in Congress with minimal opposition (a single dissenting vote in the Senate), the Patriot Act expanded the authority of U.S. law enforcement in the fight against terrorists in the United States and abroad. It also focused on eliminating the wall between law enforcement and intelligence in the sharing of information, a theme that reappeared in the Intelligence Reform and Terrorism Prevention Act. Despite being renewed on March 9, 2006, the Patriot Act's domestic intelligence provisions have raised both First and Fourth Amendment issues. Among other actions, the Act provides for "enhanced surveillance procedures" (warrantless searches to critics) and gives federal investigators the right to access such personal information as medical, telephone, student, library, and bookstore records without notification of the individual involved.

Similarly, a program approved by President Bush after 9/11, which allows NSA to intercept telephone calls and e-mails between the United States and overseas without court approval when the government suspects one party of having links to terrorism, has generated controversy and challenges in the courts. The same kinds of concerns have been raised about a Treasury-CIA program that accesses the records of international money transfers, including those made by U.S. citizens and residents. In addition, the CIA's maintenance of "secret prisons" for high-interest al Qaeda operatives, some of the interrogation techniques it has reportedly used, and the practice of "rendition," the moving of captured terrorists to countries suspected of human rights violations, have all generated varying degrees of controversy in both the American and the European press. The debate over what steps we can and should take as a government and as a nation, internally and externally, to wage the war on terrorism (or to address other, future threats), while maintaining a healthy balance between security and liberty, is not likely to go away anytime soon.

Notes

1. National Commission on Terrorist Attacks upon the United States, *Final Report* (July 22, 2004): 420, http://www.9-11commission.gov/report/index.htm. For a rigorous critique, see Richard A. Posner, *Preventing Surprise Attacks: Intelligence Reform in the Wake of 9/11* (Lanham, MD: Rowman & Littlefield, 2005).

2. See Richard A. Best, Jr., *Proposals for Intelligence Reorganization, 1949–2004* (Washington, DC: Congressional Research Service, Library of Congress, September 24, 2004), http://www.fas.org/irp/crs/RL32500.pdf; and Michael Warner and J. Kenneth McDonald, *US Intelligence Community Reform Studies since 1947* (Washington, DC: Strategic Management Issues Office, Center for the Study of Intelligence, Central Intelligence Agency, April 2005), https://www.cia.gov/csi/pubs.html.

3. Stansfield Turner, *Burn Before Reading: Presidents, CIA Directors, and Secret Intelligence* (New York: Hyperion Books, 2005), 159 (hereinafter Turner, *Burn Before Reading*).

4. U.S. Congress, Senate, *To Amend the National Security Act of 1947 to Reorganize the United States Intelligence Community to Provide for the Improved Management and Execution of United States Intelligence Activities, and for Other Purposes*, 102nd Cong., 2nd Sess., S. 2198; and U.S. Congress, House, *To Reorganize the United States Intelligence Community, and for Other Purposes*, 102nd Cong., 2nd Sess., H.R. 4165. See J. Ransom Clark,

"New Boxes for Old Tools? Considerations on Reorganizing U.S. Intelligence," *The Ohio Journal of Economics and Politics* 8(1) (Fall 1993): 1–10, http://intellit.org/reform_folder/reform90s_folder/reform90sclark.html.

5. U.S. Congress, House, Permanent Select Committee on Intelligence, Staff Study, *IC21: The Intelligence Community in the 21st Century* (Washington, DC: April 9, 1996), http://www.access.gpo.gov/congress/house/intel/ic21/index.html.

6. George W. Bush, Executive Order 13354, "National Counterterrorism Center," http://www.fas.org/irp/offdocs/eo/eo-13354.htm; "Executive Order 13355: Strengthened Management of the Intelligence Community," http://www.fas.org/irp/offdocs/eo/eo-13355.htm; and "Executive Order 13356: "Strengthening the Sharing of Terrorism Information to Protect Americans," http://www.fas.org/irp/offdocs/eo/eo-13356.htm, all dated August 27, 2004.

7. U.S. Congress, *Intelligence Reform and Terrorism Prevention Act of 2004* (Public Law 108–458), http://frwebgate.access.gpo.gov/cgi-bin/getdoc.cgi?dbname=108_cong_public_laws&docid=f:publ458.108.

8. See Privacy and Civil Liberties Oversight Board at http://www.privacyboard.gov/.

9. U.S. Congress, *Goldwater-Nichols Department of Defense Reorganization Act of 1986* (Public Law 99-433), http://www.jcs.mil/cjs/goldwater_nichol_act1986.html.

10. U.S. Congress, *Uniting and Strengthening America by Providing Appropriate Tools Required to Intercept and Obstruct Terrorism Act of 2001* (Public Law 107-56), http://frwebgate.access.gpo.gov/cgi-bin/getdoc.cgi?dbname=107_cong_public_laws&docid=f:publ056.107.

11. U.S. Congress, *Homeland Security Act of 2002* (Public Law 107–296), http://www.dhs.gov/dhspublic/interapp/law_regulation_rule/law_regulation_rule_0011.xml.

12. Commission on the Intelligence Capabilities of the United States Regarding Weapons of Mass Destruction, *Report to the President of the United States*, March 31, 2005 (hereinafter WMD Commission), http://www.wmd.gov/report/index.html; White House, "Press Release: President Bush Administrative Actions to Implement WMD Commission Recommendations," June 29, 2005, http://www.whitehouse.gov/news/releases/2005/06/20050629-5.html.

13. Turner, *Burn Before Reading*, 159–161, 252. Jimmy Carter, "Executive Order 12036: United States Intelligence Activities," January 24, 1978, http://www.fas.org/irp/offdocs/eo/eo-12036.htm.

14. Richard A. Posner, *Uncertain Shield: The U.S. Intelligence System in the Throes of Reform* (Lanham, MD: Rowman & Littlefield, 2006), 55–56.

15. Scott Shane, "Negroponte Confirmed as Director of National Intelligence," *New York Times* (April 22, 2005), http://nytimes.com; Walter Pincus, "CIA to Cede President's Brief to Negroponte," *Washington Post* (February 19, 2005): A15; WMD Commission, "Transmittal Letter," March 31, 2005, http://www.wmd.gov/report/index.html; *Associated Press*, "Goss Calls CIA Chief's Duties Overwhelming," *Washington Post* (March 3, 2005): A26.

16. Walter Pincus, "Negroponte Steps into Loop: CIA Station Chiefs Are Instructed to Include Him in Reporting," *Washington Post* (May 13, 2005): A4; Walter Pincus, "Intelligence-Transfer Proposal Withdrawn," *Washington Post* (June 8, 2005): A7; Douglas Jehl, "Bush to Create New Unit in F.B.I. for Intelligence," *New York Times* (June 30, 2005), http://www.nytimes.com; American Civil Liberties Union, "ACLU Slams Plan to Place Parts of the FBI under Control of Intelligence Agencies, Warns of Further Mixing of Law Enforcement with Intelligence Operations," Press Release, June 29, 2005, http://www.aclu.org/safefree/general/17621prs20050629.html.

17. Douglas Jehl, "Intelligence Briefing for Bush Is Overhauled," *New York Times* (July 20, 2005), http://www.nytimes.com; Director of National Intelligence, *The National Intelligence Strategy of the United States of America: Transformation through Integration and Innovation*, October 2006, http://www.dni.gov/press_releases/20051025_release.htm; "ODNI Announces Establishment of Open Source Center," ODNI News Release No. 6-05, November 8, 2005, http://www.dni.gov/; "ODNI Announces Establishment of National Counterproliferation Center (NCPC)," ODNI News Release No. 9-05, December 21, 2005, http://www.dni.gov/.

18. U.S. Congress, House Permanent Select Committee on Intelligence, Subcommittee in Oversight, *Initial Assessment on the Implementation of the Intelligence Reform and Terrorism Prevention Act of 2004*, July 27, 2006, 3, http://ciponline.org/nationalsecurity/Resources/rpts/index.htm.

19. Richard A. Posner, "Our Domestic Intelligence Crisis," *Washington Post* (December 21, 2005): A31; *Preventing Surprise Attacks: Intelligence Reform in the Wake of 9/11* (Lanham, MD: Rowman and Littlefield, 2005); *Remaking Domestic Intelligence* (Stanford, CA: Hoover Institution Press, 2005); "Remaking Domestic Intelligence," *Hoover Institution Weekly Essays*, June 16, 2005, http://www.hoover.org/pubaffairs/we/2005/posner06.html; *Uncertain Shield: The U.S. Intelligence System in the Throes of Reform* (Lanham, MD: Rowman & Littlefield, 2006); and "We Need Our Own MI5," *Washington Post* (August 15, 2006): A13.

20. John Lehman, "Five Years Later: Are We Any Safer?" *U.S. Naval Institute Proceedings* 132(9) (September 2006): 20.

21. "Letter from G. Washington (July 26, 1777)," in U.S. Central Intelligence Agency, *Intelligence in the War of Independence* (Washington, DC: 1976), https://www.cia.gov/cia/publications/warindep/index.html.

APPENDIX I

Biographies

Nathan Hale (1755–1776) and Benedict Arnold (1741–1801)

The Revolutionary War gave America its first spy-hero and its first traitor. The names Nathan Hale and Benedict Arnold remain synonymous with their acts.

Nathan Hale was born in Coventry, Connecticut, in 1755, the sixth child of Elizabeth and Richard Hale, farmer and church deacon. He graduated from Yale College in 1773 and taught school for two years, before joining the Continental Army as a lieutenant. He and his unit participated in the Siege of Boston. When the British left Massachusetts in the spring of 1776, Gen. George Washington began moving forces to New York City, where he expected the next British attack. Following the Continental Army's defeat on Long Island in August 1776, then-Captain Hale joined an elite reconnaissance unit known as Knowlton's Rangers, the American Army's first formal intelligence unit. Although records do not indicate the goal of his mission behind enemy lines, Hale clearly volunteered for the assignment. Washington certainly needed intelligence on the disposition and intentions of the British forces. Hale was captured (possibly through betrayal by someone who knew him), interrogated by Gen. William Howe, and hanged as a spy on September 22, 1776. As reported by witnesses to his death, the young spy's last words represent a ringing commitment to patriotism: "I only regret that I have but one life to lose for my country." Today, statues of Hale stand on the campus at Yale University and outside the CIA headquarters building. In 1985, the Connecticut General Assembly made Nathan Hale the state's official hero.

At the other end of the hero-villain spectrum is Gen. Benedict Arnold. Born in 1741 into a well-off Connecticut family that had lost its money by his early teens, Arnold was a businessman as war approached. Selected as a captain in the Connecticut militia, he rose to the rank of major general in the Continental Army. But for his treachery, Arnold might be remembered as a hero. Twice wounded in battle, he shares credit for the American victories at Ft. Ticonderoga (1775) and the Battle of Saratoga (1777). Arnold became disaffected by a lack of recognition from the Continental Congress. In addition, his lifestyle put him in debt and brought on some shady business dealings. The latter led to his court martial. Nonetheless, Washington gave Arnold command of the fort at West Point. Arnold conspired with British General Clinton to hand over the fort for money and a commission in the British Army. His contact with Clinton, Maj. John André, was captured in September 1780, carrying documents that revealed the plot. André was hanged as a spy, but Arnold escaped. He got his British commission and led two raids against the Americans. His later life in England was basically one of unsuccessful business dealings. Arnold died in 1801, reviled on one side of the Atlantic and ignored on the other.

Resources: John Bakeless, *Turncoats, Traitors and Heroes* (New York: Da Capo Press, 1998); Corey Ford, *A Peculiar Service: A Narrative of Espionage in and around New York during the American Revolution* (Boston: Little, Brown, 1965); and http://www.ushistory.org/valleyforge/served/arnold.html.

Allan Pinkerton (1819–1884)

Allan Pinkerton was born in Glasgow, Scotland, in 1819, and immigrated to the United States in 1842. After settling in the Chicago area and starting a barrel-making business, Pinkerton became involved in police work. Around 1850, he left the police force and established one of the nation's first private detective agencies, which became the Pinkerton National Detective Agency. During the 1850s, Pinkerton's detectives specialized in solving railroad robberies and catching counterfeiters. Hired to protect the newly elected Abraham Lincoln on his trip by rail from Illinois to Washington, DC, Pinkerton uncovered an assassination plot against the president-elect. Changing the itinerary and bringing Lincoln through Maryland at night thwarted the plot. In May 1861, Pinkerton organized an intelligence unit for Gen. George B. McClellan, then commander of the Department of the Ohio. When McClellan took over as commander of the Army of the Potomac in July 1861, Pinkerton accompanied him to Washington as his intelligence chief. Pinkerton was not a government employee but rather a private businessman on contract to provide a service. His organization performed both intelligence gathering and counterintelligence functions (overlapping with Lafayette Baker's activities for the War Department in this area). Pinkerton's most famous counterintelligence coup was breaking up the Washington espionage network centered on Rose O'Neal Greenhow. Rose Greenhow has been credited with warning the Confederates of the Union advance on Manassas, which precipitated the first Battle of Bull Run. Pinkerton's intelligence collection was generally limited to inserting transient travelers in and around the Richmond, Virginia, area and to interrogating captured Confederate soldiers, deserters, and refugees.

Historians have often commented on two interrelated aspects of McClellan's command of the Army of the Potomac: his cautiousness as a battlefield commander and his overestimations of the strength of the Confederate forces opposing him. Pinkerton has been accused of incompetence and blamed for providing McClellan grossly inflated intelligence estimates. Former intelligence officer and Civil War historian Edwin C. Fishel argues, however, that it is more likely that Pinkerton was delivering the intelligence that his commander wanted to hear. In either case, Lincoln's impatience with McClellan's lack of aggressiveness finally reached the breaking point, and the President fired the general in November 1862. Pinkerton's work in military intelligence ended with McClellan's departure, although he continued to investigate war-related claims against the government for the War Department through the end of the war. In the post-Civil War period, Pinkerton's agency would flourish as an adjunct to the bringing of law and order to the American West. Pinkerton died in 1884, but his firm continues to operate even today as Pinkerton Consulting & Investigations.

Resources: Edwin C. Fishel, *The Secret War for the Union: The Untold Story of Military Intelligence in the Civil War* (Boston, MA: Houghton Mifflin, 1996); James D. Horan and Howard Swiggett, *The Pinkerton Story* (New York: Putnam's, 1951); and http://www.americaslibrary.gov/cgi-bin/page.cgi/jb/nation/pinkerto_1.

Herbert O. Yardley (1889–1958)

Termed by his biographer "the most colorful and controversial figure in American intelligence," Herbert Osborn Yardley, was born in Worthington, Indiana, in 1889. Bright and athletic, the young man learned telegraphy from his father and poker at the hometown saloons. After graduating from high school in 1907, he worked for the railroad until becoming a code clerk with the State Department in 1912. Yardley taught himself codebreaking and proceeded to research the weaknesses (there were many) in the codes then in use by the State Department. With the coming of war in 1917, Yardley talked his way into a commission and became head of the Army's new code and cipher unit—military intelligence, section 8, or MI-8. He built an organization that handled codemaking, MI's own correspondence, foreign shorthand systems, invisible inks, and codebreaking. One message broken by MI-8 helped convict German agent Lothar Witzke, implicated in sabotage acts in the United States.

With the end of the war, Yardley convinced the Army and the State Department to jointly fund the continuation of the codebreaking section. Established in New York City, it was officially the Cipher Bureau; but, informally, it was called the American Black Chamber. However, the size and scope of Yardley's operation began to shrink as funding for the endeavor dried up in the following years. Breaking Japanese codes became the top priority. The Washington Conference on the Limitation of Armament in 1921–1922 represents the Black Chamber's finest hour. Reading Japan's diplomatic traffic made it clear that, if pressed, Japan would back down from its initial demands in the allocation of naval ratios. The U.S.

negotiators held firmly, winning the more favorable 10:6 formula. The election of 1928 brought a new administration; and the Black Chamber was shut down in 1929 when Secretary of State Henry L. Stimson, finding the practice unethical, withdrew the State Department's funding.

The out-of-work Yardley published his then-sensational and now-classic *The American Black Chamber* in 1931. In it, he revealed the extent of U.S. cryptanalytic successes in the 1920s. Although he had violated no law (two years later, a new law would establish penalties for exposing such secrets), Yardley would never again hold a position of trust with the U.S. government. To support his family, he turned to the lecture circuit and wrote articles and novels. In the late-1930s, he did cryptanalytic work for the Nationalist Chinese; and in 1941, he helped the Canadians establish a codebreaking organization. In later years, Yardley was involved in a variety of businesses, wrote another novel, and published a second classic work, *The Education of a Poker Player* (1957). He died in 1958. Despite his notoriety, Yardley was among the inaugural inductees in 1999 into the National Security Agency's Hall of Honor.

Resources: David Kahn, *The Reader of Gentlemen's Mail: Herbert O. Yardley and the Birth of American Intelligence* (New Haven, CT: Yale University Press, 2004); and Herbert O. Yardley, *The American Black Chamber* (Indianapolis, IN: Bobbs-Merrill, 1931).

William F. Friedman (1891–1969)

The man hailed by David Kahn as the world's greatest cryptologist was born Wolfe Frederick Friedman in Kishinev, Russia, in 1891. His family immigrated to Pittsburgh in 1893, and his first name was changed to William. Friedman received his B.S. degree from Cornell University in 1914, and began graduate work in genetics. He left academia to head the Genetics Department at Riverbank Laboratories, a private research endeavor established by George Fabyan. Among other projects, Fabyan was seeking proof that Francis Bacon's authorship of works attributed to William Shakespeare could be found in secret messages hidden in the texts of the plays. Friedman was drawn away from genetics by an interest in Elizebeth Smith, a cryptanalyst working on the Bacon project. The two were married in 1917.

When the United States entered World War I in 1917, the U.S. military had few cryptologists and began sending materials for Riverbank's cryptanalysts to solve. In addition, Elizebeth and William, now head of Riverbank's Ciphers Department, assisted in training Army officers in cryptography. The innovative monographs William developed to support this program are classics in the field. In mid-1918, Friedman joined the U.S. Army as a lieutenant, and worked in France with the Radio Intelligence Section. At the end of the war, the Friedmans returned to Riverbank. It was at this time that William wrote his magisterial *The Index of Coincidence and Its Applications in Cryptography*, regarded by many as the beginning of the modern science of cryptology. In 1921, he joined the Army Signal Corps as a civilian, and quickly rose to be the Corps' chief cryptanalyst. Elizebeth Friedman worked as a cryptanalyst with the Navy and later with the Treasury Department, helping catch smugglers during Prohibition. In 1929, Army codemaking and codebreaking were consolidated; and William was named head of the Signal Intelligence Service (SIS). His small, handpicked team was an extraordinary group of individuals who occupy an honored place in American cryptology.

Beginning in 1938, Friedman led the SIS team in an attack on top-level Japanese machine ciphers. The break into the diplomatic system the Americans called Purple came in August 1940. The output from SIS and similar successes by Navy cryptanalysts was disseminated under the code word of MAGIC. However, the sustained and arduous work had worn Friedman down, and he suffered a nervous breakdown. When he returned to work, it was on a limited schedule; but he remained the Army's chief cryptologist. When the National Security Agency (NSA) was formed in 1952, Friedman became its chief technical consultant, finally retiring in 1955. William Friedman died in 1969; Elizebeth, herself a cryptologic legend, died in 1980. Both were inductees when NSA began its Hall of Honor in 1999.

Resources: Ronald W. Clark, *The Man Who Broke Purple: The Life of Colonel William F. Friedman, Who Deciphered the Japanese Code in World War II* (Boston: Little, Brown, 1977); and David Kahn, *The Codebreakers: The Comprehensive History of Secret Communication from Ancient Times to the Internet*, rev. ed. (New York: Scribner, 1996). On Elizebeth Friedman, see http://www.nsa.gov/honor/honor00005.cfm.

William J. Donovan (1883–1959)

Called "the last hero" by President Eisenhower, William Joseph Donovan, was born in 1883 in Buffalo, New York. "Wild Bill" graduated from Columbia Law School in 1907 and went into private practice. In 1912, he organized a New York National Guard unit that later served on the Mexican border in the Pancho Villa campaign. In World War I, Lieutenant Colonel Donovan earned the Medal of Honor for leading an assault, in which he was wounded (one of his three Purple Hearts), against German positions. Donovan returned to the law after the war, and became involved in Republican politics in New York. He made unsuccessful bids for lieutenant governor and later for governor.

From the mid-1930s, Donovan undertook several unofficial trips to Europe and North Africa to observe and report on military matters for the War Department. In 1940, President Roosevelt sent him to Europe to assess Britain's ability to withstand the German blitz. Contact with British officials convinced Donovan that the United States needed a centralized system to manage all aspects of intelligence activities, including collection, analysis, psychological warfare, and covert action. He proposed such an organization to Roosevelt, who created something less—the position of Coordinator of Information (essentially, the President's chief intelligence adviser)—in mid-1941 and gave Donovan the job.

In June 1942, the organization Donovan had spent the previous year building was transferred to the Joint Chiefs of Staff and became the Office of Strategic Services (OSS). Donovan built his charge into America's first full-service intelligence agency. Blocked from operating in Latin America (by FBI Director Hoover), in the Pacific Theater (by Admiral Nimitz), and in the Southwest Pacific Theater (by General MacArthur), the energetic Donovan still found much for the OSS to do to further the war effort. OSS operatives were involved from the earliest use of American troops on the beaches of North Africa to the jungles of Burma. Infiltration teams, often with their British counterparts, worked with Resistance forces throughout occupied Europe. Intelligence collection against the Nazi and Fascist regimes from the neutral countries had many successes, including the work of Allen Dulles in Switzerland. In Washington, OSS had as sterling a collection of academics working as analysts as is likely to ever be assembled.

Donovan's vision of a single agency for the coordination of strategic intelligence seemingly ended with President Truman's disbanding of the OSS almost as soon as the war had ended. Nevertheless, two years later the creation of the Central Intelligence Agency brought into being the type of structure for which Donovan had argued. He retired from the Army as a major general, and returned to private practice, only to be named Ambassador to Thailand in 1953. Donovan died in 1959, and was buried with honors in Arlington National Cemetery.

Resources: Thomas F. Troy, *Donovan and the CIA: A History of the Establishment of the Central Intelligence Agency* (Frederick, MD: University Publications of America, 1981); Thomas F. Troy, *Wild Bill and Intrepid: Bill Donovan, Bill Stephenson, and the Origin of CIA* (New Haven, CT: Yale University Press, 1996); and http://www.arlingtoncemetery.net/wjodonov.htm.

Allen Welsh Dulles (1893–1969)

Born in Watertown, New York, in 1893, Allen Dulles was the grandson of a Secretary of State, the nephew of another, and the younger brother of a third. He graduated from Princeton University in 1914, taught in India for a year, and joined the State Department in 1916. After an initial posting in Austria, he moved to Bern, Switzerland, when America entered the war in April 1917. In Bern, he took over the embassy's rudimentary intelligence activities. Dulles later had assignments in Paris, Berlin, Constantinople, and Washington. After graduating from George Washington University's night law school, he resigned from the Foreign Service in 1926 and joined his older brother's New York law firm. However, Dulles continued to serve as an adviser to the State Department on arms control issues, and was part of the U.S. delegation at the 1932 Geneva disarmament conference. In 1938, he made an unsuccessful run for Congress.

Dulles established the Coordinator of Information's New York office in late 1941, and returned to Bern in November 1942 to launch the Office of Strategic Services' (OSS) station there. From that vantage point, he managed agents providing a wide range of intelligence on Italy and Germany. Intelligence from Bern included German order-of-battle; technical information on submarine production, aircraft defenses, and work on the V-1 and V-2 missiles; and early reports about Germany's research in gas and germ warfare. One agent, who worked in the German Foreign Office, provided thousands of vital military and political documents. One of Dulles' last acts in Bern was to arrange negotiations in April 1945 for the surrender of the German forces in northern Italy.

With the end of the war, Dulles returned to civilian life and the law, but was soon heading the Council on Foreign Relations' policy group on Europe. In 1946, he was elected president of the Council. The Dulles-Jackson-Correa committee was formed in 1948 to review where the newly formed CIA should be heading. In early 1951, Dulles became CIA Deputy Director for Operations and later that year Deputy Director of Central Intelligence. He took over as Director of Central Intelligence (DCI) in the new Eisenhower administration in 1953. His older brother, John Foster Dulles, became Secretary of State. The brothers were key architects of American foreign policy during the Eisenhower years, including the use of covert political, economic, and military actions. Dulles remained DCI into the Kennedy administration, until he resigned following the disastrous Bay of Pigs operation in 1961. The man affectionately known as "The Great White Case Officer" for his interest in clandestine and covert activities helped give America a modern intelligence capability. The development of the unique U-2 and SR-71 aircraft and of the CORONA and other reconnaissance satellite systems all took place during his tenure. After leaving the CIA, Dulles served on the Warren Commission investigating President Kennedy's assassination. Allen Dulles died in 1969.

Resources: Allen W. Dulles, *The Craft of Intelligence* (New York: Harper & Row, 1963); Peter Grose, *Gentleman Spy: The Life of Allen Dulles* (Boston, MA: Houghton Mifflin, 1994); and James Srodes, *Allen Dulles: Master of Spies* (Washington, DC: Regnery, 1999).

William J. Casey (1913–1987)

A native of Queens, New York, William Joseph Casey was born in 1913, graduated from Fordham University in 1934 and from St. Johns University School of Law in 1937. He went to work for the Research Institute of America, interpreting New Deal legislation for businesses, and practiced law on the side. After a stint consulting with the Board of Economic Warfare, Casey received a direct commission from the Navy in 1943 and wound up pushing paper in Washington. Looking for action, he wrangled his way into the Office of Strategic Services (OSS), applying his skills to bringing order from the chaos that was "Wild Bill" Donovan's office. In November 1943, Casey was transferred to OSS London, where he enhanced a reputation for getting things done. From late 1944, he headed OSS's intelligence-gathering arm. In the face of British doubts, Casey built an operation to infiltrate agents into the German homeland. The agents produced a stream of intelligence that led to bombing raids on important targets and revealed German troop movements.

After the war, Casey served as associate general counsel at the European headquarters of the Marshall Plan. He then returned to the practice of law. Active in Republican politics, he was appointed in 1971 as chairman of the Security and Exchange Commission. He later served as Under Secretary of State for Economic Affairs, president and chairman of the Export-Import Bank, and on the President's Foreign Intelligence Advisory Board. In 1980, he was the campaign manager for the victorious Ronald Reagan, and was named Director of Central Intelligence (DCI) in 1981, a position he held until just before his death in 1987.

Casey's tenure as DCI was controversial. The popular war against the Soviet occupation of Afghanistan, the unpopular involvement in Nicaragua, the craziness of Iran-Contra—Casey was part of all of it; how much a part will be long debated. His biographer, Joseph Persico, has suggested that Casey might be painted in several ways. There is Casey the "sinister, behind-the-scenes, above-the-law operator right out of spy fiction." Then, there is Casey the "old-fashioned patriot, an avatar of anticommunism, the director who restored a demoralized CIA." However, the middle course would portray him "as a man of considerable accomplishments who was also capable of colossal blunders, a man possessed of vision and blindness." There can be no doubt that Casey and the President he served as DCI shared the desire not just to harass the forces of communism, but also to defeat them. In many ways, Casey was the point of Reagan's spear in that struggle. Rightly or wrongly, Bill Casey was a true believer in the need to beat back the threats of fascism and communism; and he fought both the best he knew how. The Berlin Wall came down two years after his death.

Resources: Joseph E. Persico, *Casey: From the OSS to the CIA* (New York: Viking, 1990); and Bob Woodward, *Veil: The Secret Wars of the CIA, 1981–1987* (New York: Pocket Books, 1988).

Oleg Penkovsky (1919–1963) and Ryszard Kuklinski (1930–2004)

The list of Soviet and East European intelligence and military officers who provided information to the West about the internal workings of the communist system is quite long. Many fled their countries and talked freely when they were away from the repression of their former lives. A smaller number elected to stay in place and report about ongoing events; many of these—but not all—paid with their lives for their reaching out to freedom.

Oleg Vladimirovich Penkovsky was a forty-two-year-old World War II veteran and a colonel in Soviet military intelligence (GRU) when, after multiple tries, he finally made contact with Western intelligence in April 1961. A joint CIA-MI6 team managed the contacts with Penkovsky. He was a fount of intelligence on Soviet missile developments, nuclear planning, military matters generally, and Soviet designs against Berlin. The documentation photographed by Penkovsky and his reports based on high-level contacts were instrumental in changing U.S. estimates of the USSR's capabilities in advanced weapons development. His materials, reinforced by the growing U.S. capability in reconnaissance satellites, erased the so-called missile gap that had been a hot issue just a year before. This knowledge strengthened President Kennedy's hand when he had to face Khrushchev's threats about Berlin and to deal with the discovery of Soviet missiles in Cuba. Penkovsky was arrested in October 1962 in the midst of the Cuban Missile Crisis, found guilty in May 1963, and executed. His biographers may have overstated the case, but the intelligence Penkovsky supplied clearly meets the criteria for being among history's most critical.

Ryszard Kuklinski was a Polish patriot who chose to work for his country's freedom by resisting its domination by the Soviet Union. In 1972, the forty-two-year-old army colonel contacted the CIA and volunteered to provide information about the Soviets and the Warsaw Pact. His position in the Polish General Staff Headquarters provided access to highly classified documents and the discussions of senior officers. Always believing that his actions were to benefit Poland, Kuklinski lived the tension-filled life of an agent in-place for nine years. He provided tens of thousands of pages of classified documents, including the Soviet war plans for Europe, information on weapons systems, and Soviet preparations to invade Poland should that country fail to restrain Solidarity and the democracy movement. By 1981, Polish counterintelligence was beginning to close in, and the CIA exfiltrated Kuklinski and his family from Poland. Reviled by the communist regime and sentenced to death, Kuklinski lived to see the birth of a free Poland, and he visited his homeland in 1998. He died in the United States in 2004; his ashes were buried with honors at Warsaw's Powazki Cemetery.

Resources: Jerrold L. Schecter and Peter S. Deriabin, *The Spy Who Saved the World: How a Soviet Colonel Changed the Course of the Cold War* (New York: Scribner's, 1992); and Benjamin Weiser, *A Secret Life: The Polish Officer, His Covert Mission, and the Price He Paid to Save His Country* (New York: PublicAffairs, 2004).

Aldrich Hazen Ames (b. 1941)

Aldrich Hazen Ames was born in River Falls, Wisconsin, in 1941. His father worked for the CIA from 1952 until 1967. The Ames family had an overseas tour in Southeast Asia from 1953 to 1955, and young Ames spent his high-school summers as a clerk at the CIA. After dropping out of the University of Chicago, he worked at a lower-level job at the CIA until he graduated from George Washington University in 1967. He completed the CIA's Career Trainee Program, married another program participant, and received an overseas assignment as a

Clandestine Services operations officer in Ankara, Turkey. The three-year tour did not go well. Back at Headquarters for four years from 1972, he seemed more at home writing and managing paper in the Soviet-East European Division of the Directorate of Operations. However, signs of a serious drinking problem had begun to appear. He served at the CIA's New York City base from 1976 to 1981, doing well enough to rise to the mid-level grade of GS-14. He would go no higher. In 1981, he was reassigned to Mexico; but his wife stayed in New York. His job performance was mediocre, and his heavy drinking continued. While in Mexico he met the woman who became his second wife, Maria del Rosario Casas Dupuy, the cultural attaché at the Colombian Embassy.

When Ames returned to Washington in 1983, he became counterintelligence branch chief for Soviet operations. That job gave him legitimate access to all the information about the CIA's operations in the Soviet Union. Why a lackadaisical performer was placed in such a critical position continues to confound anyone studying the case. Ames's divorce settlement strained his resources, at the same time that his Colombian girlfriend had come to live with him. In 1984, Ames notified the CIA that he wanted to marry Rosario Casas. Background checks were run, and the marriage was approved. In April 1985, Ames walked into the Soviet Embassy in Washington, under cover of an approved contact with a Russian official, and offered up information for $50,000. Once committed, Ames spied, first, for the Soviets and, then, for the Russians—including during an overseas tour in Italy from 1986 to 1989—until his arrest in 1994. He ultimately gave the KGB the names of all the Soviet intelligence officers working as American agents. Ames received in excess of $2.5 million for his treachery, which resulted in the deaths of at least ten CIA sources. Following a guilty plea in April 1994, Ames forfeited his assets and was sentenced to life in prison without the possibility of parole.

Resources: Pete Earley, *Confessions of a Spy: The Real Story of Aldrich Ames* (New York: Putnam's, 1997); Frederick P. Hitz, *Unclassified Abstract of the CIA Inspector General's Report on the Aldrich H. Ames Case* (Washington, DC: CIA, 1994), http://nsi.org/Library/Espionage/Hitzreport.html; and Arthur S. Hulnick, "The Ames Case: HOW Could It Happen?" *International Journal of Intelligence and Counterintelligence* 8(2) (Summer 1995): 133–154.

John Dmitri Negroponte (b. 1939)

The first Director of National Intelligence (DNI), John Dmitri Negroponte, was born in London, England, in 1939 to the family of a Greek-American shipping magnate. He graduated from Yale University in 1960 and joined the State Department. Over a thirty-seven-year career with the Foreign Service, Negroponte served at eight different posts in Asia, Europe, and Latin America, as well as holding policy-related positions at the State Department, the National Security Council (NSC), and the United Nations. Among his assignments, he was Deputy Assistant

Secretary of State for Oceans and Fisheries (1977–1979), Deputy Assistant Secretary of State for East Asian and Pacific Affairs (1980–1981), Ambassador to Honduras (1981–1985), Assistant Secretary of State for Oceans and International Environmental and Scientific Affairs (1985–1987), Deputy Assistant to the President for National Security Affairs (1987–1989), Ambassador to Mexico (1989–1993), and Ambassador to the Philippines (1993–1996). From 1997 to 2001, Negroponte worked in the private sector as Executive Vice President for Global Markets of McGraw-Hill.

Negroponte's nomination in 2001 to be U.S. Permanent Representative to the United Nations occasioned sufficient debate to delay his confirmation for several months. He came under fire in the media and at his confirmation hearings for his role in the U.S.-supported Contra war against the Sandinista government in Nicaragua. He was specifically accused of assisting in the irregular funding of the Contras and of ignoring human rights abuses in Honduras while he was U.S. Ambassador there. His appointment was finally confirmed in mid-September 2001. Negroponte served at the United Nations until he was nominated by President Bush in April 2004 to be the U.S. Ambassador to Iraq. He was confirmed in May and took over the job in June 2004, following the transition to the new Iraqi government. He held the job for less than a year.

The Intelligence Reform and Terrorism Prevention Act, signed by President Bush on December 17, 2004, created the position of DNI, which replaced the Director of Central Intelligence (DCI) as head of the U.S. Intelligence Community. After discussions with other possible nominees, the President nominated Negroponte for the job on February 17, 2005. The human-rights issue resurfaced after Negroponte was nominated. Documents released to the media under the Freedom of Information Act (FOIA) seem to show that, as might be expected from a serving ambassador, Negroponte supported President Reagan's anticommunist offensive in Central America. He was confirmed by the Senate and sworn in as DNI on April 21, 2005. Negroponte's task was not an easy one; nor did his progress in the job please everyone. In essence, he took on a position for which expectations had been raised by legislation widely ballyhooed as reformist in nature. Nevertheless, the job is not significantly more powerful than the DCI position that the legislation abolished. In January 2007, after twenty months as DNI, Negroponte opted to return to the State Department in the number two position. To some degree, the success of the second DNI, retired Vice Admiral John M. McConnell, is connected to how well Negroponte began the process of establishing the future management of the U.S. Intelligence Community.

Resources: http://www.dni.gov/aboutODNI/bios/negroponte_bio.htm; and http://en.wikipedia.org/wiki/John_Negroponte.

APPENDIX II

Key Documents

DOCUMENT 1

NATIONAL SECURITY ACT OF 1947 (EXCERPTS)
JULY 26, 1947
(AS AMENDED)
[http://www.intelligence.gov/0-natsecact_1947.shtml]

TITLE V—ACCOUNTABILITY FOR INTELLIGENCE ACTIVITIES

GENERAL CONGRESSIONAL OVERSIGHT PROVISIONS

SEC. 501. [50 U.S.C. 413] (a) (1) The President shall ensure that the congressional intelligence committees are kept fully and currently informed of the intelligence activities of the United States, including any significant anticipated intelligence activity as required by this title.

(2) Nothing in this title shall be construed as requiring the approval of the congressional intelligence committees as a condition precedent to the initiation of any significant anticipated intelligence activity.

(b) The President shall ensure that any illegal intelligence activity is reported promptly to the congressional intelligence committees....

(d) The House of Representatives and the Senate shall each establish... procedures to protect from unauthorized disclosure all classified information... that is furnished to the congressional intelligence committees or to Members of Congress under this title....

PRESIDENTIAL APPROVAL AND REPORTING OF COVERT ACTIONS

SEC. 503. [50 U.S.C. 413b] (a) The President may not authorize the conduct of a covert action by departments, agencies, or entities of the United States Government unless the President determines such an action is necessary to support identifiable foreign policy objectives of the United States and is important to the national security of the United States, which determination shall be set forth in a finding that shall meet each of the following conditions:

> (f) Each finding shall be in writing, unless immediate action by the United States is required and time does not permit the preparation of a written finding, in which case a written record of the President's decision shall be contemporaneously made and shall be reduced to a written finding as soon as possible but in no event more than 48 hours after the decision is made.

(2) Except as permitted by paragraph (1), a finding may not authorize or sanction a covert action, or any aspect of any such action, which already has occurred.

(3) Each finding shall specify each department, agency, or entity of the United States Government authorized to fund or otherwise participate in any significant way in such action . . . .

(4) Each finding shall specify whether it is contemplated that any third party which is not an element of, or a contractor or contract agent of, the United States Government, or is not otherwise subject to United States Government policies and regulations, will be used to fund or otherwise participate in any significant way in the covert action concerned, or be used to undertake the covert action concerned on behalf of the United States.

(5) A finding may not authorize any action that would violate the Constitution or any statute of the United States.

(b) To the extent consistent with due regard for the protection from unauthorized disclosure of classified information relating to sensitive intelligence sources and methods or other exceptionally sensitive matters, the Director of Central Intelligence and the heads of all departments, agencies, and entities of the United States Government involved in a covert action—

> (f) shall keep the congressional intelligence committees fully and currently informed of all covert actions which are the responsibility of, are engaged in by, or are carried out for or on behalf of, any department, agency, or entity of the United States Government, including significant failures; and

(2) shall furnish to the congressional intelligence committees any information or material concerning covert actions . . . which is requested by either of the congressional intelligence committees in order to carry out its authorized responsibilities.

(c) (1) The President shall ensure that any finding approved pursuant to subsection (a) shall be reported to the congressional intelligence committees as soon as possible after such approval and before the initiation of the covert action authorized by the finding, except as otherwise provided in paragraph (2) and paragraph (3).

(2) if the President determines that it is essential to limit access to the finding to meet extraordinary circumstances affecting vital interests of the United States, the finding may be reported to the chairmen and ranking minority members of the congressional intelligence committees, the Speaker and minority leader of the House of Representatives, the majority and minority leaders of the Senate, and such other member or members of the congressional leadership as may be included by the President.

(3) Whenever a finding is not reported pursuant to paragraph (1) or (2) of this section, the President shall fully inform the congressional intelligence committees in a timely fashion and shall provide a statement of the reasons for not giving prior notice.

(4) In a case under paragraph (1), (2), or (3), a copy of the finding, signed by the President, shall be provided to the chairman of each congressional intelligence committee . . . .

(d) The President shall ensure that the congressional intelligence committees, or, if applicable, the Members of Congress specified in subsection (c) (2), are notified of any significant change in a previously approved covert action, or any significant undertaking pursuant to a previously approved finding, in the same manner as findings are reported pursuant to subsection (c) . . . .

(f) No covert action may be conducted which is intended to influence United States political processes, public opinion, policies, or media.

DOCUMENT 2

INTELLIGENCE REFORM AND TERRORISM PREVENTION ACT OF 2004 (Edited Excerpts)
December 17, 2004

[http://frwebgate.access.gpo.gov/cgi-bin/getdoc.cgi?dbname=108_cong_public_laws&docid=f:publ458.108]

TITLE I—REFORM OF THE INTELLIGENCE COMMUNITY

SEC. 1011. REORGANIZATION AND IMPROVEMENT OF MANAGEMENT OF INTELLIGENCE COMMUNITY.

(a) IN GENERAL.—Title I of the National Security Act of 1947 (50 U.S.C. 402 et seq.) is amended by striking sections 102 through 104 and inserting the following new sections:

"Sec. 102. (a) DIRECTOR OF NATIONAL INTELLIGENCE.—(1) There is a Director of National Intelligence [DNI] who shall be appointed by the President, by and with the advice and consent of the Senate . . . .

"(2) The [DNI] shall not be located within the Executive Office of the President.

"(b) PRINCIPAL RESPONSIBILITY.—Subject to the authority, direction, and control of the President, the [DNI] shall—

"(1) serve as head of the intelligence community;

"(2) act as the principal adviser to the President, to the National Security Council, and the Homeland Security Council for intelligence matters related to the national security; and

"(3) . . . oversee and direct the implementation of the National Intelligence Program [NIP] . . . .

"Sec. 102A . . . . (c) BUDGET AUTHORITIES.—(1) With respect to budget requests and appropriations for the [NIP], the [DNI] shall—

"(A) based on intelligence priorities set by the President, provide to the heads of departments containing agencies or organizations within the intelligence community, and to the heads of such agencies and organizations, guidance for developing the [NIP] budget pertaining to such agencies and organizations;

"(B) based on budget proposals provided to the [DNI] by the heads of agencies and organizations within the intelligence community . . . develop and determine an annual consolidated [NIP] budget; and

"(C) present such consolidated [NIP] budget, together with any comments from the heads of departments containing agencies or organizations within the intelligence community, to the President for approval . . . .

"(3) (A) The [DNI] shall participate in the development by the Secretary of Defense of the annual budgets for the Joint Military Intelligence Program [JMIP] and for Tactical Intelligence and Related Activities [TIARA].

"(B) The [DNI] shall provide guidance for the development of the annual budget for each element of the intelligence community that is not within the [NIP] . . . .

"(d) ROLE OF [DNI] IN TRANSFER AND REPROGRAMMING OF FUNDS.—(1) (A) No funds made available under the [NIP] may be transferred or reprogrammed without the prior approval of the [DNI] . . . .

"(B) The Secretary of Defense shall consult with the [DNI] before transferring or reprogramming funds made available under the [JMIP].

"(2) Subject to the succeeding provisions of this subsection, the [DNI] may transfer or reprogram funds appropriated for a program within the [NIP] to another such program . . . .

"(e) TRANSFER OF PERSONNEL.—(1) (A) . . . [I]n the first twelve months after establishment of a new national intelligence center, the [DNI] . . . may transfer not more than 100 personnel authorized for elements of the intelligence community to such center . . . .

"(2) (A) The [DNI] . . . may transfer personnel authorized for an element of the intelligence community to another such element for a period of not more than 2 years . . . .

"(f) TASKING AND OTHER AUTHORITIES.—(1) (A) The [DNI] shall—

"(i) establish objectives, priorities, and guidance for the intelligence community . . . ;

"(ii) determine requirements and priorities for, and manage and direct the tasking of, collection, analysis, production, and dissemination of national intelligence by elements of the intelligence community . . . .

"(2) The [DNI] shall oversee the National Counterterrorism Center and may establish such other national intelligence centers . . . .

"(g) INTELLIGENCE INFORMATION SHARING.—(1) The [DNI] shall have principal authority to ensure maximum availability of and access to intelligence information within the intelligence community . . . .

"(h) ANALYSIS.—To ensure the most accurate analysis of intelligence is derived from all sources to support national security needs, the [DNI] shall—

"(1) implement policies and procedures—

"(A) to encourage sound analytic methods and tradecraft . . . ;

"(B) to ensure that analysis is based upon all sources available; and

"(C) to ensure that the elements of the intelligence community regularly conduct competitive analysis of analytic products . . . ;

"(2) ensure that resource allocation for intelligence analysis is appropriately proportional to resource allocation for intelligence collection systems and operations . . . ;

"(3) ensure that differences in analytic judgment are fully considered and brought to the attention of policymakers; and

"(4) ensure that sufficient relationships are established between intelligence collectors and analysts to facilitate greater understanding . . . .

"(k) COORDINATION WITH FOREIGN GOVERNMENTS.—Under the direction of the President . . . , the [DNI] shall oversee the coordination of the relationships between elements of the intelligence community and the intelligence or security services of foreign governments or international organizations on all matters involving intelligence related to the national security or involving intelligence acquired through clandestine means. . . .

"(q) ACQUISITIONS OF MAJOR SYSTEMS.—(1) For each intelligence program within the [NIP] for the acquisition of a major system, the [DNI] shall—

"(A) require the development and implementation of a program management plan that includes cost, schedule, and performance goals and program milestone criteria, except that with respect to Department of Defense programs the Director shall consult with the Secretary of Defense;

"(B) serve as exclusive milestone decision authority, except that with respect to Department of Defense programs the Director shall serve as milestone decision authority jointly with the Secretary of Defense or the designee of the Secretary. . . .

"(2) If the [DNI] and the Secretary of Defense are unable to reach an agreement on a milestone decision . . . , the President shall resolve the conflict. . . .

"(r) PERFORMANCE OF COMMON SERVICES.—The [DNI] shall, in consultation with the heads of departments and agencies of the United States Government containing elements within the intelligence community and with the Director of the Central Intelligence Agency, coordinate the performance by the elements of the intelligence community within the [NIP] of such services as are of common concern to the intelligence community. . . .

"Sec. 103. (a) OFFICE OF [DNI].— . . .

"(d) STAFF.— . . . The staff of the Office of the [DNI] . . . shall include the staff of the Office of the Deputy Director of Central Intelligence for Community Management that is transferred to the Office of the [DNI] . . . .

"(e) LIMITATION ON CO-LOCATION WITH OTHER ELEMENTS OF INTELLIGENCE COMMUNITY.—Commencing as of October 1, 2008, the Office of the [DNI] may not be co-located with any other element of the intelligence community.

"Sec. 103A. (a) PRINCIPAL DEPUTY [DNI].—(1) There is a Principal Deputy [DNI] who shall be appointed by the President, by and with the advice and consent of the Senate. . . .

"(b) DEPUTY DIRECTORS OF NATIONAL INTELLIGENCE.—(1) There may be not more than four Deputy Directors of National Intelligence who shall be appointed by the [DNI] . . . .

"(c) MILITARY STATUS OF [DNI] AND PRINCIPAL DEPUTY [DNI].—

(1) Not more than one of the individuals serving in the[se] positions . . . may be a commissioned officer of the Armed Forces in active status. . . .

"Sec. 103B. (a) NATIONAL INTELLIGENCE COUNCIL [NIC].— . . . (1) The [NIC] shall be composed of senior analysts within the intelligence community and substantive experts from the public and private sector, who shall be appointed by, report to, and serve at the pleasure of, the [DNI] . . . .

"(c) Duties and Responsibilities.—(1) The [NIC] shall—

"(A) produce national intelligence estimates . . . , including alternative views held by elements of the intelligence community . . . ;

"(B) evaluate community-wide collection and production of intelligence . . . and the requirements and resources of such collection and production. . . .

"(d) SERVICE AS SENIOR INTELLIGENCE ADVISERS.—Within their respective areas of expertise and under the direction of the [DNI], the members of the [NIC] shall constitute the senior intelligence advisers of the intelligence community for purposes of representing the views of the intelligence community. . . .

"Sec. 103C. (a) GENERAL COUNSEL.—There is a General Counsel of the Office of the [DNI] who shall be appointed by the President, by and with the advice and consent of the Senate . . . .

"Sec. 103D. (a) CIVIL LIBERTIES PROTECTION OFFICER.—(1) Within the Office of the [DNI], there is a Civil Liberties Protection Officer who shall be appointed by the [DNI] . . . .

"(b) Duties.—The Civil Liberties Protection Officer shall—

"(1) ensure that the protection of civil liberties and privacy is appropriately incorporated in the policies and procedures developed for and implemented by the Office of the [DNI] and the elements of the intelligence community within the [NIP];

"(2) oversee compliance by the Office and the [DNI] with requirements under the Constitution and all laws, regulations, Executive orders, and implementing guidelines relating to civil liberties and privacy;

"(3) review and assess complaints and other information indicating possible abuses of civil liberties and privacy in the administration of the programs and operations of the Office and the [DNI] and, as appropriate, investigate any such complaint or information;

"(4) ensure that the use of technologies sustain, and do not erode, privacy protections relating to the use, collection, and disclosure of personal information . . . .

"Sec. 103E. (a) DIRECTOR OF SCIENCE AND TECHNOLOGY.—There is a Director of Science and Technology within the Office of the [DNI] who shall be appointed by the [DNI] . . . .

"(c) DUTIES.—The Director of Science and Technology shall—

"(1) act as the chief representative of the [DNI] for science and technology;

"(2) chair the [DNI]Science and Technology Committee . . . .

"Sec. 103F. (a) NATIONAL COUNTERINTELLIGENCE EXECUTIVE.—The National Counterintelligence Executive . . . is a component of the Office of the [DNI] . . . .

"Sec. 104A. (a) DIRECTOR OF CENTRAL INTELLIGENCE AGENCY [DCIA].—There is a [DCIA] who shall be appointed by the President, by and with the advice and consent of the Senate.

"(b) SUPERVISION.—The [DCIA] shall report to the [DNI] regarding the activities of the Central Intelligence Agency . . . .

"(d) RESPONSIBILITIES.—The [DCIA] shall—

"(1) collect intelligence through human sources and by other appropriate means, except that the [DCIA] shall have no police, subpoena, or law enforcement powers or internal security functions;

"(2) correlate and evaluate intelligence related to the national security and provide appropriate dissemination of such intelligence;

"(3) provide overall direction for and coordination of the collection of national intelligence outside the United States through human sources by elements of the intelligence community authorized to undertake such. . . .

"(f) COORDINATION WITH FOREIGN GOVERNMENTS.—Under the direction of the [DNI] . . . , the [DCIA] shall coordinate the relationships between elements of the intelligence community and the intelligence or security services of foreign governments or international organizations on all matters involving intelligence related to the national security or involving intelligence acquired through clandestine means . . . ."

SEC. 1013. JOINT PROCEDURES FOR OPERATIONAL COORDINATION BETWEEN DEPARTMENT OF DEFENSE AND CENTRAL INTELLIGENCE AGENCY.

(a) DEVELOPMENT OF PROCEDURES.—The [DNI], in consultation with the Secretary of Defense and the [DCIA], shall develop joint procedures to be used by the Department of Defense and the Central Intelligence Agency to improve the coordination and deconfliction of operations that involve elements of both the Armed Forces and the Central Intelligence Agency . . . .

SEC. 1014. ROLE OF DIRECTOR OF NATIONAL INTELLIGENCE IN APPOINTMENT OF CERTAIN OFFICIALS RESPONSIBLE FOR INTELLIGENCE-RELATED ACTIVITIES.

Section 106 of the National Security Act of 1947 (50 U.S.C. 403-6) is amended by striking all after the heading and inserting the following:

"(a) RECOMMENDATION OF DNI IN CERTAIN APPOINTMENTS.—(1) In the event of a vacancy in a position referred to in paragraph (2), the [DNI] shall recommend to the President an individual for nomination to fill the vacancy.

"(2) . . . (A) The Principal Deputy [DNI].

"(B) The [DCIA].

"(b) CONCURRENCE OF DNI IN APPOINTMENTS TO POSITIONS IN THE INTELLIGENCE COMMUNITY.—(1) In the event of a vacancy in a position referred to in paragraph (2), the head of the department or agency having jurisdiction over the position shall obtain the concurrence of the [DNI] . . . .If the Director does not concur in the recommendation, the head of the department or agency concerned may not fill the vacancy or make the recommendation to the President . . . .

"(2) . . . (A) The Director of the National Security Agency.

"(B) The Director of the National Reconnaissance Office.

"(C) The Director of the National Geospatial-Intelligence Agency.

"(D) The Assistant Secretary of State for Intelligence and Research.

"(E) The Director of the Office of Intelligence of the Department of Energy.

"(F) The Director of the Office of Counterintelligence of the Department of Energy.

"(G) The Assistant Secretary for Intelligence and Analysis of the Department of the Treasury.

"(H) The Executive Assistant Director for Intelligence of the Federal Bureau of Investigation or any successor to that position.

"(I) The Assistant Secretary of Homeland Security for Information Analysis.

"(c) CONSULTATION WITH DNI IN CERTAIN POSITIONS.—(1) In the event of a vacancy in a position referred to in paragraph (2), the head of the department or agency having jurisdiction over the position shall consult with the [DNI] before appointing an individual to fill the vacancy or recommending to the President an individual to be nominated to fill the vacancy.

"(2) . . . (A) The Director of the Defense Intelligence Agency.

"(B) The Assistant Commandant of the Coast Guard for Intelligence. . . . "

SEC. 1021. NATIONAL COUNTERTERRORISM CENTER.

Title I of the National Security Act of 1947 (50 U.S.C. 402 et seq.) is amended by adding at the end the following new section:

"NATIONAL COUNTERTERRORISM CENTER"

"Sec. 119. (a) ESTABLISHMENT OF CENTER.—There is within the Office of the [DNI] a National Counterterrorism Center [NCTC].

"(b) DIRECTOR OF [NCTC].—(1) There is a Director of the [NCTC] . . . who shall be appointed by the President, by and with the advice and consent of the Senate . . . .

"(c) REPORTING.—(1) The Director of the [NCTC] shall report to the [DNI] with respect to matters described in paragraph (2) and the President with respect to matters described in paragraph (3).

"(2) . . . (A) The budget and programs of the [NCTC].

"(B) The activities of the Directorate of Intelligence of the [NCTC] under subsection (h).

"(C) The conduct of intelligence operations implemented by other elements of the intelligence community; and

"(3) The matters described in this paragraph are the planning and progress of joint counterterrorism operations (other than intelligence operations)." . . .

"(e) DOMESTIC COUNTERTERRORISM INTELLIGENCE.—(1) The Center may, consistent with applicable law, the direction of the President, and the guidelines referred to in section 102A (b), receive intelligence pertaining exclusively to domestic counterterrorism from any Federal, State, or local government or other source necessary to fulfill its responsibilities and retain and disseminate such intelligence . . . .

"(g) LIMITATION.—The Director of the [NCTC] may not direct the execution of counterterrorism operations . . . .

"(i) DIRECTORATE OF INTELLIGENCE.—The Director of the [NCTC] shall establish and maintain within the [NCTC] a Directorate of Intelligence which shall have primary responsibility within the United States Government for analysis of terrorism and terrorist organizations (except for purely domestic terrorism and domestic terrorist organizations) from all sources of intelligence, whether collected inside or outside the United States.

"(j) DIRECTORATE OF STRATEGIC OPERATIONAL PLANNING.—(1) The Director of the [NCTC] shall establish and maintain within the [NCTC] a Directorate of Strategic Operational Planning which shall provide strategic operational plans for counterterrorism operations conducted by the United States Government . . . .

SEC. 1022. NATIONAL COUNTER PROLIFERATION CENTER.

Title I of the National Security Act of 1947, as amended by section 1021 of this Act, is further amended by adding at the end the following new section:

"Sec. 119A. (a) ESTABLISHMENT.—Not later than 18 months after the date of the enactment of the National Security Intelligence Reform Act of 2004, the President shall establish a National Counter Proliferation Center. . . .

SEC. 1023. NATIONAL INTELLIGENCE CENTERS.

Title I of the National Security Act of 1947, as amended by section 1022 of this Act, is further amended by adding at the end the following new section:

"Sec. 119B. (a) AUTHORITY TO ESTABLISH.—The [DNI] may establish one or more national intelligence centers to address intelligence priorities . . . .

SEC. 1031. JOINT INTELLIGENCE COMMUNITY COUNCIL.

Title I of the National Security Act of 1947 (50 U.S.C. 402 et seq.) is amended by inserting after section 101 the following new section:

"Sec. 101A. (a) JOINT INTELLIGENCE COMMUNITY COUNCIL. . . .

"(b) Membership.—The Joint Intelligence Community Council shall consist of the following:

"(1) The [DNI], who shall chair the Council.

"(2) The Secretary of State.

"(3) The Secretary of the Treasury.
"(4) The Secretary of Defense.
"(5) The Attorney General.
"(6) The Secretary of Energy.
"(7) The Secretary of Homeland Security.
"(8) Such other officers of the United States Government as the President may designate from time to time.

"(c) FUNCTIONS.—The Joint Intelligence Community Council shall assist the [DNI] in developing and implementing a joint, unified national intelligence effort to protect national security . . . .

SEC. 1052. OPEN-SOURCE INTELLIGENCE.

(a) SENSE OF CONGRESS.—It is the sense of Congress that–

(1) the [DNI] should establish an intelligence center for the purpose of coordinating the collection, analysis, production, and dissemination of open-source intelligence to elements of the intelligence community . . . .

SEC. 1061. PRIVACY AND CIVIL LIBERTIES OVERSIGHT BOARD.

(a) FINDINGS.— . . . Congress makes the following findings:

(1) In conducting the war on terrorism, the Federal Government may need additional powers and may need to enhance the use of its existing powers.

(2) This potential shift of power and authority to the Federal Government calls for an enhanced system of checks and balances to protect the precious liberties that are vital to our way of life.

(b) ESTABLISHMENT OF BOARD.—There is established within the Executive Office of the President a Privacy and Civil Liberties Oversight Board . . . .

(c) FUNCTIONS.—(1) ADVICE AND COUNSEL ON DEVELOPMENT AND IMPLEMENTATION OF POLICY . . . .

(2) OVERSIGHT.—The Board shall continually review—

(A) regulations, executive branch policies, and procedures (including the implementation of such . . .), related laws pertaining to efforts to protect the Nation from terrorism, and other actions by the executive branch related to efforts to protect the Nation from terrorism to ensure that privacy and civil liberties are protected; and

(B) the information sharing practices of the departments, agencies, and elements of the executive branch to determine whether or not such practices appropriately protect privacy and civil liberties and adhere to the information sharing guidelines under subsections (d) and (f) of section 1016 and to applicable laws, regulations, and executive branch policies regarding the protection of privacy and civil liberties . . . .

(e) MEMBERSHIP.— . . .

(A) IN GENERAL.—The Board shall be composed of a chairman, a vice chairman, and three additional members appointed by the President.

(B) CHAIRMAN AND VICE CHAIRMAN.—The chairman and vice chairman shall each be appointed by the President, by and with the advice and consent of the Senate . . . .

SEC. 1091. TRANSFER OF COMMUNITY MANAGEMENT STAFF . . . . There shall be transferred to the Office of the [DNI] such staff of the Community Management Staff . . . as the [DNI] determines to be appropriate, including all functions and activities discharged by the Community Management Staff . . . .

SEC. 1092. TRANSFER OF TERRORIST THREAT INTEGRATION CENTER . . . . There shall be transferred to the [NCTC] the Terrorist Threat Integration Center (TTIC) or its successor entity, including all functions and activities discharged by the [TTIC] . . . .

TITLE II—FEDERAL BUREAU OF INVESTIGATION

SEC. 2001. IMPROVEMENT OF INTELLIGENCE CAPABILITIES OF THE FEDERAL BUREAU OF INVESTIGATION [FBI]

(a) FINDINGS.—Congress makes the following findings:

(1) The National Commission on Terrorist Attacks Upon the United States in its final report . . . urged that the [FBI] fully institutionalize the shift of the Bureau to a preventive counterterrorism posture.

(b) IMPROVEMENT OF INTELLIGENCE CAPABILITIES.—The Director of the [FBI] shall continue efforts to improve the intelligence capabilities of the [FBI] and to develop and maintain within the Bureau a national intelligence workforce.

(c) NATIONAL INTELLIGENCE WORKFORCE.—(1) . . . [T]he Director of the [FBI] shall develop and maintain a specialized and integrated national intelligence workforce consisting of agents, analysts, linguists, and surveillance specialists who are recruited, trained, and rewarded in a manner which ensures the existence within the [FBI] an institutional culture with substantial expertise in, and commitment to, the intelligence mission of the Bureau . . . .

(f) Budget Matters.—The Director of the [FBI] shall, establish a budget structure of the [FBI] to reflect the four principal missions of the Bureau as follows:

(1) Intelligence.

(2) Counterterrorism and counterintelligence.

(3) Criminal Enterprises/Federal Crimes.

(4) Criminal justice services . . . .

SEC. 2002. DIRECTORATE OF INTELLIGENCE OF THE [FBI].

(a) DIRECTORATE OF INTELLIGENCE OF [FBI].—The element of the [FBI] known as of the date of the enactment of this Act as the Office of Intelligence is hereby redesignated as the Directorate of Intelligence . . . .

(c) RESPONSIBILITIES.—The Directorate of Intelligence shall be responsible for the following:

(1) Supervision of all national intelligence programs, projects, and activities of the Bureau.
(2) The discharge by the Bureau of the requirements in section 105B of the National Security Act of 1947 (50 U.S.C. 403-5b).
(3) The oversight of Bureau field intelligence operations.
(4) Coordinating human source development and management by the Bureau.
(5) Coordinating collection by the Bureau against nationally determined intelligence requirements.
(6) Strategic analysis.
(7) Intelligence program and budget management.
(8) The intelligence workforce . . . .

DOCUMENT 3

THE NATIONAL INTELLIGENCE STRATEGY OF THE UNITED STATES OF AMERICA: TRANSFORMATION THROUGH INTEGRATION AND INNOVATION
October 2005 [Excerpts]

[http://www.dni.gov/press_releases/20051025_release.htm]

Our Vision—What we will become:

A unified enterprise of innovative intelligence professionals whose common purpose in defending American lives and interests, and advancing American values, draws strength from our democratic institutions, diversity, and intellectual and technological prowess.

Our Mission—What we must do:

* Collect, analyze, and disseminate accurate, timely, and objective intelligence, independent of political considerations, to the President and all who make and implement US national security policy, fight our wars, protect our nation, and enforce our laws.
* Conduct the US government's national intelligence program and special activities as directed by the President.

* Transform our capabilities in order to stay ahead of evolving threats to the United States, exploiting risk while recognizing the impossibility of eliminating it.
* Deploy effective counterintelligence measures that enhance and protect our activities to ensure the integrity of the intelligence system, our technology, our armed forces, and our government's decision processes.
* Perform our duties under law in a manner that respects the civil liberties and privacy of all Americans.

Our Strategy—How we will succeed:

The stakes for America in the 21st Century demand that we be more agile and resourceful than our adversaries. Our strategy is to integrate, through intelligence policy, doctrine, and technology, the different enterprises of the Intelligence Community. It encompasses current intelligence activities as well as future capabilities to ensure that we are more effective in the years ahead than we are today. The fifteen strategic objectives outlined in this strategy can be differentiated as mission objectives and enterprise objectives.

Mission objectives relate to those efforts to predict, penetrate, and pre-empt threats to our national security and to assist all who make and implement US national security policy, fight our wars, protect our nation, and enforce our laws in the implementation of national policy goals.

Enterprise objectives relate to our capacity to maintain competitive advantages over states and forces that threaten the security of our nation.

Transformation of the Intelligence Community will be driven by the doctrinal principle of integration. Our transformation will be centered on a high-performing intelligence workforce that is:

* Results-focused
* Collaborative
* Bold
* Future-oriented
* Self-evaluating
* Innovative

These six characteristics are interdependent and mutually reinforcing. They will shape our internal policies, programs, institutions, and technologies.

Strategic Objectives

Mission Objectives: To provide accurate and timely intelligence and conduct intelligence programs and activities directed by the President, we must support the following objectives drawn from the *National Security Strategy*:

1. Defeat terrorists at home and abroad by disarming their operational capabilities and seizing the initiative from them by promoting the growth of freedom and democracy.
2. Prevent and counter the spread of weapons of mass destruction.
3. Bolster the growth of democracy and sustain peaceful democratic states.
4. Develop innovative ways to penetrate and analyze the most difficult targets.
5. Anticipate developments of strategic concern and identify opportunities as well as vulnerabilities for decision-makers.

Enterprise Objectives: To transform our capabilities faster than threats emerge, protect what needs to be protected, and perform our duties according to the law, we must:

1. Build an integrated intelligence capability to address threats to the homeland, consistent with US laws and the protection of privacy and civil liberties.
2. Strengthen analytic expertise, methods, and practices; tap expertise wherever it resides; and, explore alternative analytic views.
3. Rebalance, integrate, and optimize collection capabilities to meet current and future customer and analytic priorities.
4. Attract, engage, and unify an innovative and results-focused Intelligence Community workforce.
5. Ensure that Intelligence Community members and customers can access the intelligence they need when they need it.
6. Establish new and strengthen existing foreign intelligence relationships to help us meet global security challenges.
7. Create clear, uniform security practices and rules that allow us to work together, protect our nation's secrets, and enable aggressive counterintelligence activities.
8. Exploit path-breaking scientific and research advances that will enable us to maintain and extend our intelligence advantages against emerging threats.
9. Learn from our successes and mistakes to anticipate and be ready for new challenges.
10. Eliminate redundancy and programs that add little or no value and re-direct savings to existing and emerging national security priorities. . . .

Next Steps

These strategic objectives will guide Intelligence Community policy, planning, collection, analysis, operations, programming, acquisition, budgeting, and execution. They will be overseen by senior officials of the Office of the Director of National Intelligence, but will be implemented through an integrated Intelligence Community effort to capitalize on the comparative advantages of constituent organizations . . . .

The Fiscal Year 2008 planning, programming, and performance guidance will reflect these mission and enterprise objectives. Ongoing program and budget activities for Fiscal Years 2006 and 2007 will adjust to these objectives to the maximum extent possible.

Chronology of Events

1775	Continental Congress establishes Committee of Secret Correspondence
September 22, 1776	Nathan Hale hanged by British for spying
1790	Congress creates Contingency Fund for President Washington
1861	Allen Pinkerton joins General McClellan's staff; resigns in 1862
1861	First U.S. balloon reconnaissance; balloon corps disbanded in 1863
1862	Lafayette Baker forms counterintelligence unit in War Department
1863	Col. George H. Sharpe sets up Bureau of Military Information for Army of the Potomac
1865	Secret Service formed in Treasury Department
1882	Navy establishes Office of Naval Intelligence (ONI)
1885	Army establishes Military Information Division (MID)
1888	Congress authorizes military attachés to diplomatic posts abroad
1898	Spanish-American War; Spain's Montreal Spy Ring broken up
1908	Bureau of Investigation established in Justice Department
1916	Congress gives the Bureau of Investigation authority to conduct counterintelligence investigations

January 1917	British intercept and decipher "Zimmermann Telegram"
April 1917	United States enters World War I
1921	Washington disarmament conference
1924	Navy establishes OP-20-G under Laurance F. Safford
1929	Yardley's "Black Chamber" shut down
1929	Army Signal Corps consolidates codemaking and codebreaking activities under the leadership of William F. Friedman
1935	Bureau of Investigation becomes Federal Bureau of Investigation (FBI)
1940	President Roosevelt expands the FBI's responsibilities to collecting nonmilitary foreign intelligence for the western hemisphere
1940	Japanese Purple machine-cipher system solved by Friedman's Signal Intelligence Service
July 1941	President Roosevelt creates Coordinator of Information (COI); names William J. Donovan to the position
December 7, 1941	Japanese attack Pearl Harbor
May 1942	Battle of the Coral Sea
June 1942	Battle of Midway
June 1942	Office of Strategic Services (OSS) created with William J. Donovan as head
November 1942	British-American invasion of North Africa
June 6, 1944	Allied forces land in France
1945	World War II ends; OSS disbanded
1947	National Security Act creates Department of Defense, National Security Council, Air Force, and Central Intelligence Agency
1949	USSR explodes a nuclear device
1949	Armed Forces Security Agency (AFSA) established
June 1950	Korean War begins

1952	National Security Agency established by Executive Order
1953	President Eisenhower appoints Allen Dulles as Director of Central Intelligence
1953	CIA-backed coup d'etat in Iran returns the Shah to power
1954	CIA-backed coup d'etat ousts Guatemalan president
October-November 1956	Suez crisis and Hungarian uprising
1956	U-2 flights over Soviet Union begin
1958	CIA assigned responsibility for Project CORONA—developing a photographic reconnaissance satellite
1958	Failed covert action in Indonesia
1959	Covert action begins in Tibet
May 1960	Francis Gary Powers' U-2 shot down over Soviet Union
August 1960	Successful mission of CORONA reconnaissance satellite
1960	President Eisenhower establishes National Reconnaissance Office
1961	CIA-sponsored invasion of Cuba at the Bay of Pigs fails
August 1961	Defense Secretary McNamara creates Defense Intelligence Agency
October 1962	Cuban Missile Crisis
1967	Israeli attack on SIGINT ship USS *Liberty*
1968	North Koreans seize SIGINT ship USS *Pueblo*
1974	Hughes-Ryan Amendment restrains spending on covert action without President's finding such is important to national security
1975	House (Pike) and Senate (Church) committees investigate intelligence agencies
November 4, 1979	U.S. Embassy staff in Teheran taken hostage
December 25, 1979	Soviet Union invades Afghanistan

January 28, 1980	U.S. diplomats hidden by Canadians escape from Teheran
April 24, 1980	Iranian hostage rescue mission fails
1982	Boland Amendment prohibits use of funds for overthrowing Nicaraguan government
April 18, 1983	Terrorist car bomb attack on U.S. Embassy in Beirut
October 23, 1983	Terrorist attack on U.S. Marine barracks in Beirut
February 1989	Soviet Union completes withdrawal from Afghanistan
November 1989	Berlin Wall comes down
1991	Persian Gulf War ousts Iraq from Kuwait
December 26, 1991	Demise of the Soviet Union
1992	Existence of NRO officially recognized
February 26, 1993	Terrorists explode van in parking garage of World Trade Center
1993	Defense HUMINT Service created in DIA
February 1994	CIA officer Aldrich Ames arrested for spying
1996	National Imagery and Mapping Agency created as Defense Department component (renamed National Geospatial-Intelligence Agency in 2003)
June 25, 1996	Terrorists explode truck bomb at U.S. military compound in Dhahran, Saudi Arabia
August 7, 1998	Terrorists bomb U.S. embassies in Nairobi, Kenya, and Dar es Salaam, Tanzania
October 12, 2000	Terrorists attack USS *Cole* during refueling stop in the port of Aden, Yemen
February 2001	FBI counterintelligence officer Robert Philip Hanssen arrested for spying
September 11, 2001	Al Qaeda terrorists attack World Trade Center and Pentagon; fourth hijacked aircraft crashes in Pennsylvania
September 19, 2001	CIA team leaves to begin U.S. support for attacking the Taliban and al Qaeda in Afghanistan
October 2001	President signs the USA Patriot Act

November 2001	Kabul falls to U.S.-supported forces
November 2002	CIA-controlled Predator UAV kills al Qaeda leader in Yemen
November 2002	Congress creates Department of Homeland Security
March 2003	U.S. invades Iraq to remove Saddam Hussein from power
July 2004	9/11 Commission issues its public *Final Report*
December 2004	President signs Intelligence Reform and Terrorism Prevention Act creating position of Director of National Intelligence
March 2005	WMD Commission issues its *Report*
November 2005	DNI Open Source Center established
December 2005	National Counterproliferation Center formally inaugurated
July 2006	HPSCI staff report critical of progress being made in intelligence reform

Glossary

Analysis. The stage in the intelligence cycle where information is subjected to systematic examination in order to identify meaning and derive conclusions.

Briefing. Often means an informational presentation, usually oral. May refer to preparation of an individual or group for a specific assignment or operation. Also, can be the process of introducing someone into a classified, compartmented program.

Collection. Obtaining information in any manner and delivering it to the appropriate processing unit for use in the production of intelligence.

Command, Control, Communications, and Intelligence (C3I). An integrated system of doctrine, procedures, organizational structure, personnel, equipment, facilities, communications, and supporting intelligence activities that provides authorities at all levels with data to plan, direct, and control their activities.

Compromise. Unauthorized disclosure of information.

Confidential source. Any individual or organization that provides information to the U.S. government on matters pertaining to the national security and expects, in return, that the information or relationship, or both, will be held in confidence.

Consumers. The term used by the producers of intelligence to identify their target audience. It includes both the users within the decision making process and those who produce other intelligence.

Coordination. The process of seeking concurrence from other agencies regarding a proposal or an activity for which there is some shared responsibility. The result may be contributions, concurrences, or dissents. Intelligence producers seek the views of other producers on the adequacy of a specific draft assessment, estimate, or report. The goal is to increase a product's factual accuracy, clarify its judgments, and resolve or sharpen statements of disagreement on contentious issues.

Covert operation. An operation planned and executed so as to conceal the identity of, or permit plausible denial by, the sponsor. Covert operations differ from clandestine operations in that emphasis is placed on concealment of the identity of the sponsor, rather than on concealment of the operation.

Critical intelligence. Information of such urgent importance to U.S. national security that it is directly transmitted at the highest precedence to the President and other national decision making officials before passing through regular evaluative channels. In the military it is intelligence that requires the immediate attention of the commander.

Damage assessment. In intelligence usage, an evaluation of the impact of a compromise in terms of loss of intelligence information, sources, or methods. The goal is to identify the measures needed to minimize damage and prevent future compromises. In military usage, an appraisal of the effects of an attack on one or more elements of a nation's strength (military, economic, and political). The goal is to determine residual capability for further military action.

Deception. Measures designed to mislead an adversary by manipulation, distortion, or falsification of evidence in order to induce a reaction that is prejudicial to the adversary's interests.

Declassification. Removal of official information from the protective status afforded by security classification. It requires an official determination that disclosure no longer would be detrimental to national security.

Dissemination. Part of the intelligence cycle; refers to the distribution of the various intelligence products to departmental and/or agency consumers.

Electronic Warfare. A military action involving the use of electromagnetic and directed energy to control the electromagnetic spectrum or to attack the enemy.

Espionage. Spying or using spies to obtain protected intelligence.

Evaluation. Appraisal of the value of an intelligence activity, information, or product in terms of its contribution to a specific goal or intelligence need. Elements in the appraisal include credibility, reliability, pertinence, accuracy, and/or usefulness.

Exploitation. In general, the process of obtaining intelligence information from a source and taking advantage of it. In signals intelligence, it refers to the production of information from messages that are encrypted in systems the basic elements of which are known. Exploitation includes decryption, translation, and the solution of specific controls.

Finding. A determination made by the President stating that a particular intelligence operation is important to U.S. national security in compliance with the Foreign Assistance Act of 1961, as amended by the 1974 Hughes-Ryan Amendment.

Finished intelligence. The product that results from the collection, processing, integration, analysis, evaluation, and interpretation of information concerning foreign countries or areas or national security issues. The end product of the production step of the intelligence cycle—that is, the intelligence product.

Foreign Intelligence Surveillance Court (FISC). Created by the Foreign Intelligence Surveillance Act of 1978 (FISA), the FISC can authorize electronic surveillance and physical searches absent consent, which occur within the United States, for the purpose of collecting "foreign intelligence." The Court has seven U.S. District court judges who are appointed by the Chief Justice of the Supreme Court and who serve for seven years. The Foreign Intelligence Surveillance Court of Review, comprised of three U.S. District or Appeals court judges, may review FISC decisions.

Information Warfare. Actions taken to adversely affect an adversary's information, information-based processes, and/or information systems while defending one's own information, information-based processes, and/or information systems.

Intelligence cycle. The process by which information is acquired and converted into intelligence and made available to users.

National security. A country's territorial integrity, sovereignty, and international freedom of action. Intelligence activities relating to national security include the military, economic, political, scientific, technological, and other aspects of foreign developments that may pose a threat to national interests.

Need-to-know. A determination made by an authorized holder of controlled information as to whether a prospective recipient requires access to the information in order to perform or assist in an authorized governmental function.

Psychological operations. Operations to convey information and indicators to foreign audiences to influence their emotions, motives, objective reasoning, and, ultimately, the behavior of foreign governments, other groups, and individuals. The purpose is to induce or reinforce foreign attitudes and behavior favorable to the originator's objectives.

Raw intelligence. Collected information that still needs to be converted into finished intelligence.

Special Access Program. A program established for a specific class of information that imposes handling and access requirements beyond those normally required for information at the same classification level.

Note

Adapted from U.S. Central Intelligence Agency, *A Consumer's Guide to Intelligence* (Washington, DC: n.d.); U.S. Intelligence Community, "Intelligence Terms and Definitions," http://www.intelligence.gov/0-glossary.shtml; and Interagency OPSEC Support Staff, "OPSEC Glossary of Terms," http://www.ioss.gov/docs/definitions.html.

Annotated Bibliography

Intelligence Web Sites

Government

Air Force: http://www.aia.af.mil/.
Army: http://www.inscom.army.mil/.
Central Intelligence Agency: https://www.cia.gov.
Coast Guard: http://www.intelligence.gov/1-members_coastguard.shtml.
Defense Intelligence Agency: http://www.dia.mil/index.htm.
Director of National Intelligence: http://www.dni.gov.
Drug Enforcement Administration: http://www.intelligence.gov/1-members_dea.shtml.
Energy Department: http://www.intelligence.gov/1-members_energy.shtml.
Federal Bureau of Investigation: http://www.fbi.gov/.
Homeland Security Department: http://www.intelligence.gov/1-members_dhs.shtml.
Marine Corps: http://hqinet001.hqmc.usmc.mil/DirInt/default.html.
National Geospatial-Intelligence Agency: http://www.nima.mil.
National Reconnaissance Office: http://www.nro.gov.
National Security Agency: http://www.nsa.gov/.
Navy: http://www.nmic.navy.mil/.
State Department: http://www.state.gov/s/inr/.
Treasury Department: http://www.intelligence.gov/1-members_treasury.shtml.

Non-Government

Federation of American Scientists Intelligence Resource Program: http://www.fas.org/irp/. [Official and unofficial materials on intelligence policy, structure, and operations.]

The Literature of Intelligence: A Bibliography of Materials, with Essays, Reviews, and Comments: http://intellit.muskingum.edu/. [Annotated listings by topics and authors of books and articles on intelligence from ancient times to the present.]

Loyola College Political Science Department Strategic Intelligence Site: http://www.loyola.edu/dept/politics/intel.html. [Useful for links to additional sites. Regularly updated. Excellent starting point for Web searches.]

Encyclopedias

O'Toole, George J.A. *The Encyclopedia of American Intelligence and Espionage: From the Revolutionary War to the Present*. New York: Facts on File, 1988. [Excellent for U.S. intelligence and the time period. Usually accurate, thoughtful selection criteria, and avoids polemics.]

Polmar, Norman, and Thomas B. Allen. *Spy Book: The Encyclopedia of Espionage*, 2nd ed. New York: Random House, 2004. [Most accurate and comprehensive intelligence encyclopedia available. Reliable but not perfect in all its detail.]

General

Andrew, Christopher. *For the President's Eyes Only: Secret Intelligence and the American Presidency from Washington to Bush*. New York: HarperCollins, 1995. [Mostly how modern presidents used or misused intelligence. Strong on intelligence in presidential decision making during the Cold War.]

Bozeman, Adda B. *Strategic Intelligence and Statecraft: Selected Essays*. Washington, DC: Brassey's, 1992. [Eight intellectual and intelligent essays that illustrate the theme that strategic intelligence is the key to success in foreign affairs.]

Dulles, Allen W. *The Craft of Intelligence*. Guilford, CT: Lyons Press, 2006. [Classic piece of intelligence literature, first published in 1963; remains worth reading.]

O'Toole, George J.A. *Honorable Treachery: A History of U.S. Intelligence, Espionage, and Covert Action from the American Revolution to the CIA*. New York: Atlantic Monthly Press, 1991. [Well-done history of U.S. intelligence from Revolution to 1962. Reads well; presents subject matter in an informed fashion.]

Powers, Thomas. *Intelligence Wars: American Secret History from Hitler to Al-Qaeda*, rev. ed. New York: New York Review of Books, 2004. [Collection of book reviews. Thoughtful comments on key intelligence and national security subjects.]

Shulsky, Abram N., and Gary Schmitt. *Silent Warfare: Understanding the World of Intelligence*, 3rd ed. New York: Brassey's, 2001. [Among the best general books on intelligence. Short on history, military intelligence, and intelligence-policy relationship.]

Revolutionary War

Allen. Thomas B. *George Washington, Spymaster: How the Americans Outspied the British and Won the Revolutionary War*. Washington, DC: National Geographic, 2004. [Not "heavy" history. Well-written, interesting look at George Washington as a spymaster and user of intelligence.]

U.S. Central Intelligence Agency. *Intelligence in the War of Independence*. Washington, DC: 1976. [https://www.cia.gov/cia/publications/warindep/index.html.] [Excellent introduction to the subject. Issued as part of the Bicentennial.]

Civil War

Feis, William B. *Grant's Secret Service: The Intelligence War from Belmont to Appomattox*. Lincoln, NE: University of Nebraska Press, 2002. [Focuses on Grant's use of intelligence, first, in command in the western theater and, then, in command of the Army of the Potomac.]

Fishel, Edwin C. *The Secret War for the Union: The Untold Story of Military Intelligence in the Civil War*. Boston, MA: Houghton Mifflin, 1996. [Monumental work covering military intelligence in the eastern theater, predominantly on the Union side, through Gettysburg.]

Rose, P.K. "The Civil War: Black American Contributions to Union Intelligence." *Studies in Intelligence* (Winter 1998–1999): 73–80. [https://www.cia.gov/cia/publications/dispatches/index.html.] [Intelligence from frontline tactical debriefings of former slaves. Also, behind-the-lines missions and agent-in-place operations.]

Spanish-American War

O'Toole, George J.A. *The Spanish War: An American Epic*. New York: Norton, 1984. [Good coverage of intelligence aspects of an often-ignored war.]

World War I

Tuchman, Barbara W. *The Zimmermann Telegram*. New York: Ballantine, 1986. [This history of a British intelligence success reads like a thriller.]

Interwar

Parker, Frederick D. *Pearl Harbor Revisited: United States Communications Intelligence, 1924–1941*. Ft. George G. Meade, MD: Center for Cryptologic History, National Security Agency, 1994. [Meticulous analysis of U.S. COMINT efforts between the wars.]

World War II

Brown, Anthony Cave, ed. *The Secret War Report of the OSS*. New York: Berkley, 1976. [Edited version of official report prepared immediately after the war and declassified in 1976. Dry reading, but regarded as generally accurate.]

History Channel. "Secrets of War: Sworn to Secrecy—Breaking the Japanese Codes." [http://www.secretsofwar.com.] [A fifty-minute program in History Channel's fifty-two-part "Secrets of War" series. Uses photos and film to tell the story of U.S. codebreaking.]

McIntosh, Elizabeth P. *Sisterhood of Spies: The Women of the OSS*. Annapolis, MD: Naval Institute Press, 1998. [Served with OSS in the Far East. An illuminating look at women at war in the field of intelligence, without overdoing the drama.]

Warner, Michael. *The Office of Strategic Services: America's First Intelligence Agency*. Washington, DC: Central Intelligence Agency, [n.d]. [https://www.cia.gov/cia/publications/oss/.] [Excellent brief overview of the OSS's contribution to waging World War II, and its heritage for intelligence in the years that followed.]

Korean War

Haas, Michael E. *In the Devil's Shadow: U.N. Special Operations during the Korean War*. Annapolis, MD: Naval Institute Press, 2000. [Provides a broad picture. Places on-the-ground activities within their political-military context.]

Vietnam

Ford, Harold P. *CIA and the Vietnam Policymakers: Three Episodes, 1962–1968*. Washington, DC: History Staff, Center for the Study of Intelligence, Central Intelligence Agency, 1998. [Former Vice Chairman of the National Intelligence Council skillfully lays out CIA's assessments concerning Vietnam.]

Shultz, Richard H., Jr. *The Secret War against Hanoi: Kennedy and Johnson's Use of Spies, Saboteurs, and Covert Warriors in North Vietnam*. New York: HarperCollins, 1999. [Superb work outlining activities of Studies and Observation Group (SOG); puts its role into broader perspective of Vietnam War.]

Cold War and Beyond

Allison, Graham T., and Philip Zelikow. *Essence of Decision: Explaining the Cuban Missile Crisis*, 2nd ed. New York: Longman, 1999. [This scholarly work offers a unique theoretical perspective on the crisis. It is excellent for students interested in developing their analytical skills.]

Bearden, Milt, and James Risen. *The Main Enemy: The Inside Story of the CIA's Final Showdown with the KGB*. New York: Random House, 2003. [Among his Cold War battles, Bearden headed CIA field operations in Afghanistan in the 1980s. This book reads easily.]

Gates, Robert M. *From the Shadows: The Ultimate Insider's Story of Five Presidents and How They Won the Cold War*. New York: Simon & Schuster, 1996. [Interesting, well-written book by former DCI. Stresses extraordinary continuity of U.S. policy from Nixon to George H.W. Bush.]

Johnson, Loch K. *A Season of Inquiry: The Senate Intelligence Investigation*. Lexington, KY: University Press of Kentucky, 1985. [Former Church Committee staff member details the committee's inner workings and the inception of today's Congressional oversight.]

Murphy, David E., Sergei A. Kondrashev, and George Bailey. *Battleground Berlin: CIA vs. KGB in the Cold War*. New Haven, CT: Yale University Press, 1997. [Authoritative and well written. Murphy is a former head of CIA Soviet operations, while Kondrashev headed the KGB's German Department.]

Post-9/11

Schroen, Gary C. *First In: An Insider's Account of How the CIA Spearheaded the War on Terror in Afghanistan*. Novato, CA: Presidio, 2005; and Berntsen, Gary, and Ralph Pezzullo. *Jawbreaker: The Attack on Bin Laden and Al Qaeda: A Personal Account by the CIA's Key Field Commander*. New York: Crown, 2005. [These two books should be read together and in the order listed. They tell the story of the post-9/11 attack on al Qaeda and its Taliban patrons, and represent a stunningly detailed view of a major paramilitary operation.]

Analysis

Grabo, Cynthia M. *Anticipating Surprise: Analysis for Strategic Warning*. Washington, DC: University Press of America, 2005. [Defines steps in warning process and discusses guidelines for assessing the meaning of gathered information.]

Heuer, Richards J., Jr. *Psychology of Intelligence Analysis*. Washington, DC: Center for the Study of Intelligence, Central Intelligence Agency, 1999. [https://www.cia.gov/csi/books/19104/index.html.] [Explores the cognitive biases that can affect analysts and the act of perception.]

Steury, Donald P., ed. *Sherman Kent and the Board of National Estimates: Collected Essays*. Washington, DC: History Staff, Center for the Study of Intelligence, Central Intelligence Agency, 1994. [https://www.cia.gov/csi/books/shermankent/toc.html.] [Kent chaired the Board of National Estimates 1952–1967. "The Law and Custom of the National Intelligence Estimate" is particularly significant.]

Central Intelligence Agency

Colby, William E., with Peter Forbath. *Honorable Men: My Life in the CIA*. New York: Simon & Schuster, 1978. [Covers career from OSS to DCI. Colby remains controversial. Gives judicious discussion of role of intelligence in democratic society.]

Holm, Richard L. *The American Agent: My Life in the CIA*. With a new introduction by the author. London: St. Ermin's, 2005. [The author exemplifies bravery and human endurance, but his story is about the life of a CIA operations officer over a multifaceted career.]

Powers, Thomas. *The Man Who Kept the Secrets: Richard Helms and the CIA*. New York: Knopf, 1979. [One of the best books written about U.S. intelligence. Powers worked hard to tell his story accurately; the telling of it is easy to read.]

Richelson, Jeffrey T. *The Wizards of Langley: Inside the CIA's Directorate of Science and Technology*. Boulder, CO: Westview, 2002. [Filled with details of technical accomplishments and bureaucratic struggles with the Defense Department; not an easy read but worth the effort.]

Troy, Thomas F. *Donovan and the CIA: A History of the Establishment of the Central Intelligence Agency*. Frederick, MD: University Publications of America, 1981. [Magnificently documented account of how the CIA came into existence.]

Turner, Stansfield. *Burn Before Reading: Presidents, CIA Directors, and Secret Intelligence*. New York: Hyperion Books, 2005. [Despite the silly title, the former DCI provides perceptive commentary and an easy read.]

Weiser, Benjamin. *A Secret Life: The Polish Officer, His Covert Mission, and the Price He Paid to Save His Country*. New York: Public Affairs, 2004. [Best book on human intelligence. Polish patriot/spy Kuklinski and his CIA handlers are real people. Great story, told beautifully.]

Counterintelligence

Benson, Robert Louis. *The VENONA Story*. Ft. George G. Meade, MD: National Security Agency, Center for Cryptologic History, [n.d.]. [http://www.nsa.gov/publications/publi00039.cfm.] [An excellent overview of the VENONA materials.]

U.S. Department of Defense. *Espionage Cases, 1975–2004: Summaries and Sources*. Monterey, CA: Defense Personnel Security Research Center, 2004. [http://www.dss.mil/training/espionage/.] [Factual case summaries of thirty years of spy cases.]

Weinstein, Allen, and Alexander Vassiliev. *The Haunted Wood: Soviet Espionage in America—the Stalin Era*. New York: Random House, 1999. [Exceptional addition to intelligence literature. Not easy reading, but rounds out previously less-supported stories of Soviet spies.]

Covert Action

Daugherty, William J. *Executive Secrets: Covert Action and the Presidency*. Lexington, KY: University Press of Kentucky, 2004. [Overview of nature and use of covert action operations as tool of U.S. Presidents in executing national security policy.]

Grose, Peter. *Operation Rollback: America's Secret War Behind the Iron Curtain*. Boston, MA: Houghton Mifflin, 2000. [Well-researched and short (222 pages) account of sabotage, espionage, and covert action against postwar Eastern Europe and the Soviet Union.]

Knott, Stephen F. *Secret and Sanctioned: Covert Operations and the American Presidency*. New York: Oxford University Press, 1996. [Focuses on use by Presidents of covert operations 1776–1882. Finds that covert operations date back to the Founders.]

Treverton, Gregory F. *Covert Action: The Limits of Intervention in the Postwar World*. New York: Basic Books, 1987. [Dated but still useful. Concludes that major covert actions increasingly will become public.]

Cryptography

Kahn, David. *The Codebreakers: The Comprehensive History of Secret Communication from Ancient Times to the Internet*, rev. ed. New York: Scribner, 1996. [Monumental work with everything you ever wanted to know about cryptology up to 1967.]

Federal Bureau of Investigation

Cumming, Alfred, and Todd Masse. *Intelligence Reform Implementation at the Federal Bureau of Investigation: Issues and Options for Congress*. Washington, DC: Congressional Research Service, Library of Congress, August 16, 2005. [http://www.fas.org/sgp/crs/intel/RL33033.pdf.] [Less than positive assessment of the FBI's efforts to implement intelligence reform initiatives.]

Powers, Richard Gid. *Broken: The Troubled Past and Uncertain Future of the FBI*. New York: Free Press, 2004. [The author reviews the FBI's history and finds today's difficulties rooted in the past.]

Wannall, W. Raymond. *The Real J. Edgar Hoover: For the Record*. Paducah, KY: Turner Publishing, 2000. [The former FBI Assistant Director takes on Hoover's critics to paint a more nuanced picture of the man who led the FBI from 1924 to 1972.]

Imagery Intelligence

Day, Dwayne A., John M. Logsdon, and Brian Latell, eds. *Eye in the Sky: The Story of the Corona Spy Satellites*. Washington, DC: Smithsonian Institution Press, 1998. [Pioneers in the space-intelligence field share their perspectives and recollections of the U.S. satellite programs.]

Pedlow, Gregory W., and Donald E. Welzenbach. *The CIA and the U2 Program, 1954–1974*. Washington, DC: History Staff, Center for the Study of Intelligence, Central Intelligence Agency, 1998. [https://www.cia.gov/csi/books/U2/index.htm.] [Excellent review of the U-2 program. Contains substantial detail, and an assessment of the program's accomplishments.]

Richelson, Jeffrey T. *America's Secret Eyes in Space: The U.S. Keyhole Spy Satellite Program*. New York: HarperCollins, 1990. [Comprehensive, thoroughly researched introduction to photographic and imaging satellites. Includes a good bibliography.]

Intelligence Reform

Best, Richard A., Jr. *Proposals for Intelligence Reorganization, 1949–2004*. Washington, DC: Congressional Research Service, Library of Congress, September 24, 2004. [http://www.fas.org/irp/crs/RL32500.pdf.] [Provides objective details on and the results from the recommendations of the numerous reviews of U.S. intelligence since 1947.]

Posner, Richard A. *Preventing Surprise Attacks: Intelligence Reform in the Wake of 9/11*. Lanham, MD: Rowman & Littlefield, 2005; and Posner, Richard A. *Uncertain Shield: The U.S. Intelligence System in the Throes of Reform*. Lanham, MD: Rowman & Littlefield, 2006. [These slim volumes are a devastating critique of the 9/11 Commission and the Intelligence Reform and Terrorism Prevention Act of 2004.]

National Security Agency

Bamford, James. *Body of Secrets: Anatomy of the Ultra-Secret National Security Agency from the Cold War through the Dawn of a New Century*. New York: Doubleday, 2001. [Most of what a reader might want to know about NSA is somewhere in this book.]

Burns, Thomas L. *The Quest for Cryptologic Centralization and the Establishment of NSA: 1940–1952*. Ft. George G. Meade, MD: Center for Cryptologic History, National Security Agency, 2005. [http://www.fas.org/irp/nsa/quest.pdf.] [Declassified version of in-house history that documents the evolution of NSA into a national signals intelligence organization.]

Index

About the Author

J. RANSOM CLARK, a twenty-five-year veteran of the Central Intelligence Agency (CIA), has worked assignments from Asia, Europe, Latin America, to the Middle East, and Washington, DC. He retired in 1990 as a member of the CIA's Senior Intelligence Service. From 1990 until his second retirement in 2005, Clark taught and held administrative positions at Muskingum College in New Concord, Ohio. His honors include the CIA's Intelligence Medal of Merit and Muskingum College's Excellence in Teaching and Faculty Service awards. Clark maintains an extensive Web site on intelligence—The Literature of Intelligence: A Bibliography of Materials, with Essays, Reviews, and Comments at http://intellit.muskingum.edu.

Recent Titles in
Contemporary Military, Strategic, and Security Issues

Military Base Closure: A Reference Handbook
David S. Sorenson

Military Education: A Reference Handbook
Cynthia A. Watson

Strategic Defense in the Nuclear Age: A Reference Handbook
Sanford Lakoff